INTRODUCING
COGNITIVE ANALYTIC THERAPY

INTRODUCING COGNITIVE ANALYTIC THERAPY

Principles and Practice

Anthony Ryle DM, FRCPsych

Honorary Consultant Psychotherapist and Senior Research Fellow,
South London and Maudsley NHS Trust and Guy's,
King's, St Thomas'(GKT) Medical School, Munro Clinic,
Guy's Hospital, London, UK

Ian B. Kerr MD, MRCPsych Mem. ACAT,
Ass.Mem.BAP

Consultant Psychiatrist and Psychotherapist and Honorary Senior
Lecturer, Community Health Sheffield NHS Trust, Sheffield, UK

JOHN WILEY & SONS, LTD

Other Wiley Editorial Offices

John Wiley & Sons Inc., 111 River Street, Hoboken, NJ 07030, USA

Jossey-Bass, 989 Market Street, San Francisco, CA 94103-1741, USA

Wiley-VCH Verlag GmbH, Boschstr. 12, D-69469 Weinheim, Germany

John Wiley & Sons Australia Ltd, 33 Park Road, Milton, Queensland 4064, Australia

John Wiley & Sons (Asia) Pte Ltd, 2 Clementi Loop #02-01, Jin Xing Distripark, Singapore
129809

John Wiley & Sons Canada Ltd, 22 Worcester Road, Etobicoke, Ontario, Canada M9W 1L1

British Library Cataloguing in Publication Data

A catalogue record for this book is available from the British Library

ISBN 0 471 89273 4

Typeset in 10/12pt Palatino by Saxon Graphics Ltd., Derby
Printed and bound in Great Britain by Antony Rowe Ltd, Chippenham, Wiltshire
This book is printed on acid-free paper responsibly manufactured from sustainable forestry
in which at least two trees are planted for each one used for paper production.

CONTENTS

LIST OF FIGURES

ABOUT THE AUTHORS

Anthony Ryle qualified in medicine in 1949 and worked successively as a founding member of an inner city group practice, in Kentish Town, London, as Director of Sussex University Health Service and as a Consultant Psychotherapist at St Thomas's Hospital, London. Since retiring from the NHS he has worked part-time in teaching and research at Guy's Hospital. While in general practice he carried out epidemiological studies of the patients under his care and the experience of demonstrating the high prevalence and family associations of psychological distress influenced his subsequent interest in the development of forms of psychological treatment which could realistically be provided in the NHS. Studies of the process and outcome of psychotherapy followed and from these grew the elaboration of an integrated psychotherapy theory and the development of the time-limited model of treatment which became cognitive analytic therapy.

Ian B. Kerr graduated in medicine from the University of Edinburgh in 1977. After several junior hospital posts he worked for many years in cancer research. He subsequently completed dual training in psychiatry and psychotherapy at Guy's, Maudsley and St George's Hospitals in London. Currently he is Consultant Psychiatrist and Psychotherapist and Honorary Senior Lecturer, Community Health Sheffield NHS Trust, Sheffield, UK.

PREFACE

This book offers an updated introduction and overview of the principles and practice of cognitive analytic therapy (CAT). The last such book appeared over ten years ago and was the first systematic articulation of a new, integrative model which had been developed over a period of many years. Although there have been two specialist volumes since then (Ryle, 1995a; 1997a) it is significant that a restatement of the model and its applications is now necessary. There are many reasons for this. They include the fact that as a young, genuinely integrative model, (as acknowledged in the influential Roth and Fonagy report (1996)), it is still evolving and developing both in terms of its theoretical base and its range of applications. In this book a further exposition of the CAT model of development is given, stressing in particular an understanding of the social formation of the self based on Vygotskian activity theory and Bakhtinian 'dialogism'. We also outline an ever-expanding range of practical applications of CAT as an individual therapy as well as its application as a conceptual model for understanding different disorders and informing approaches to their management by staff teams. This trend has been described (Steve Potter) as 'using' CAT, as opposed to 'doing' it. Newer or preliminary applications of CAT reviewed here include CAT in old age, with learning disabilities, in anxiety-related disorders, in psychotic disorders, CAT for self-harming patients presenting briefly to casualty departments, CAT with the 'difficult' patient in organisational settings and CAT in primary care. In part these also reflect theoretical developments of the model which are also reviewed. Its gradually expanding evidence base is also reviewed, along with some of the difficulties, both scientific and political, inherent in research in this area.

CAT evolved initially as a brief (usually 16-session) therapy. This was partly for pragmatic reasons and related to the search for the optimum means of delivering an effective treatment to the kind of patients being seen in under-resourced health service settings. However, it also arose from consideration and evaluation of which aspects of therapy, including its duration, were actually effective. This aspect of research is fundamental to the model and continues to be important in its continuing evolution. We suggest, incidentally, that a brief treatment like CAT, within the course of which profound psychological change can be achieved, genuinely merits the description of 'intensive' as opposed to much longer-term therapies usually described as such, which we suggest might better be called 'extensive'.

Despite the effectiveness of brief CAT for very many patients it is clear that not all patients can be successfully treated within this length of time. However, it is also evident from some very interesting work, with, for example, self-harming patients but also less damaged 'neurotic' patients, that effective work can also be done in a few, or even one session. The length of treatment has thus been modified to adapt to the needs of differing patients. Longer-term therapy may need to be offered to those with severe personality disorder, long-standing psychotic disorder, or those with histories of serious psychological trauma. Thus, there will be some patients for whom the reparative and supportive aspect of therapy over a longer period of time may be an important require-ment. Similarly, more extended treatments may be offered in settings such as a day hospital, where the treatment model may be informed by CAT, as an alter-native to offering it as an individual therapy.

A further reason for the present book is the ever increasing popularity of CAT with mental health professionals and the demand from trainees and others for a comprehensive but accessible introduction to it. The rapidly increasing popu-larity of CAT with both professionals and patients is, we feel, a further indica-tion of the effectiveness and attractiveness of the model. In part, we see this popularity as arising from the congruence of CAT with the increasing demand for 'user participation' in mental health services; the explicitly collaborative nature of the model offers and requires active participation on the part of the client or patient. This 'doing with' therapeutic position, in addition to being demonstrably effective, appears to be very much more appropriate and welcome to a younger generation of trainees and potential therapists. This 'power-sharing' paradigm has overall, in our view, radical implications for mental, and other, health services.

The CAT understanding of the social and cultural formation of the self also highlights the role of political and economic forces in the genesis of many psychological disorders. The external conditions of life and the dominant values of current society, internalised in the individual, are seen as active deter-minants of psychological health or disorder. Recognising this, we suggest that, as therapists, we should strive to avoid describing psychological disorders as simply 'illnesses' and should also play our part in identifying and articulating whatever social action may be called for in response.

The book is the result of the collaborative work of two authors who share responsibility for the text. Our contributions were different, in part because AR was the initiator of the CAT model and has a much longer history of writing about it. In so far as this conferred authority it also risked complacency which, he felt, needed to be challenged. IK brought a more recent experience of psychiatry and psychotherapy in the NHS, reflected in particular in the discussion of psychosis and of the 'difficult' patient and contextual reformulation. He also wished to emphasise the importance of a full biopsychosocial perspective. Our longest and most fruitful arguments were involved in writing the theoretical chapters (3 and 4).

THE STRUCTURE OF THE BOOK

Chapters 1 and 2 will give a brief account of the scope and focus of CAT and how it evolved and will spell out the main features of its practice. Most of CAT's relatively few technical terms will appear in these chapters; they and other general terms which may have a different meaning in CAT are listed in a glossary. In order to flesh out this introductory survey and give readers a sense of the unfolding structure of a time-limited CAT, Chapter 2 also offers a brief account of a relatively straightforward therapy. Chapters 3 and 4 consider the normal and abnormal development of the self and introduce the Vygotskian and Bakhtinian concepts which are part of the basic theory of individual development and change. Subsequent chapters describe selection and assessment (Chapter 5), reformulation (Chapter 6), the course of therapy (Chapter 7), the 'ideal model' of therapist interventions and its relation to the supervision of therapists (Chapter 8), applications of CAT in various patient groups and settings (Chapter 9) and in treating personality disorders (Chapter 10), and the concept of the 'difficult' patient and approaches to this problem, including the use of 'contextual reformulation' (Chapter 11). Each chapter commences with a brief summary of its contents and most conclude with suggestions for further reading. References to CAT published work and to the work of others are provided in the text. In addition, Appendix 1 contains a list of all CAT research-related publications available at the time of going to press. Appendix 2 contains the CAT Psychotherapy File, Appendix 3 the Personality Structure Questionnaire and Appendix 4 a description of repertory grid basics and their use in CAT.

Case material derived from audiotaped sessions is used with the permission of both patients and therapists; we gratefully acknowledge their help. Other illustrative material is either drawn from composite sources or disguised in ways preventing recognition. We have, on the whole, referred to patients rather than clients, although we use the term interchangeably.

FURTHER INFORMATION

Further information about CAT and about the Association for Cognitive Analytic Therapy (ACAT) may be obtained from The Administrator, ACAT,

Academic Division of Psychiatry, St Thomas' Hospital, London SE1 7EH (Tel: 020 7928 9292 ext. 3769) or through the website www.acat.org.uk, which also lists other CAT-related events and activities.

May 2001

ACKNOWLEDGEMENTS

We should like to thank the many colleagues and patients who have contributed material to this book and who have been named in it. There are also innumerable others who have made important contributions to its production both recently and over a period of many years. They are too many to name but we should like to express our gratitude to them collectively. We would like to acknowledge the support provided by the staff at John Wiley and, in particular, the early encouragement offered by Michael Coombs. Finally, we should like to thank our partners Flora and Jane for making, in various and important ways, the writing of this book possible.

Chapter 1

THE SCOPE AND FOCUS OF CAT

SUMMARY

CAT evolved as an integration of cognitive, psychoanalytic and, more recently, Vygotskian ideas, with an emphasis on therapist–patient collaboration in creating and applying descriptive reformulations of presenting problems. The model arose from a continuing commitment to research into effective therapies and from a concern with delivering appropriate, time-limited, treatment in the public sector. Originally developed as a model of individual therapy, CAT now offers a general theory of psychotherapy with applicability to a wide range of conditions in many different settings.

In order to locate cognitive analytic therapy (CAT) in the still expanding array of approaches to psychotherapy and counselling and to indicate the continuing developments in its theory and practice, its main features will be briefly summarised in this introductory chapter.

CAT IS AN INTEGRATED MODEL

One source of CAT was a wish to find a common language for the psychotherapies. While there is a place for different perspectives and different aims in psychotherapy, the use by the different schools of virtually unrelated concepts and languages to describe the same phenomena seems absurd. It has resulted in a situation where discussion is largely confined to the parish magazines of each of the different churches or to the trading of insults between them. Despite the growth of interest in integration and the spread of technical eclecticism in recent years the situation has not radically altered; CAT remains one of the few models to propose a comprehensive theory which aims to integrate the more robust and valid findings of different schools of psychotherapy as well as those of developmental psychology and observational research.

The process of integration in CAT originated in the use of cognitive methods and tools to research the process and outcome of psychodynamic therapy. This involved the translation of many psychoanalytic concepts into a more accessible language based on the new cognitive psychology. This led on to a consideration of the methods employed by current cognitive-behavioural and psychodynamic practitioners. While cognitive-behavioural models of therapy needed to take more account of the key role of human relationships in development, in psychopathology and in therapy, their emphasis on the analysis and description of the sequences connecting behaviours to outcomes and beliefs to emotions made an important contribution. Psychoanalysis offered three main important understandings, namely its emphasis on the relation of early development to psychological structures, its recognition of how patterns of relationship derived from early experience are at the root of most psychological distress and its understanding of how these patterns are repeated in, and may be modified through, the patient–therapist relationship.

Neither cognitive nor psychoanalytic models acknowledge adequately the extent to which individual human personality is formed and maintained through relating to and communicating with others and through the internalisation of the meanings developed in such relationships, meanings which reflect the values and structures of the wider culture. In CAT, the self is seen to be developed and maintained in the course of such interactions.

CAT IS A COLLABORATIVE THERAPY

The practice of CAT reflects these theoretical developments. It has been suggested that, in contrast to the traditional polarisation of health care professionals between those who are good at 'doing to' their patients (e.g. surgeons and perhaps some behaviour therapists) and those who are good at 'being with' their patients (e.g. many dynamic psychotherapists or nurses involved in long-term care), the CAT therapist is good at *'doing with'* their patients (Kerr, 1998b). This highlights the fact that CAT involves hard work for both patients and therapists and also the fact that much of this work is done together and that the therapy relationship plays a major role in assisting change.

The ways therapists describe their patients have implications for the value they accord to them and the nature of the therapeutic relationship conveys more than any particular technique. The techniques used and how they are employed must convey human acknowledgement and value. CAT therapists therefore encourage patients to participate to the greatest possible extent in their therapies; therapists do know useful ways of thinking and, in some sense, are experts involved in activities which parallel parenting or remedial teaching, but our patients are not pupils or children and their capacities need to be respected, mobilised and enlarged through the joint creation of new understandings.

CAT IS RESEARCH BASED

One reason, or excuse, for the underfunding of psychotherapy in the National Health Service (NHS) has been the failure of dynamic therapists to evaluate seriously the efficacy of their work. The outcome research which led on to the development of CAT pre-dated the present insistence on evidence-based practice, originating in a programme dating back to the 1960s which aimed to develop measures of dynamic change. While the research base remains inadequate, the evolution of the model over the last 20 years has been accompanied by a continuous programme of largely small-scale research into both the process and outcome of therapy and this continues on an expanding scale.

CAT EVOLVED FROM THE NEEDS OF WORKING IN THE PUBLIC SECTOR AND REMAINS IDEALLY SUITED TO IT

Despite the proliferation of treatment models, a considerable proportion of psychologically distressed people in the UK (and in most other developed nations, let alone in the developing world) do not have access to effective psychological treatment. CAT, by providing a therapy which can be delivered at reasonable cost while being effective across a wide spectrum of diagnoses and a wide range of severity, is a contribution to meeting their needs. Most CAT therapists have worked in the NHS as nurses, occupational therapists, social workers, psychologists or psychiatrists; we are experienced in, and largely committed to, work in the public sector. We share a social perspective which assumes that psychotherapy services should take responsibility for those in need in the populations we serve, and should not be reserved for those individuals who happen to find (or buy) their way to the consulting room. It does, however, appear, not surprisingly perhaps, that CAT is becoming a very popular model of therapy in the private sector where many therapists make their living. Here, its time-limited but radical approach appeals to many clients who may have, possibly serious, psychological difficulties but who do not wish to spend protracted periods of time in long-term therapies of uncertain efficacy. As a model of brief therapy it is of course, for very different reasons, attractive to health insurance companies.

Our own social perspective is not new. The following description of the NHS was sent to demobilised servicemen in 1950: 'It will provide you with all medical, dental and nursing care. Everyone, rich, poor, man, woman or child, can use it or any part of it. There are no charges except for a few special items ... . But it is not a charity. You are all paying for it, mainly as taxpayers and it will relieve your money worries in times of illness.' (Quoted in Wedderburn, 1996.) Despite the chronic underfunding of mental health services and of psychotherapy in particular, we believe that these principles can still be fought for and that CAT can contribute to their realisation.

CAT IS TIME-LIMITED

CAT is delivered in a predetermined time limit. While this time limit is clearly one important way of being cost-effective, the important argument in its favour rests on the fact that, for most people, time-limited therapy is as clinically effective as many much more prolonged interventions. The time limit is usually of 16 sessions but this can be extended in treating more disturbed and damaged patients or shortened where the threshold to consultation is low and mildly disturbed patients are seen.

CAT OFFERS A GENERAL THEORY, NOT JUST A NEW PACKAGE OF TECHNIQUES

The book aims to describe and illustrate the methods, techniques and tools developed in CAT. While largely concerned with individual therapy, applications in other modalities are considered, as are the wider implications for psychotherapy theory. While some CAT techniques could be incorporated in other treatment approaches, the model and the method involve more than these. Psychotherapy patients can make use of a great many different psychotherapy techniques and there would be no point in simply offering a new combination of these under a new label. So why do we need theory?

One robust finding from psychotherapy research is that the patient's perception of the therapist as helpful is associated with a good outcome. This being so, a major part of any therapy model must be concerned with how to achieve this, given that the central problem for many patients is that they are damaging or incompetent in their personal relationships and are mistrustful and destructive of offers of help from others. Overcoming these tendencies is never easy and becomes increasingly important and difficult as more disturbed patients are considered. Being helpful means more than being nice, indeed it may sometimes involve being 'nasty' or at least confronting; the crucial quality required is to respect the patient enough to be honest. Techniques therefore need to be understood in relation to the complex human issues which are at the heart of therapy. Those used in CAT, whether adapted from other approaches or specific to CAT, have, as their main aim, the development of the patients' capacities to know, reflect on and ultimately control their negative actions and experiences.

Other tools and techniques are designed to maintain the therapist's adherence to the methods and values of the approach; they provide a framework within which a sincere and often intense working relationship can flourish. Practice embedded in theoretical clarity must be combined with accurate empathy if therapists are to be able to reach and maintain an understanding of their patients' experiences and at the same time be fully aware of their role in encouraging change.

CAT HAS APPLICATIONS IN MANY CLINICAL SETTINGS

The book is primarily addressed to those working with psychologically disturbed adults including those who, while not 'doing therapy', have important therapeutic responsibilities. We believe that psychological understandings should play a larger part than is now the case in the management of groups such as psychiatric patients with major mental illness, forensic patients and the mentally handicapped. We believe that psychotherapists should take more responsibility for supporting staff in these fields. In addition, psychotherapists should involve themselves both directly and in supporting staff in the treatment of patients with personality disorders who are currently so poorly served by mental health services. In all these fields, and in work with adolescents, experience is accumulating of applying CAT and the model is proving to be accessible and useful to patients and clinical staff. While both psychoanalysis and cognitive therapy have contributed to these fields neither, in our view, adequately mobilises the therapeutic power of the relationship between patients and those looking after them. We believe that CAT has a major contribution here, offering a distinct, coherent and teachable model of social and interpersonal interaction which can help individuals and staff groups respond helpfully, rather than react collusively, to their patients, and which may have applications outside clinical practice.

Chapter 2

THE MAIN FEATURES OF CAT

SUMMARY

The practice of CAT is based on a collaborative therapeutic position, which aims to create with patients narrative and diagrammatic reformulations of their difficulties. Theory focuses on descriptions of sequences of linked external, mental and behavioural events. Initially the emphasis was on how these procedural sequences prevented revision of dysfunctional ways of living. This has been extended more recently to a consideration of the origins of reciprocal role procedures in early life and their repetition in current relationships and in self-management. This model—the Procedural Sequence Object Relations Model—has been further modified by the introduction of Vygotskian and Bakhtinian ideas on the social formation of mind. Practice involves early reformulation followed by work designed to recognise and then revise dysfunctional procedures in daily life and in the therapy relationship. The model of practice is illustrated by a brief case history.

This chapter will describe the development of CAT and will introduce most of the 'technical' terms employed. Although it was not defined and named as a separate model until the mid-1980s, it was derived from practice and research carried out during the previous twenty years. As this pre-history explains many of its features, this chapter will begin by summarising these sources.

Thirty years ago, there was hardly any evidence to show whether psychodynamic therapy worked. To measure the effectiveness of therapy it is necessary to declare at the start what the aims are, a task easily accomplished by behaviourists where these are defined as the relief of symptoms or modification of behaviours, but more difficult for psychodynamic therapists whose aims are complex and are often poorly articulated or only emerge in the course of the therapy. Two small studies were carried out to address this problem. The first involved a careful reading of the notes of a series of completed therapies with the aim of finding out how early in therapy the key problems had been identified. This revealed that most therapies were concerned with only one or two key themes and that these had usually been evident early on, often in the first session. It also showed that much of the work of therapy had been directed to trying to understand why the patient had not revised the ways of thinking and ·acting which maintained these problems. On this basis the 'dynamic' aims of therapy could be defined early on as the revision of the identified, repetitive, maladaptive patterns of thought and behaviour.

Three patterns explaining this non-revision were identified; these were labelled dilemmas, traps and snags. Dilemmas prevent revision because the possibilities for action or relationships are seen to be limited to polarised choices; the only apparent options are to follow the less objectionable choice or to alternate between them. Traps represent the maintenance of negative beliefs by the way they generate forms of behaviour which lead to consequences (usually the responses of others) which appear to confirm the beliefs. In snags, appropriate goals are abandoned or sabotaged, because (or as if) it is believed that their achievement would be dangerous to self or others or otherwise disallowed.

The second study involved the use of repertory grid techniques. (The basic principles of this technique are summarised in Appendix 4). At the start of therapy patients completed such grids by rating how far a range of descriptions (constructs), partly elicited and partly supplied, were true of a range of elements consisting of significant people. In the case of the dyad grid (Ryle and Lunghi, 1970) the elements are the relationships between the self and significant people. Analysis of such grids provided a number of measures of the individual's way of construing self and other. Measures that reflected the issues which had been noted clinically and described in psychodynamic terms could be identified and the changes in these seen to be desirable in terms of the aims of therapy could be specified. Repeating the grid after therapy showed how far such changes had occurred. Through the use of such repertory grids, described in Ryle (1975, 1979, 1980), it became possible to derive measures of change between pre- and post-therapy testing indicating how far dynamic aims had been achieved.

What started as an exercise designed to provide evidence of the effectiveness of dynamic therapy was therefore successful; outcome research could now be based on identifying and measuring change in patients' 'dynamic' problems, described as patterns of traps, dilemmas and snags at the start of therapy, and on measuring change in the associated repertory grid measures. But the main effect was incidental to this aim, for this process, which involved explicit, joint work with the patient to identify and describe problems, had such a powerful positive effect on the course of therapy that conventional dynamic therapy was abandoned. The joint reformulation of the patient's problems became a key feature of what developed into CAT.

THE EARLY DEVELOPMENT OF CAT PRACTICE

The first specific CAT tool was developed at this stage, the 'Psychotherapy File'; a version of this is reproduced in Appendix 2. This is usually given to patients to take away at the end of the first session. It gives explanations and examples of dilemmas, traps and snags and invites patients to consider which may apply to them; these will be discussed with the therapist at the next session. The File also gives instructions in self-monitoring of mood changes and symptoms, based on cognitive therapy practice, and contains screening questions concerning instability of the self; positive answers to these suggest borderline features. The use of the File introduces patients to active participation in the therapy process and initiates them to the task of learning self-reflection. At this point readers may find it useful to go through the File with a patient, and perhaps with themselves, in mind.

Practice diverged from the psychodynamic model and was now based on the active, joint creation and use of the reformulation. Thereafter, daily life and the evolving therapy relationship were understood in terms of this reformulation and patients were involved in homework on issues related to recognition and revision of the identified patterns. Self-monitoring of symptoms and behaviours to identify when they were activated contributed to the creation of a written list of target problems (TPs) and target problem procedures (TPPs), the latter in the form of dilemmas, traps and snags. Changes in TPs and TPPs were rated by patients on visual analogue scales and discussed at each session. This procedure was not popular with therapists from psychodynamic backgrounds, but for them and for many patients it served to maintain the focus and it contributed to the accuracy of the patient's self-observation.

Despite the introduction of these 'cognitive' practices the main form of early sessions was exploratory and unstructured and particular attention was paid to transference–countertransference events and feelings and to their relation to the identified patterns. Change in therapy was seen to be the result of the patient's heightened, conscious, focused ability to recognise and in due course revise the negative patterns and of the therapist's ability to avoid reinforcing them. In addition, within the framework defined by the descriptive reformulation, a wide range of specific techniques might be employed towards the revision of problem procedures and their integration.

THE THEORETICAL MODEL

The theoretical basis of practice was now formalised in the Procedural Sequence Model (PSM). This offered a general model of how events are responded to, how intentional aims are pursued and of how revision might or might not occur. The procedure or procedural sequence became the basic unit of description, providing the understandings needed to elucidate repetitive circular patterns of activity, including those problematic ones (dilemmas, traps and snags) which were not revised. The sequence traces out and describes the following stages:

1. External factors: events, cues and context.
2. Mental processes: (a) appraising the situation and the possibilities for action, (b) relating these to (possibly conflicting) existing beliefs, values and aims and (c) the selection of a response or action plan or role on the basis of predictions of its efficacy and outcome.
3. Action, including playing a role in a relationship.
4. Mental processes: (a) evaluating the consequences of the role or action, (b) confirming or revising the aim and/or the means used.

This model (described in Ryle, 1982) was compatible with current cognitive models but offered a more comprehensive description of the ways in which problem procedures remained unrevised. Affect, cognition, meaning and action were seen to be intimately linked and were not studied in isolation from each other and the individual was understood in relation to past and present relationships with others. Many psychoanalytic concepts, including the relation of development to structure, could be restated in terms of it. But it differed from both cognitive and analytic theories in its emphasis on the way in which the individual's engagements with others constantly reflect and largely maintain their self processes.

This basic theory needed further development in order to explain the formation of the self in early life and to clarify the problems in self-management and relationships which are the main concern of psychotherapy. This initially involved bringing into the model ideas derived from object relations theories. All procedures involve predicting or seeking to achieve certain outcomes. In seeking relationships with another, one plays a role based on the expectation of, wish for, or the attempt to elicit, one particular outcome, namely their acknowledgement and reciprocation (see Ryle, 1985). These procedures were therefore named reciprocal role procedures (RRPs), and this concept became of key importance in the revised model—the Procedural Sequence Object Relations Model (PSORM). It should be emphasised that 'role', as used here, implies action linked to memory, meaning, affect and expectation. The subjective experience of playing a role can be described as a state of mind or state of being, terms which must be distinguished from reciprocal role procedure, which is essentially a theoretical construct.

THE DEVELOPMENT OF THE BASIC MODEL OF PRACTICE

The habit of showing patients the accounts of their assessment interviews and of writing down the agreed list of identified problems and problem procedures had been established from the beginning as part of the attempt to be as open and non-mysterious as possible. This led on to the present practice of covering the same ground in a reformulation letter addressed directly to the patient. (These were initially referred to as 'prose reformulations' to distinguish them from the TP and TPP lists—not because verse was an option!) These letters are reconstructions of the often jumbled narratives told by patients. They summarise key events in the past and suggest, in a non-blaming way, how the negative patterns learned from early experiences are being repeated or how alternative patterns developed in order to avoid these early ones have themselves become restrictive or damaging.

Working on the basis of the PSORM, the patterns identified as traps, dilemmas and snags will be linked to the individual's repertoire of reciprocal roles. In some cases deriving the dilemmas, traps and snags from the history and the discussion of responses to the Psychotherapy File is the best way to start the reformulation process. In other cases, an immediate consideration of the role patterns evident in the patient's account of early experiences and current relationships and of 'in the room' feelings and enactments is more effective.

THE DEVELOPMENT OF SEQUENTIAL DIAGRAMMATIC REFORMULATION

The description of problematic sequences is a central aspect of reformulation but clear verbal descriptions of complex processes can be difficult to construct and remember. With experience, they were increasingly supplemented or replaced by the use of sequential diagrammatic reformulation (SDR). Detailed discussion of the construction of these diagrams, with illustrative examples, can be found in Chapter 6. In their simplest form they are flow charts, which may arise from an initial, joint sketch of a patient's core 'subjective self', linking aims to outcomes and indicating how problem procedures fail to achieve the intended aim. With the development of the PSORM they came to be drawn in a way which demonstrated the generation of problem procedures from the patient's reciprocal role repertoire, which was listed in a box as the core of the diagram.

An idea of hierarchy was implicit in the model, in that the very general patterns described in reformulation were seen to be manifested in a variety of detailed actions and roles. (The patterns themselves are, of course, generalisations arrived at during reformulation from the consideration of such detailed examples.) Also implicit was the assumption that procedures were mobilised appropriately in terms of the situation and according to the individual's aims, through the largely unconscious operation of metaprocedures which also served to link together and harmonise the array of available procedures.

That harmonious and appropriate mobilisation does not always occur, however, became clear through work with patients with borderline personality disorder (BPD). Many borderline features are best explained as the result of the partial dissociation of the patient's core reciprocal role repertoire, dissociation being understood as discontinuities in, and incomplete access between, different reciprocal role procedures. These are seen to be due to the disruption or maldevelopment of the metaprocedural system in subjects genetically predisposed to dissociate (see Chapter 10). This borderline structure is depicted in diagrams by describing separate cores to the diagram indicating what are best described as dissociated RRPs (self states). This clumsy title helps to prevent confusion between the theoretical concept of the self state and the subjective experience of a state of mind or state of being. At any one time, a borderline individual's behaviour and experience are determined by only one of these self states. The switches between, and the procedures generated by, these discrete states are mapped in self state sequential diagrams (SSSDs). Similar structures are found in many patients who do not meet full criteria for borderline personality disorders (see the case at the end of this chapter).

Recognising and describing the reciprocal role repertoire provides a new basis for the patient's self-reflection and is of particular value in helping therapists to avoid reciprocating (colluding with) the patient's damaging role procedures. In contrast to most short-term therapies, CAT does not select a limited focus but seeks rather to identify and describe these general, high level procedural patterns. Such 'strategic' patterns will have been formed by, and will be manifest in, a range of detailed 'tactical' behaviours. People are often only dimly aware of these general patterns, which are developed in early childhood, but they are not 'dynamically repressed' (that is, their inaccessibility does not have the function of avoiding painful or forbidden memories and desires) and their description and recognition can allow rapid change over a wide spectrum. An essential CAT therapist skill during reformulation is to be good at seeing what overall patterns are suggested by detailed events or repetitions; discussing with a patient whether a particular episode is an example of a more general pattern nearly always elicits parallel examples which may confirm or modify the pattern.

Verbal or diagrammatic descriptions of these patterns must be made in joint work using, as far as possible, the patient's own words and images. These are essentially descriptions abstracted with the therapist's help from the patient's witnessed or reported strategies. It is often possible to identify the repertoire without discussing early developmental history in any detail, although therapists may make suggestions such as 'do you think this pattern comes from your relationship with your father?' The recollected patterns of interaction in the childhood family (even though their historical accuracy may be uncertain) are often the clear precursors of key current procedures. The aim of historical inquiries is not to reconstruct the past so much as to explore what conclusions have been drawn from it, conclusions which may be based on partial or distorted memory but are seldom pure fantasy. CAT therapists base their comments on what can be seen or has been reported; they do not offer interpretations of 'the unconscious', although comments like 'you seem to act as if everyone is bound to leave you' might well be appropriate. The vast majority of relevant mental processes are unconscious, but claiming to know what the patient could not know, as in so-called 'deep' interpretations, plays no part in CAT practice. Such interpretations are likely to be reflections of theory at least as much as they are linked to the patient's processes. They are in any case redundant because relevant unconscious processes causing restrictive and damaging procedures will be manifest in the shaping or blocking of activity, in omissions from memory or perception or in intrusions into consciousness, all of which can be described.

THE COURSE OF THERAPY

By the end of the first four sessions a sequential model of problem procedures and a narrative reconstruction of their origins in the reformulation letter has usually been jointly constructed and recorded. This demanding and often intense phase usually creates a strong working alliance. As patients feel understood and 'contained' by the reformulation they are frequently able to recall memories and experience feelings which have been muted or denied. Such memories, feelings or dreams may be supplemented by biographical writing or other forms of exploration such as drawing. Direct challenges to avoidant behaviours are seldom called for and the phrase 'coping strategy' is preferable to the potentially pejorative word 'defence'. Symptoms, mood swings and unwanted behaviours which had been monitored since the first session are increasingly understood in terms of their relation to the identified procedural patterns which are in need of revision. At this stage the need to recognise the problem procedures as they are manifest is emphasised and the focus of self-monitoring and diary keeping shifts from recording symptoms or moods to the identification of enacted problem procedures. The three Rs of CAT are, in order, Reformulation, Recognition and Revision. It is important to establish recognition before directing attention to revision, for one cannot reflect on or change what has not been identified.

The phase of uncomplicated commitment to the tasks of therapy usually fades out around the tenth session out of sixteen, as termination becomes a more real prospect and as disappointments in the limits of what has been achieved in the therapy accumulate. Both the early cooperation and this emergence of negative feelings need to be identified and named and linked to the reformulation. Failure to discuss and accept transference feelings and failure to link them to the reformulation is a wasted opportunity and is associated with dropping out and poor outcome, while the matter-of-fact acceptance, description but non-reciprocation of hostility or emotional withdrawal—and equally of idealisation—are powerfully healing.

TIME LIMITS

The time-limited nature of CAT owed a lot to the work of James Mann (1973) and his emphasis on the importance of naming the session number, especially as termination approaches, is a part of CAT practice. Working to predetermined time limits is not the same as using long-term techniques for a short time. The process is heightened and most of the problems addressed in long-term dynamic psychotherapy can be satisfactorily dealt with. Indeed some patients with more severe disorders are more responsive and more safely helped in time-limited work where the dangers of over-dependence are much reduced and where the realistic disappointment which allows separation is evident from the beginning.

Termination is always an issue, however, and the last sessions are seldom easy for the patient or the therapist. In CAT, the practice was introduced of exchanging 'goodbye letters' at the penultimate or last session. The aim of the therapist's letter is to offer an accurate (not blandly optimistic) account of what has and has not been achieved in terms of modifying problem procedures and relieving problems and to identify where further work is needed. The existence of disappointment despite what has been achieved is expressly noted or predicted. This letter gives the patient a reminder of the unidealised person of the therapist and of the tools of the therapy and is intended to help the internalisation of the experience. In the same way the letter from the patient (always suggested but not always produced) invites accurate reflection and plain speaking. Follow-up at about three months is usually arranged; in most cases change is maintained more thoroughly than either therapist or patient expect. If this is not the case further follow-up or 'top up' sessions may be arranged. Decisions about further treatment of whatever kind are best postponed until the effects of the therapy have become stabilised and the experience of termination has been completed.

THE DEVELOPMENT OF A VYGOTSKIAN OBJECT RELATIONS THEORY

By the mid-1980s the CAT model of self processes incorporated ideas concerning procedural sequences linking internal (mental) and external events, but the origins of these in early development were not clearly described. Current theories appeared unsatisfactory. On the one hand, the dominant object relations school, largely derived from theory-based hypotheses based on the psychoanalysis of adults, emphasised innate conflicting drives, neglected the role of experience and paid little attention to the expanding body of observational studies of early development. On the other hand, simple cognitive descriptions, such as were included in the original procedural sequence model, while useful as guides to identifying negative patterns did not offer an adequate understanding of structure or of development.

The introduction into CAT of Vygotsky's understandings of the social and historical formation of higher mental processes and of the key importance in human learning of sign mediation, linked with Bakhtin's illuminating understandings of the role of interpersonal and internal dialogue, allowed a radical restatement of object relations ideas. The theoretical language now referred to reciprocal role relationships learned in interaction with caretakers and others and mediated by signs which are used first in outer and then in inner dialogue. The theory supported the use of the concrete mediating signs created in the reformulation process in CAT, such mediation being the medium of the internalisation through which transformation of the patient's internal structures could be achieved. Informed also by Bakhtin's explorations of literature, the theory replaces the traditional model of an internal world peopled by objects or part objects derived from ego and others and operating like little 'ghosts in the machine' with a model of internal 'voices'. These have been learned in activity and conversation with others but are now equally involved in external and internal communication and control—the model of the 'dialogic self'. Fuller accounts of the development of CAT will be found in Ryle (1995a) and Leiman (1994a). The introduction of Vygotsky's ideas is described in Ryle (1991) and Leiman (1992). The relation of Vygotsky to current developmental psychology is discussed in Wertsch and Tulviste (1992) and reviewed in Burkitt (1991). Holquist (1990) provides an introduction to the ideas of Bakhtin.

THE SCOPE OF CAT

Time-limited CAT is by no means a superficial treatment for mild disorders. It has a wider scope and at least as great an impact as do most currently available longer-term models. There is no reason to believe that, for most people, open-ended dynamic psychotherapy, from which there is a massive drop-out in the course of the first year, achieves more and there is reason to believe that CAT is a better intervention for more fragmented and disturbed patients. The CAT therapist works with the therapeutic relationship in a way which is more immediate and accessible to patients than are psychoanalytic interpretations and uses understandings which are not available to most cognitive therapists. Decisions to offer long-term work are best made after the impact of a time-limited intervention can be assessed.

The aims of CAT therapists are, in a sense, modest: we seek to remove the 'roadblocks' which have maintained restriction and distress and have prevented the patient's further growth and we assist in the development of more adequate route maps. But we do not offer to accompany the patient along the road. Obstacles to change are of three main kinds: self-reinforcing ineffective procedures, restricted, avoidant or symptomatic procedures and disconnected, dissociated self processes. Unlike some psychoanalysts, we do not seek to explain, let alone claim to share or replace, the wisdom and creativity of artists, writers and philosophers. As well as being modest in our aims we are pragmatic: knowing that resources will always be limited, our main aim is to give the minimum sufficient help to those in need. In an inner city outpatient service CAT seems to be a satisfactory treatment for over two-thirds of patients and of some benefit to many of the remainder. Some of these go on to further treatment such as more CAT, group therapy or cognitive-behavioural work on unrevised procedures (Dunn et al. 1997). CAT might be more effective for some patients if given over a somewhat longer time or in separate blocks with intervals. Its combination or alternation with other interventions such as art therapy or psychodrama or group work would almost certainly be helpful for patients who are hard to engage emotionally or who need more time to explore alternatives. The paucity of such resources has not allowed these possibilities to be explored systematically so far.

Which aspects of CAT are the effective ingredients in successful therapy has not been fully demonstrated, but research summarised later in the book has shown that the reformulation process can produce accurate summaries of key issues and that systematic linking of transference enactments to the reformulation is associated with good outcome. Our belief is that the two main factors are (1) the joint creation and use of reformulation tools and their availability in written and graphic form and (2) the internalisation of these as the signs developed in the course of a collaborative and non-collusive relationship. These factors cannot be isolated from the other features of the theory and practice which allow intense but contained connections between patients and therapists.

To end this chapter we present an abbreviated and revised account of a typical CAT therapy in order to illustrate its stages and the use of the various tools.

CASE HISTORY: BOBBY (Therapist Steve Potter)

Bobby, a mature student in his early thirties, presented to a lunchtime on-call session at a student counselling service with depression and 'agitation'. Since the break-up of a four-year relationship over the previous two years he had been sleeping badly, drinking and smoking excessively despite having asthma, eating irregularly and neglecting his studies while indulging in fantasies of becoming a famous musician. He had had two previous experiences of therapy and felt he would need it always.

Background

Bobby was the youngest of a large family, alternately spoiled (especially on the many occasions when he was ill) and neglected; in part this was because his mother was frequently away in hospital. He recalled frequently lying in his bed calling quietly for his mother, crying into his pillow and feeling inconsolable but afraid of a telling-off from his brother, by whom he was frequently bullied. He was also bullied later on at school although he had one best mate there with whom he shared fantasies of becoming a famous pop star.

Assessment and reformulation

After two assessment sessions he was offered 16 sessions of CAT. He was given the Psychotherapy File (see Appendix 2) and he started to keep a symptom diary. The Psychotherapy File and some of his diary keeping confirmed the initial patterns he had described and also set him thinking that perhaps he was not as bad as he used to be. We identified what he wanted to change (target problems) and how his patterns of relating to others and self-neglect and self-comfort fed into these. By session 4 Bobby felt much improved in morale. He had used the provisional diagram, begun self-monitoring and was keeping a diary.

At session 4, a letter was read to him which is reproduced in part:

Dear Bobby,
Here, in writing, is what we have talked about in recent weeks. I hope it can help us keep on track in the weeks ahead and serve as a reminder to you of what we have been working on.
… One thing you remember of your childhood is either feeling especially loved and trea-sured, or being a nuisance and ignored and smacked and told to shut up and go to sleep (for example by your brother). You felt you were cared for if ill but otherwise ignored by your older brothers and sisters. You tried to please them and win them over but always felt scared.
This pattern seems to have been echoed in your close relationships with women and with a therapist previously, as well as in the way you either neglect and ignore your own needs or seek comfort through drink or smoking dope … You are usually neglectful of your body and have not seen a doctor or got proper care (for asthma and other ailments) …
We have named a number of patterns of feeling, thinking and behaving:
1. *You long for special care but fear it won't last, so you tend to cling anxiously and alien-ate others (as with Elizabeth your partner), leaving you still uncared for.*
2. *Feeling depressed leads you to drink or smoke dope and ignore problems which then build up making you feel low and even more depressed.*
3. *You receive care, but only if 'special', so you strive to create special claims but feel you must suffer to deserve it and so neglect yourself and become 'agitated' and drink or smoke dope.*
These patterns undoubtedly arose from the ways you coped with the limited options of your childhood; they seem to have given you some intimacy and relief but they have been costly …
Already in our relationship we have seen how you push to get me to provide comfort and hold you through this difficult time when you are no longer in a relationship with a woman who will rescue you. By learning to recognise these patterns in therapy you will be better able to explore more satisfactory ways of doing things.
You have said you have been impressed with my help (a bit like the honeymoon phase in one of your relationships), but I suspect it will be hard to imagine how short and limited

our relationship is (16 sessions), and how you will cope with tolerating the disappointment when I cannot meet your current pattern of neediness …

Our aims in therapy will include:
— *learning to be less clinging and demanding in relationships*
— *getting help with your health*
— *focusing on working for your degree and on more concrete 'out there' activities and achievements.*

With best wishes

He was moved and tearful as the letter was read out. He said he had learnt more in five sessions than in four years of previous therapy. He began to see his helplessness within a wider emotional narrative. The state of forlorn 'agitation'— which seemed deeply part of him and just swept over him, especially at night-time, had hitherto seemed beyond his understanding. Now it began to be seen as part of an emotional story. However, he did not like the ending being mentioned in the letter. He asked if he would be better after 16 sessions.

The course of therapy

Before the next session he left a note in which he said his relationship with Elizabeth his partner was definitely over and could he have an extra session? I said I couldn't see him for an additional session and he later left a letter saying he wanted to stop the therapy:

I think I am going to have to stop the therapy for now. It has been very revealing but is too much at the moment and I must concentrate on my studies. I am writing so you can allocate tomorrow's session to someone else but if you would like to see me I am on the phone. If not, then I 'd like to thank you for all your hard work and for helping me to see so many things about myself which need to be changed.

On the telephone I said I felt strongly that we should have one session to review how his wish to end fitted into the patterns we had already identified. At the next session he said that he had felt very relieved by my telephone call. He wanted to continue and had had a 'breakthrough' by seeing all the places on the diagram where he could do different things. In particular he had made a feature of having 15 minutes' self-care time when he felt most agitated. He had other plans of self-care such as going to the gym and not smoking at night. He described what he called his third person perspective as a way of standing back and looking at himself: not being in a state but looking at the state he was in. A simplified version of the diagram showing the enactment of a key reciprocal role procedure is shown in Figure 2.1.

From session 4, Bobby had rated his progress on his aims of recognising and revising his identified problematic procedures (TPPs). Figure 2.2 shows a rating sheet for the first of these.

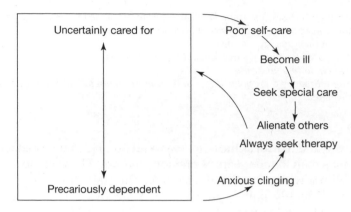

Figure 2.1 Simplified version of SDR for Bobby showing one key RRP

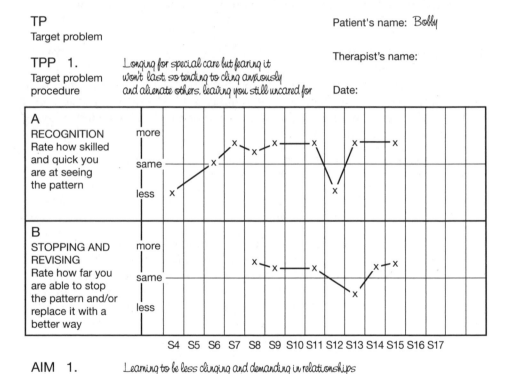

Figure 2.2 Rating sheet for target problem procedure 1 for Bobby

Termination

In session 11, he noted he had five more sessions and asked if I could spread them out to make them last. We talked about his continuing health problems (a recurring theme) and wondered if he might now seek medical help. We looked at it in terms of the diagram and linked this to the old pattern of having to suffer to achieve or get love. We discussed how he could continue to work after therapy on how my 'abandonment' might be a helpful experience. He seemed helped by the idea of asking for realistic care from self and others. We wondered what a realistic 'okay' relationship with Elizabeth might be like. He talked about me abandoning him and how maybe he could learn from it. He paid detailed attention to his not sleeping pattern and noted that the 'agitation' was provoked by thoughts about how forlorn and neglected he was. We wondered what he could do to change his going to bed routines and how to promote self talk whenever he did wake in the night so as to dispute the forlorn feeling.

Bobby rang two days before the final session asking if it had to be the last. I restated that it was tough, but asked how he would learn about managing on his own, using what he had learnt with me, if he did not end the therapy. In the final session, as he read out his goodbye letter, he was in tears and had to stop several times. He wrote:

> *I can see how I throw myself in and expect too much. I don't know how to hold back. I tried to rope you in to make it impossible for you to reject me, but you were having none of it and I appreciate that. I can't give my whole self to people and expect to be looked after. I have to look after myself. I am beginning to look after myself. The few months we have been seeing each other have seen possibly the biggest changes in me, at least in my way of thinking. I have worked hard at it and will continue to do so because I have seen that it is possible to change. I'm feeling more able to live in the 'external reality' and this seems to have come from protecting my 'self' a bit more.*

Follow-up

In the follow-up session after his final exams, Bobby said he could now see the revised diagram in his head and use it. He could now tolerate shifts in mood, which still came but were now less extreme. There had been some tough times and he had rung Samaritans once just to talk to someone. Things were not all resolved and there were still times of despair, but he felt he could survive and work his way out of, or into, relationships with more mutual understanding.

He had seen his GP and was seeing the asthma nurse regularly. He had resumed a more balanced relationship with Elizabeth, was sleeping better and living a more healthy, self-caring lifestyle. He had been able to sustain academic work with a more normal sleep pattern, obtained a degree and had a more realistic career goal not based on fame. He no longer thought he needed long-term therapy and was on better terms with his mother, brother and sisters.

FURTHER READING

Key papers marking the evolution of CAT are Ryle (1979, 1985, 1991, 1997b) and Leiman (1992, 1997). The main developments are reviewed in Leiman (1994a). The early integration of cognitive and behavioural ideas and the transformed account of some psychoanalytic notions incorporated in the Procedural Sequence Model is described in Ryle (1982). Further CAT critiques and modifications of psychoanalytic ideas are presented in Ryle (1991, 1994, 1996, 1997b). The present volume is the last of a series in which the initial process of integration has been followed by the increasingly clear articulation of a distinct theory and practice. To date, no systematic critiques of CAT have been published. Many other integrative models exist, of course, the majority being described in Stricker and Gold (1993).

Chapter 3

DEVELOPMENT OF THE SELF:
BACKGROUND CONSIDERATIONS

SUMMARY

The theory and practice of CAT are based upon a consideration of current evolutionary psychology, genetics and developmental neurobiology and psychology. The CAT understanding of developmental psychopathology takes, in particular, detailed account of the role of experiences of emotional deprivation and trauma. Early interpersonal experience is seen to be fundamental to the development of the self and in particular to the acquisition of a repertoire of reciprocal role procedures. The development of this repertoire is partly influenced by individual temperament and occurs on the basis of our innate predisposition to intersubjectivity and joint sign-mediated activity.

The theory and practice of CAT is based on a clearly defined and radically social concept of the self. The mature self in this view represents the outcome of a process of development during which a genotypic self with a set of inherited psychological characteristics, including an evolutionary predisposition to intersubjectivity, interacts reciprocally with care-givers in a given culture and in the process 'internalises' that experience. In CAT the social meanings and cultural values intrinsic to such interactions are seen as contributing fundamentally to the dynamic structure of the self. This developmental process and its implications for psychological change is seen as critical in determining the focus of psychotherapy and will be considered in some detail in the next chapter. Before doing so we shall outline some of the background factors which play a role in determining and influencing the outcome of that process.

EVOLUTIONARY PSYCHOLOGY

There is an increasingly large and at times rather contradictory literature on the acknowledged effects of our evolutionary inheritance on our mental functions (Donald, 1991; Gilbert, 1992; Rose, 1995; Plotkin, 1997; Slavin and Kriegman, 1992; Tooby and Cosmides, 1992; Stevens and Price, 1996; McGuire and Troisi, 1998; Evans and Zarate, 1999). Since we are, in evolutionary terms, simply another product of that process, it is accepted increasingly that we carry within us certain evolutionarily more 'primitive' although originally adaptive predispositions to behave in certain ways at certain times and in certain circumstances. However, unlike 'lower' order species whose activities may be determined almost exclusively by stimulus-evoked, 'all or nothing', instinctual patterns, our species is characterised by a remarkable capacity, consequent to the development of our large frontal cerebral cortex (Innocenti and Kaas, 1995), to reflect upon and modify such patterns. In addition, our evolutionary development has given us the potential to acquire a capacity for intersubjectivity and an extraordinary ability, acquired through the process of socially meaningful, joint and reciprocal interactions, to 'read' or 'be in' the minds of others. It has been suggested (see Evans and Zarate, 1999) that this ability enabled our ancestors to exist effectively and advantageously in large groups, which have, for some time, been our 'environment of evolutionary adaptedness'. It is suggested that the ability to understand each other's minds and motives has been and continues to be of critical importance for our species and is reflected in our preoccupation with social intercourse and communication—including our predilection for gossip! More seriously, this also implies that whatever meaning or fulfilment there is in our lives is fundamentally social, a position with important implications for both psychotherapy and politics in our view.

However, discussion of our capacity to develop a 'theory of mind' by some of these authors within evolutionary psychology does not appear to have included serious consideration of the important role played during individual development by the internalisation of socially meaningful, interpersonal experience in generating mental structures and capabilities. Likewise, there is little explicit discussion of how natural selection occurred while people lived collectively and hence favoured what was adaptive to social life, nor the contribution of this process to the formation of mind, despite the stress on the general importance of culture in human evolution by many authors (see below). Most evolutionary psychologists, in common with even more recent psychodynamic theorists, propose an understanding of mind and self which is characterised by a cognitive, or at best an intersubjective, monadism. In this formulation, interpersonal experience is seen as 'mapped' or 'represented' within fundamentally individual, mental structures. Curiously, this very Western view of the self would almost certainly be incomprehensible to most members of traditional or 'primitive' societies. In this respect, the CAT model may well have something important to contribute to a dialogue with evolutionary psychology.

These various features of our evolutionary inheritance, in particular our capacity to be shaped by developmental experience and the internalisation of social meanings and cultural values, has largely contributed to the historic conceptual conflict between the protagonists of the effects of 'nature' and 'nurture'. This 'for or against' argument should, by now, be essentially redundant. As Plomin (1994) has remarked, the 'nature-nurture' debate is centred nowadays around the hyphen.

THE EVOLUTION OF COGNITIVE CAPACITIES AND OF CULTURE

In the view proposed here, although humans retain their biological characteristics, the sources of their evolutionary success are to be found in the ways in which they are radically *unlike* animals. These include notably (1) the enormously enlarged brains which enabled our ancestors to replace stereotypic and predetermined techniques with flexible, intelligent solutions in the struggle to wrest a living from nature and (2) the development of faculties, eventually speech, which enhanced their ability to work together and to pass on knowledge from one generation to the next. As a result of these changes, cultural evolution became a dominant factor in how humankind evolved biologically. As new social forms radically altered the behaviours and qualities of individuals likely to aid survival of the group, individuals evolved who could learn the skills and values of the particular group they were born into, that is, people whose nature it was to be formed by nurture. There is also direct biological evidence for the social formation of mind, namely the shaping of neural pathways which occur during early development. To quote a review of the field by Eisenberg (1995) 'Major brain pathways are specified by the genome; detailed connections are fashioned by, and consequently reflect, socially mediated experience in the world.'

How evolution led to the remarkably flexible and capable mind of modern humans will now be considered in more detail. Much of the following account is drawn from Donald (1991) who, by adding understandings drawn from cognitive psychology to the traditional sources in archaeological, anthropological and biological studies, offers, in our view, a convincing and fascinating reconstruction of the main stages in the evolution of the modern mind.

Four million years ago, our ancestors the australopithecines already shared food and labour and formed nuclear family structures. One and a half million years ago *Homo erectus*, blessed with a much larger brain, managed to build shelters, use fire, and develop better tools. Over the following period the size of the brain compared to that of other mammals continued to increase markedly, with a last period of rapid growth occurring 0.3 million years ago. These changes were accompanied by another significant anatomical development: the evolution of the human vocal tract, with its capacity for the rapid generation of differentiated sounds allowing speech.

Donald describes how contemporary chimpanzees are capable of flexible and non-stereotypical ways thinking and of relating and how their social organisation is dependent on their capacity to remember 'large numbers of distinctly individual learned dyadic relationships'. The development of the human brain from an equivalent level went through a number of intermediate stages, each conveying greater cognitive and social advantages. During the first of these (the Mimetic culture), non-linguistic skills in representing, differentiating, rehearsing and communicating were elaborated. Knowledge could now be contained and communicated using metaphoric activities; both tool-using and sign-using were established. This allowed the greater cohesion of social groups, which developed complex structures sustained by group rituals. The semantic and social structures that developed over the million or more years of this phase were accompanied by developments in the brain which prepared the way for the addition of symbolic language, but it appears that this developed independently, existing alongside the mimetic modes which persisted and are still a powerful aspect of human communication. The evolution of the larynx and the acquisition of language in the Mythic age provided the individual with the basis for the conscious mobilisation of mental capacities. It also enormously enhanced the cohesion and purposefulness of human society by linking, in stories and myths, the guiding values and meanings of the group. The power of oral transmission is illustrated by the account of an Australian aboriginal myth which incorporates accurate descriptions of a terrain, recently identified, which has been under the sea for the past 8,000 years (Tudge, 1996). Another example is provided by New Zealand Maoris, whose ancestors arrived in a small number of boats. Traditional accounts trace the ancestry of different groups to one or other of these boats and genetic studies have provided confirmation of the groupings.

Speech is now the dominant mental function because, with it, both memories of events and descriptions of the skills and sequences which can be conveyed mimetically can be described and communicated in abstract, generalised forms. Language opened the way for the theoretic culture we now inhabit, where we are capable of analytic, de-contextualised forms of thinking which the earlier systems could not sustain. These functions were sustained in turn by the manufacture of pictorial or sculpted artefacts, perhaps initially serving mythic functions, and the development of external, physical mnemonic devices such as notched sticks, indicators of astronomical events, maps and eventually, 8,000 years ago, writing. The development of written records greatly increased the accumulation and transmission of information. External symbolic storage, vaster than any single mind could conceivably hold, has now become a dominant factor in human thought. Just as the development of tools and machines enormously extended people's physical capacity to change material objects so the brain developed the capacity to extend enormously the power of thought.

EVOLUTIONARILY PRE-PROGRAMMED PSYCHOLOGICAL TENDENCIES

Many authors (reviewed in Gilbert, 1992; Stevens and Price, 1996; McGuire and Troisi, 1998) suggest that pre-programmed patterns, analogous to those triggered by the 'innate releasing mechanisms' described by ethologists, may underlie our tendency to think and act in certain ways in certain circumstances. The Jungian concept of archetypes can be seen as similar. Whilst requiring careful attention as partial, possible determinants of human behaviour, we consider that to exaggerate their importance can be as reductive and misleading as some of the attempts by earlier sociobiologists to explain culture in terms of the enactment of 'hard-wired' biological tendencies. However, according to these writers there are highly stereotyped, ritual behaviours seen throughout the animal kingdom associated with, for example, aggression, status-seeking, mating or care-eliciting and care-giving. The power and apparent 'irrationality' of such responses is well exemplifed by the experience of falling in love or the dedicated preoccupation of a nursing mother with her baby. Gilbert (1992) has described the predisposition to enact such phyogenetically evolved 'biosocial goals' as 'mentalities'. This concept combines affects, action tendencies and cognitive and attentional structures. These are manifest in social life from early on and could be seen as analogous to or contributing to the formation of RRPs. But since Gilbert does not consider the formative role of interpersonal experience or the processes of internalisation and cultural transmission, it is not clear that these 'mentalities' can be attributed exclusively to innate, inherited structures.

The behavioural patterns (for example care- or proximity-seeking behaviour) described by attachment theorists can also be seen to be subsumed within such repertoires. However, as pointed out by Gilbert (1992), they would be, phylogenetically, only one of many adaptive developmental behaviours rather than the all-important one as some writers in that tradition have more recently tended to suggest. However, attachment theorists (Bowlby, 1988) have properly pointed to the life-long importance of negotiation of issues relating to attachment and loss. In parallel, writers such as Stevens and Price (1996) have described the concept of 'frustration of archetypal intent', by analogy with the ethological phenomenon of the 'search for the object never known'. This could manifest, for example, in the case of someone who never had the experience of a good mother, as a life-long search for this never-experienced, perhaps idealised, relationship. This phenomenon can be recognised clinically and described in terms of role enactments and can be important to identify and work with.

Primitive, stereotypic responses to highly stressful situations provide perhaps more definite examples of such pre-programmed predispositions. These would include freezing or attacking responses to threat, the sensitivity to shame which we share with other social animals and the resort to dichotomous, 'black and white' thinking derived in evolution from the critical need to distinguish friend from foe, or safe from dangerous situations. Some of these responses, particularly dichotomous thinking, may be a focus of psychotherapy, as may the stereotypic consequences of prolonged stress or trauma on the developing self (Kalsched, 1998). Primitive responses such as these are most often elicited in those who have been subject to threat and abuse during their own upbringing and can manifest in social phenomena such as racism, aggressive nationalism and stigmatising behaviour (see Zulueta, 1993). Expression of these will also be determined by the history, power relations and dominant ideology of different societies. By contrast, those who have been treated with love and respect tend to re-enact those roles and are capable of more considered responses to stressful situations. It should be noted, despite the history of our past century, that the dominant tendencies enacted by our species have been, and potentially are, those of cooperation, creativity and mutual interdependence.

GENETICS AND TEMPERAMENT

It is well documented by behavioural geneticists, as well as by evolutionary psychologists, that we arrive in this world with a considerable psychological 'baggage' in the form of both individual temperamental characteristics and also more general evolutionary predispositions to behave in certain ways in certain situations (Plomin, 1994; Aitken and Trevarthen, 1997; Stevens and Price, 1996; Gilbert, 1992; McGuire and Troisi, 1998). Thus, the human infant is very far from being a completely malleable and motiveless, naive being or 'tabula rasa'. Much of the variance in observed patterns of human behaving and thinking (personality) is due to variation in inherited temperamental factors. Of these, the so-called 'big 5' (neuroticism, extraversion–introversion, openness to experience, conscientiousness and agreeableness) are perhaps the best known and documented (Costa and McCrae, 1992; Deary and Power, 1988). It is similarly clear that a varying but significant amount of the variance in the prevalence of frank mental disorders is due to genetic factors. This may range from about 0.5 (i.e. about half) for manic depression and the schizophrenias (as tested in identical twins reared apart), to much lower but still significant figures for 'neurotic' disorders such as depression and anxiety (Plomin, 1994). These figures indicate the need to understand what sort of factors contribute to the remainder of the variance.

The implications of this for psychotherapy are considerable since it implies that a certain amount of what may be described as personality may be the effects of temperament rather than of developmental experience. As such they may be relatively immutable, raising the question of whether, in that case, the task of psychotherapy may be, in part, to help an individual to live with and manage their particular temperamental characteristics as well as to make sense of their consequences. The effects of temperament are rarely direct and will, importantly, include the complex effects whereby the behaviour of a child will actually modify the responses of others and so their experience (Plomin, 1994), which will then, in turn, be internalised. Thus a demandingly aggressive or a highly anxious child will elicit very different responses from a parent compared to a more placid sibling. This mechanism ('non-shared family environment') accounts in part for the very different developmental experience which siblings may have had within the same family.

These inherited characteristics may be usefully conceived of overall in terms of 'vulnerability' and 'resilience' factors (Rutter et al., 1997; Plomin, 1994; and see Figure 4.1), although it does seem that some factors could operate as one or the other depending on circumstances. Thus, an increased predisposition to anxiety (broadly speaking 'neuroticism' in terms in the 'big 5') could compound the damaging effects of growing up in an abusive family resulting in a severely damaged self. However, lack of anxiety in another dangerous setting, such as a primitive jungle or a modern motorway, could result in disastrous consequences. Similarly, a degree of temperamental disinhibition could be invaluable in a creative artist or business entrepreneur but in a chronically stressful, unsupported setting could result in overt manic depression in someone so predisposed. It has been suggested that an important resilience factor may be an innate capacity for self-reflection or 'mentalisation' and the ability, for example as a child, to imagine beyond an immediately stressful or traumatic family situation (Fonagy and Target, 1997). It is not yet clear, however, how far such inabilities are innate and how far a consequence of developmental deprivation or damage. Genetic variability may also account for a tendency to dissociation (Silk, 2000). This may also have been evolutionarily adaptive in the face of overwhelming anxiety or stress, but if chronically and excessively endured during a traumatic childhood may have catastrophic effects on the developing self. It has also been suggested that individuals with a predisposition to obsessional or perfectionistic behaviour are more vulnerable to developing disorders such as anorexia. Although these factors are not the immediate focus of psychotherapy, we suggest that it is important to bear them in mind, especially given a common psychotherapeutic tendency to attribute difficulties or psychopathology entirely to an individual's developmental history and to think that personality is malleable and 'mendable' in all cases.

Developmental neurobiology

Neurobiological processes are involved in the developmental mediation and internalisation of experience through the processes of perception, cognition and memory and the neurophysiological substrates of these are beginning to be a described in some detail (Schore, 1994; Glover, 1997; Toth and Cicchetti, 1998). However, it is inconceivable that the attempt to describe and account for higher mental function solely in physico-chemical terms will be successful. This was of course Freud's great aspiration a century ago as described in his 'Project for a Scientific Psychology'. This attempt is based on the fallacious belief that highly complex systems can be understood by assembling models of their component parts. In reality, when new properties emerge new paradigms are required. More recent versions of this attempt to account for mental functions in terms of disordered biology by describing abnormal molecules, anatomical structures or functional brain scans has been described as simply 'referential connectionism' (McGuire and Troisi, 1998). The limits of this project are further determined by the fact that essential aspects of higher mental functions represent also the internalisation of cultural values and relate to issues of meaning and purpose. The 'emergent property' that is mind (Post and Weiss, 1997), characterised by consciousness, a sense of self, and the experience of free will and of 'spirit' (Samuels, 1985) points to the need for understandings beyond those based on physico-chemical laws (Solms, 1995). Such understandings we see as implicit in the aims of psychotherapy.

It is well known that the first few years of life (including intrauterine life) are a period of particular neural plasticity when processes of neurological development and maturation are still occurring (Schore, 1994; Eisenberg, 1995; Fox et al., 1994). Hence, this is a period of particular vulnerability. It has been documented in increasing detail in both animal experiments and in humans that early experiences of deprivation, stress and trauma can have profound and long-lasting biological effects. These in turn will clearly distort or restrict the internalisation and subsequent enactment of the reciprocal role procedures central to the CAT model of development even if they do not fully account for their subtlety and complexity. Damaged relationship patterns have, for example, been reported in socially deprived primates whose social and cognitive development is severely impaired and in whom apparently permanent abnormalities of neurotransmitter function are seen (Schneider et al., 1998). In rats, post-natal or intrauterine stress has been observed to lead to lifetime vulnerability to states of anxiety and hyper-arousal (Glover, 1997). Chronic stress may generate permanent homeostatic abnormalities in the developing hypothalamo-pituitary-adrenal (HPA) system whilst in the extreme case of post-traumatic stress disorder (PTSD) in humans, gross anatomical abnormalities ('scarring') of the hippocampus have been seen on brain scan (Bremner et al., 1995). The latter are said to be mediated by the toxic effects of elevated levels of glucocorticoid hormones and of various neurotransmitters. These also have powerful effects on emotional memory and also on the re-experiencing and re-enactment of traumatic situations when triggered. Clearly such reactions will affect an individual's reciprocal role repertoire. As such it clearly needs to be borne in mind that some of the role enactments encountered in therapeutic and other situations may be determined in part by such biological damage. They may also be relatively refractory to insight-oriented therapeutic work and possibly need more behavioural techniques to treat and modify them (e.g. the recently introduced EMDR—eye movement desensitisation and reprocessing)

(Van Etten and Taylor, 1998; MacCulloch, 1999). It is not yet clear how far such neurobiological abnormalities are reversible or modifiable by treatment, whether psychological or pharmacological, although there are reports (see Robertson, 2000) that the brain, even at later stages of life, may remain more plastic than at first thought. It is of interest that the functional brain scan abnormalities reported in the orbito-frontal cortex in severe obsessive-compulsive disorder revert to a more normal picture following both drug and psychological (cognitive-behavioural) treatment (Baxter et al., 1992). This raises the fascinating possibility that, as well as neurobiological damage occurring through psychological causes such as stress or emotional deprivation, conversely, neurological changes may be brought about by psychological treatments. This is a further argument against any mutually exclusive biological or psychological models of mental disorder (see also Gabbard, 2000).

Implications of a trauma/deficit based model of psychopathology

This emerging body of neurobiological evidence, combined with sociological evidence such as the pioneering work of Brown and Harris on the social origins of depression (Brown and Harris, 1978), indicates that an important cause of psychological disorder is actual experience of trauma, abuse or deprivation. This also supports the hypotheses of various writers in, broadly speaking, the 'deficit' tradition of theories of psychopathology (see discussion in Bateman and Holmes, 1995). This would include historic figures such as Ferenczi (see Stanton, 1990), discredited at the time for holding such views on the importance of real life trauma and on the reparative aspects of psychotherapy, Sullivan (1953) with his emphasis on the damaging effects of stress and anxiety on development, some of the British object relations school such as Guntrip, Winnicott, Sutherland (see review by Sutherland, 1980) and Khan (1973) with his theory of subtle, 'cumulative' trauma. Bowlby (1988) and the attachment theory tradition he engendered produced important evidence on the developmental significance of adversity and trauma. Kohut's (1977) self psychology model departed radically from classical psychoanalytic theory in stressing the importance of empathic care-giving in development and therapy. Recent findings in the field of infant observation have also confirmed the damaging developmental effects of early deprivations (e.g. through maternal depression) (see review by Murray, 1992). This area overall is well reviewed in Zulueta (1993) and Mollon (1993).

In addition to the overt effects of early deprivation and trauma on mental health, more subtle, damaging effects on general health and well-being have also been demonstrated as a result of psychological 'attitudes' acquired during an upbringing in low status socio-economic groups (Bosma et al., 1999). These 'attitudes' can well be understood in terms of reciprocal role enactments.

Such a model of psychopathology also points up the need for strategies to identify developmental trauma and deprivation as it happens and to undertake preventative action. This has important social and political implications and has been in recent years an area of increasing interest in studies of child development and psychiatric epidemiology. Increasingly sophisticated analyses of populations at various degrees of risk are being undertaken along with definition of possible types of intervention which might reduce it (Mrazek and Haggerty, 1994; Albee, 1998). Some of these will be social rather than psychological. Apart from direct intervention with children, psychotherapy may, however, also play an important role in, for example, treatment of parents who may be at risk of damaging their children through their own disorders. Such models of developmental psychopathology may also play an important role in suggesting what sort of interventions, social or psychological, may be helpful. An innovative, CAT-based, early intervention for youngsters at risk of developing borderline personality disorder is currently being evaluated in Australia, the results of which will be of some considerable interest (Chanen, 2000).

IMPLICATIONS OF OUR EVOLUTIONARY PAST AND BIOLOGY FOR PSYCHOTHERAPY

Human personality is determined by the interaction between individual variations in the human genome and the practices, beliefs and language of the culture into which the individual is born. The scope for individual differentiation is huge, allowing genetically similar infants to grow into all the diverse contemporary and historical cultures. However, these cultural influences do not always prepare individuals well for the world into which they are born, and psychotherapists are engaged in trying to correct the resulting deformations. This may also involve them in identifying some of the requirements of the culture as damaging; the aim of therapy cannot be adaptation to every kind of political system.

The relationship of psychotherapy theory to the dominant beliefs and values of our contemporary societies is an area with political and moral implications which deserves more attention. The biological versus cultural debate is related to this: while psychotherapists need to accept the power of those biological factors which cannot be influenced by therapy, whether due to genetic or organic factors, theories which exaggerate biological and minimise cultural influences generate forms of treatment which in reality impose or justify a diminished status for the patient.

All therapies rely heavily on speech but few make much use of the concrete semiotic artefacts which, in evolutionary history, played so important a part in intellectual development. CAT makes use of writing and diagrams in the reformulation process just as our ancestors 10,000 years ago used their mnemonic devices, because the availability of these for re-reading and repeated application to events provides a much more powerful input than do purely verbal comments. One main purpose of reformulation is to make explicit, and therefore available to reflection, the patient's unreflected-upon interpersonal and internalised reciprocal role procedures. As mentioned above, chimpanzees can differentiate between a range of dyadic relationship patterns; through descriptive reformulation CAT opens these early learned patterns in humans to discussion and reflection, The use of words and symbolic devices does not mean that other forms of communication are left out, however, for much of the 'chemistry' of an established therapeutic relationship depends on 'mimetic' communication. What are often described by dynamic therapists as intuitive responses to 'the unconscious' are more probably reactions to unidentified mimetic communications, especially those not congruent with what is said, of which the patient may or may not be aware. The use of words or diagrams to explore and describe these can bring them into full awareness and into the therapeutic conversation.

The evolutionary story also suggests some ways in which CAT practice might be extended. For some people, as group therapists are aware, group experiences, with their capacity to mobilise parallel mimetic communications, have powerful alternative or additional effects to the dominantly verbal interchanges of individual therapy. For others, drawing and painting may provide a more powerful form of externalisation and symbolisation than language or the abstract diagrams of CAT; some CAT therapists do in fact combine the more 'conventional' tools with these methods. Role play and psychodrama, with their ritual components, combine the use of mimetic communication with the permitted expression of inhibited or forbidden affects. More active bodily involvement through dance, rhythmic exercises and music-making, which are essentially mimetic modes, have a long history as healing rituals in 'less developed' societies but are little used in ours. In treating psychological distress accompanied by somatic symptoms the fuller integration of physical treatments might be of value. These would address what in CAT terms would be seen as the incorporation and enactment of RRPs in body states and 'language'. This would also constitute a recognition of the way in which somatic symptoms may be understood as signs. The most widely applied methods in current use are those seeking to ease the secondary somatic effects of anxiety through relaxation, a procedure at once bringing ease and restoring some sense of control to the patient. Forms of meditation usually include physical relaxation as a means of diminishing symbolic mode thinking. These various procedures, it should be noted, are normally provided in therapeutic contexts which convey permission, acceptance or membership and serve to ease the demands and remedy the isolation experienced by many in our individualistic culture. It is to be hoped that, in the future, the indications for combining some of these methods with CAT will be evaluated.

Before considering in detail the therapeutic applications of CAT we shall next review its model of normal and abnormal development.

FURTHER READING

The issues considered in this chapter concern both evidence and interpretation. The extensive references in the text point to recent writing from various viewpoints. Of these, Donald (1991) provides an excellent synthetic account of the evolution of human mental processes, the paper by Eisenberg (1995) summarises the evidence for the impact of social experiences on the development of neural tracts and Stern (1985) provides a thoughtful and comprehensive consideration of observational studies and of their relation to psychoanalytic ideas. The paper by Aitken and Trevarthen (1997) offers an understanding of the early development of the self which has contributed to the position incorporated in CAT.

Chapter 4

NORMAL AND ABNORMAL DEVELOPMENT OF THE SELF AND ITS IMPLICATIONS FOR PSYCHOTHERAPY

SUMMARY

CAT is based upon a radically social concept of the self, which has important implications for psychotherapy. The mature 'phenotypic' self is understood to be the result of a process of development through which an original 'genotypic' self engages and interacts with others and 'internalises' the social meanings and cultural values implicit in these interactions. From a Vygotskian perspective, 'internalisation' is seen to involve sign mediation and, as it proceeds, to result in modification of the psychological structures involved. Such learning takes place optimally in the infant's 'zone of proximal development'. The CAT model also developed from a consideration of Kellyian personal construct theory, cognitive therapy and psychoanalytic object relations theory but differs increasingly from these in its emphasis on the social formation of mind, based on consideration of Vygotskian activity theory and Bakhtinian concepts of the dialogic self. These differentiate CAT from cognitive schema-based approaches or from psychoanalytic models of 'representation' of interpersonal experience and of the development of 'theory of mind', which, from a CAT perspective, are both seen as still essentially monadic and Cartesian. Abnormal development is understood in CAT as the internalisation of dysfunctional role procedures, the development of avoidant, defensive and symptomatic role procedures and failures or disruptions of integration of self processes. Therapeutic change is seen to depend on the creation of a non-collusive relationship with the patient informed by the joint creation of mediating tools such as letters and diagrams within a phased, time-limited relationship. By this means a long-standing repertoire of RRPs may be described and revised.

Psychotherapists aim to help their patients change how they experience, make sense of and manage their lives, seeking to free them from maladaptive, damaging or restrictive self processes. Psychotherapy is concerned principally, although by no means exclusively, with changing the consequences of early developmental experience. Different therapies have different understandings of these consequences and of how therapy may influence them. In this chapter we shall describe in some detail the CAT model of development of the self and its implications for psychotherapy.

THE CAT CONCEPT OF SELF

CAT is based on a clearly defined and radically social concept of the self. In this view the mature, individual, 'phenotypic' self is formed through a process of development during which an original, infant 'genotypic' self, with a set of inherited characteristics and certain evolutionary predispositions, interacts reciprocally with care-giver(s) in a given culture and in time psychologically internalises that experience and their 'voices'. These 'voices' and the patterns of relationship established, convey the values of the immediate family and the wider culture and contribute to the formation of a repertoire of reciprocal role patterns embodying action, thinking, feeling and meaning.

The processes of internalisation as described by Vygotsky, and introduced into CAT by Leiman (1992), will be presented later in this chapter. Combined with the ideas of Bakhtin they offer a transformation of object relations theories by embodying social, cultural and semiotic understandings. This 'dialogic' Bakhtinian view of the mature self is one which has come increasingly to influence the CAT model of development and mental activity. Leiman, in particular, by means of his technique of 'dialogical sequence analysis' (Leiman, 1997) has demonstrated that it is possible and productive to work explicitly with such 'voices' in psychotherapy. As he pointed out, an interest in the nature of the voices implicit in the phenomena of transference and countertransference has been of considerable interest to some object relations-oriented psychoanalysts, although the Vygotskian implications for psychotherapy of such a view of the self have not been pursued within that tradition.

The process of development of the self is depicted diagrammatically in Figure 4.1. This stresses the interaction between a genotypic self predisposed to inter-subjectivity and reciprocal role enactments (shown as protruding half circles). The outcome of this process of development is a mature, phenotypic self characterised by a repertoire of more or less adaptive reciprocal role procedures in which knowledge, memory, feeling, meaning and action are linked. These role procedures (shown as completed circles in Figure 4.1) operate internally ('self–self') as well as in interpersonal, 'self–other' relationships. In the healthy self these procedures would co-exist and complement each other in a seamless and integrated fashion. This also results in the unique, subjective sense of

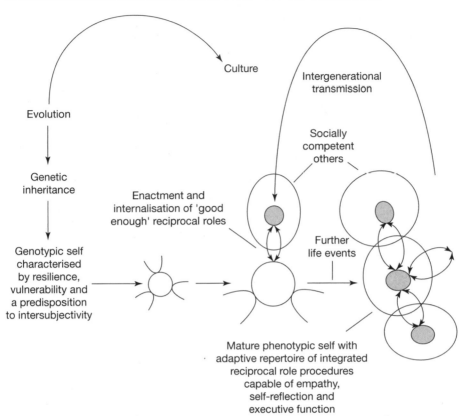

Culture

Intergenerational
transmission

Evolution

Socially
competent
others

Genetic
inheritance

Enactment and
internalisation of 'good
enough' reciprocal roles

Further
life events

Genotypic self
characterised
by resilience,
vulnerability and
a predisposition
to intersubjectivity

Mature phenotypic self with
adaptive repertoire of integrated
reciprocal role procedures
capable of empathy,
self-reflection and
executive function

Figure 4.1 CAT-based diagrammatic sketch of normal development of the self

continuous and integrated existence that most of us take for granted but which is so strikingly and distressingly disrupted in individuals suffering from severe personality disorder and more radically in acute psychotic disorders. This subjective sense of self is accompanied by a need to experience and achieve a sense of personal and social meaning embodied in narrative. This view of the importance of the narrative self, which we share with others (Spence, 1982; Schafer, 1992; White, 1995; Crits-Christoph, 1998; Holmes, 1998b; Meares, 1998), is explicitly addressed in CAT though reformulation. Ultimately, the process of development of self in relation to others results in an emergent capacity for self-reflection, empathy and executive function.

In CAT, many self processes are described in terms of relationships or dialogue with internalised figures or voices, for example the 'voice of conscience', although not every role has its recognisable figurehead. Nor is it clear how far the 'I' is unitary rather than a federation or from where, in the infant–caretaker conversation, it (I) finds its (my) voice; if individuals come to know themselves through early reciprocal relationships with others, with which role or voice is the 'I' identified? One might expect that in the internal dialogue with others the child would identify 'I' with the child's voice. But given that the 'I' is more a federation than a single nation, the internalised voices of others can dominate the dialogue, defining reality and providing a running commentary of judgement which may determine what aims may be pursued.

A fully centred, integrated self is a rare achievement, as famously noted by Fairbairn (1952). Through the course of adult life the inner conversation comes to include voices from all stages of life, embodying feared, hated, admired and loved others, each capable of representing systems of value and belief. 'I' may relate to, or be constituted by, all or any of these; the therapist's task is to identify the restrictive and damaging voices and to encourage the emergence of a more reflective, independent, superordinate and complex 'I'. To indicate this, CAT therapists often include in the diagram an image of an observing eye of the patient which is outside the system: the eye which becomes an 'I'. This underlines the central emphasis in CAT on extending and equipping conscious, self-reflective thought.

Several tensions or paradoxes are clearly also evident in such a conception of the self, similar to those which in the end dissuaded writers such as Kohut from attempting any formal definition of such an entity. The concept of 'self' is of course a reification of a complex set of dynamic phenomena and functions. It combines, as William James (1890) noted, the joint existence of the 'I' as unitary knower, experiencer and agent and the 'me' as an aggregate of bodily, social, spiritual and other aspects. It is thus, as Rycroft (1991) put it, 'not only an experiencing subject, but also its own object'. The 'self' is both a structural and an experiental, narrative-based, fluid entity (de Waele, 1995; Meares, 1998; Holmes, 1998b) capable of, although later very resistant to, change.

THE PERMEABILITY OF THE SELF

Although we have a strong sense of our individuality and separateness, we argue here that this individuality is essentially rooted and maintained in relationships with others. In this historical period, in which individualism is a dominant belief, this view is felt to be counter-intuitive. The full understanding of the ways in which external social and internal psychological processes are mutually influenced will require continuing empirical work but for this to be productive we believe the Vygotskian and Bakhtinian perspective or paradigm needs to be taken on board. The following notes written by Bakhtin (1986) provide, from a literary source, a persuasive and poetic account of the apparent paradox of the self's dependence on the other: 'I am conscious of myself and become myself only while revealing myself for another. The most important acts constituting self-consciousness are determined by a relationship toward another consciousness (toward a thou) ... not that which takes place within, but that which takes place on the boundary between one's own and someone else's consciousness, on the threshold … a person has no internal sovereign territory; he is wholly and always on the boundary; looking inside himself, he looks into the eyes of another or with the eyes of another.'

CONTRASTS WITH OTHER PSYCHODYNAMIC CONCEPTS OF SELF

The CAT model of self and its formation shares much with the different conceptions of self formulated historically by various writers. These would include notably Jung (see Samuels, 1985), although Jungians have tended to neglect the social dimensions of the self, Sullivan (1953) within the American 'interpersonal' tradition, and Kohut (1977). CAT shares with Kohut an emphasis on the damage which can be done to the developing self by empathic failure or overt neglect but places more emphasis on active abuse and trauma. CAT also shares a central interest in social conceptions of the self with group analysts. Foulkes, for example, saw individuals in a social fashion as being nodes in a 'social matrix' (Foulkes and Anthony, 1957). Later group analytic writers (e.g. Pines, 1996; Brown and Zinkin, 1994) have also developed an interest in the (Bakhtinian) dialogic aspects of the self.

Although object relations theorists were a major influence on the development of CAT, they were on the whole little interested in the concept of self. However, the current CAT model is close to some later authors in the object relations tradition such as Sutherland (1980), Ogden (1990), Sandler and Sandler (1998). It is also close to Bowlby (1988) and subsequent workers in the attachment theory tradition such as Fonagy and Target (1997) in their descriptions of the role of internalisation of early interpersonal experience. However, these authors do not take the further, and, in our view, important, conceptual leap of seeing the self as being essentially *constituted* by early, socially meaningful, sign-mediated interpersonal experiences, as opposed to 'representing' them mentally.

CULTURAL RELATIVITY OF MODELS OF SELF

Although the depiction of the self in Figure 4.1 reflects the individualistic concerns of our present culture, the CAT model should nonetheless be able to account for cultural variance in its development. The detached individualism of the Western world would be inconceivable in more traditional societies. The distinction between these extremes has been described in anthropological terms as that between 'egocentric-contractual' and 'sociocentric-organic' modes of social being (Shweder and Bourne, 1982). In terms of the model outlined, the self, its procedures and sense of narrative would be experienced in a traditional, closed culture as largely defined by existing relationships with others, implying both powerful attachments and restrictions (see review of these issues in Stevens, 1996). This contrasts with the 'inflation' of the detached self in our contemporary culture, manifest pathologically in those with, for example, 'narcissistic' disorders. Many recent authors have highlighted this 'narcissistic' trend as a feature of our 'post-modern' culture and have expressed concern about its deleterious effects on our (common) well-being (e.g. Frosh, 1991; Tacey, 1997; Symington, 1999; Gordon, 1998).

Models of psychotherapy must consider these issues if not resolve them. We believe that this is an area where the CAT model may have something to offer. Any model of psychotherapy should be able to generate some meaningful account of cultural and ethnic diversity as manifest in the range of individuals and their problems who may, or may not, present for treatment (Dalal, 1992; Krause, 1998; Bhugra and Bhui, 1998; Burman et al., 1998). In some cultures emotional distress may be experienced as somatic symptoms, in some as overt anxiety or depression. In others, including our own, distress may be 'repressed' through 'coping' or 'soldiering on' role procedures. Another example of how culture is manifest in terms of self-identity is evident in the ways in which meaning is ascribed to gender. The diversity and acceptability of gender-related role enactments is a clear, and in the West rapidly changing, example of how cultural values are internalised and enacted and one which again requires an appropriately sensitive model to address it. We would argue that some form of 'culture mapping' should be at least implicit within any model of psychother-apy and that psychotherapists should aim to be free of normative cultural values. CAT's practice of collaborative reformulation aims to reflect and under-stand what each patient brings to therapy, including their cultural assumptions and formation.

STUDIES OF INFANT DEVELOPMENT

One important influence on CAT has been the body of literature which has emerged over the past couple of decades from the observational work of infant researchers and developmental psychologists, notably Stern (1985), Murray (1992), Trevarthen (1993), Aitken and Trevarthen (1997), Tronick (1998), Brazelton and Cramer (1991); see also the review by Rutter et al. (1997). Many of the findings emerging from this fascinating body of work have illuminated in unexpected ways our understandings of early infant experience, abilities and development. In particular, they have contradicted and disconfirmed many of the speculative ideas developed previously within the psychoanalytic tradition. This work describes an infant busily engaged from birth in a process of recog-nising, remembering and interacting with significant others, notably mother, capable of perception and demonstrating an increasingly dominant intersubjec-tive focus. An important feature of this process is a collaborative playfulness which, from the beginning, is imbued with social meaning and makes use of

signs, as in Winnicott's famous 'transitional object'. The developmental importance of play, its role in creativity as well as its relevance to therapy was stressed
historically by Winnicott (1971). These issues have been further emphasised
and explored by later writers such as Trevarthen (1993), Meares (1993) and,
from a CAT perspective, parallels with the work of Winnicott have been noted
by Leiman (1992). The psychological predisposition to behave in these ways has
been described by Aitken and Trevarthen (1997) as an innate or 'intrinsic motive
formation' (IMF). These studies demonstrate a rudimentary, preverbal, sense of
self existing from birth. This sense of self is developed and transformed in the
context of a constant interaction with others, resulting eventually in a capacity
for self-reflection and a subtle awareness of others. This culminates normally in
the development of an empathic, imaginative understanding of others (a
'theory of mind') by the age of three to four years. These observations refute
earlier theories which suggested 'fused' or 'symbiotic' states in early development; rather than 'fusion', the presence of an exquisite intersubjectivity
between baby and mother is now stressed.

The predominant affects reported in these studies of infants and children are
those such as joyfulness and curiosity, albeit tempered by intermittent frustration, shame or depression (Trevarthen, 1993). These observational studies
provide no evidence for such postulated entities as a 'death instinct' or any
innate predisposition to destructiveness or to pervasive, endogenous anxiety.
They also refute the idea that infants can undertake the complex, mental opera-
tions such as 'splitting' or 'projection', postulated by Kleinian writers. The
damaging effects of insecurity and of externally generated anxiety on infant
development are, however, stressed in this literature and CAT would regard
this as a critically important developmental issue. Such damage would include
the effects of maternal depression and other ways in which the infant's need for
interaction are denied (Murray, 1992). Some of these effects are described in the
disturbed patterns of attachment behaviour observed in the 'strange situation'
experimental tests as developed by Ainsworth (Ainsworth et al., 1978). These
observational studies overall confirm the importance of real, social experience
in the formation of mind. They also confirm the Vygotskian emphasis (see
below) on the importance of a competent and enabling other in development
and on the active, collaborative participation of the infant in this process.

THE CONTRIBUTION OF VYGOTSKY'S IDEAS

Many of the criticisms made of psychoanalytic theory and practice during the
evolution of the CAT model and many features of the specific methods
employed were grounded in a wider perspective with the incorporation of a
Vygotskian perspective into CAT theory (Ryle, 1991; Leiman, 1992, 1994b, 1997).
Useful reviews of these ideas are given in Volosinov (1973), Burkitt (1991) and
Stevens (1996). This involved the application of ideas originally concerned with

intellectual development to the formation of the self. Four distinctive aspects of Vygotsky's thought which have been important for CAT theory will now be summarised:

1. The social formation of mind

Individuals are not self-generated or self-maintained. Born with a unique genetic endowment, their individuality is shaped and maintained through their relationships with others. This rejection of the monadic view of personality is shared with Mead and many others (see Burkitt, 1991, for a useful survey of the field). It emphasises that the activities of learning and becoming a person take place essentially in relation to others. In this process our activity and the acquisition of facts and of their meanings are inseparable. We do not store representations to which we apply a mayonnaise of meaning, representations are inextricably imbued with the meanings acquired in the course of our activity in an intersubjective universe, through our relation to others, notably parents, whose own meanings in turn will reflect those of the wider society. Child-rearing practices are guided by deliberate educational intent to a small extent only and their impact on the growth of the self is registered without conscious reflection on the part of the child.

Just as the realisation that the world was not the centre of the cosmos was resisted for a long time, so to think of the individual self as being formed and maintained in this social, interpersonal way, rather than as being the central source of thought and action, does seem to present major conceptual difficulties to many trainees and many members of our contemporary professional culture. This point is returned to at the end of this chapter.

2. Sign mediation

Long before language is acquired children are active in the presence of others who, by gesture, expression, movement, rhythms, mimicry, sounds and by jointly created rituals and symbols, communicate wishes, intentions and meanings. Repeated parental responses which reflect, amplify, control or ignore the child's actions and expressions offer a commentary on the child's activity, whether its object is a part of its own or its mother's body or a pattern of light or a spoon or a toy. These responses shape the child's understanding of the world and also constitute a defining example of the parent–child relationship and are hence a source of the sense of self.

From a Vygotksian viewpoint signs are created and used between people or within cultures. A well-known example of the creation of meaning and intention is provided by Clark's (1978) extension of Vygotsky's account of what happens when a child attempts to reach an object beyond its range. Whether it elicits from the caretaker assistance, encouragement or removal from possible harm, the fact of the response transforms the attempt into a gesture which, with repetition, can come to serve as a statement of intent and as a means of influ-encing the caretaker, that is to say it becomes a jointly elaborated interpsycho-logical sign (see Leiman, 1992).

Within psychoanalysis, Winnicott's understanding of the transitional object as standing for the mother in her absence was an example of such an interpsy-chological sign and was related to his insistence that the mother–baby dyad was the proper focus of attention for developmental psychology. Language is a shared system of signs which is 'de-contextualised' and hence flexible, allowing more abstract and theoretical forms of thought. It creates for the individual (as it did, in the course of evolution, for the species) the possibility of conscious self-knowledge and it represents the main human way of making sense of the world.

3. Internalisation

One of Vygotsky's well-known statements was: 'What the child does with an adult today she will do on her own tomorrow'. In this he was proposing a two-stage learning process whereby interpersonal activity, involving the develop-ment and use of skills and the acquisition of concepts which convey meaning, always precedes internalisation. In this way speech, which is first acquired in conversation with others, is practised in conversation with the self (the instruc-tions and commentaries and judgements of their own actions of young children bearing witness to this) before finally 'going underground' as the internal speech which is a main component of conscious thought. It is important to recognise that the 'protoconversations' between mother and infant (see Braten, 1988 and Trevarthen, 1993), and the reciprocal role relationships they embody, which are major determinants of the development of personality, involve pre-linguistic mediating tools and are, as a result, largely unavailable to conscious reflection. It will be clear from this account that internalisation of external inter-personal activities takes place by way of signs conveying meanings and is quite distinct from representation. An important feature of Vygotsky's concept of internalisation is that the process is also understood to transform the psycho-logical structures which mediate it.

4. The zone of proximal development (ZPD)

This is defined as the gap between what a child is able to do alone and what he or she could learn to do with the provision of appropriate help from a more competent other, who may be parent, teacher or peer. The good teacher will aim to work in the ZPD, not assuming that current performance is a measure of capacity, by providing what Bruner (Wood et al., 1976) described as a 'scaffold-ing' in the form of support and the provision and development of the appropri-ate conceptual tools which are then 'handed over' to the pupil. Importantly, this also implies a 'prospective' view of development (and of therapy). The aim is to explore where one can get to rather than describe where one came from, as in classical psychoanalysis. This has some commonality with the 'synthetic' and prospective therapeutic position stressed in analytical (Jungian) psychology (Samuels, 1985). It is clear that individual therapists must work within the ZPD but the same is true of the opportunities for learning through peers as provided in groups.

Vygotskian ideas in CAT

The Vygotskian ideas of relevance to therapy are those which are derived from the understanding of the formation of self processes. They indicate the need for the therapist to (1) 'scaffold' learning in the patient's ZPD (perhaps better labelled here the zone of proximal personality development, ZPPD), (2) provide a significant, empathic relationship in which (3) appropriate mediating 'tools' are created. The relevance of this fertile concept of scaffolding to therapy was noted in Ryle (1982) and had some influence on the later development of CAT; through this, the object relations ideas in CAT were modified in a way emphasising actual experience.

In their exploration of the world children constantly encounter a reality which is imbued with the meanings conveyed by others. Through the early joint, and the later, increasingly sign-mediated, activity of the mother–infant dyad (Leiman, 1994b), children learn both the meanings of reality and the definitions of self and other. The 'learning' involved in personality development differs from intellectual learning in many ways. Formal rules of conduct and explicit social norms have a small and late impact compared to the indirect transmission of values and assumptions about the world and the self through the child's joint activities with others in the early years. These formative experiences are the source of most of the issues addressed in psychotherapy. What is learned through them is, to a greater or lesser degree, unreflected upon. This is not to say that later experiences of deprivation, adversity or frank abuse and trauma may not also have profound or catastrophic effects on mental health.

The child's sense of self and emergent repertoire of reciprocal roles will largely reflect the style in which the scaffolding for early learning is supplied. For example, this may be sensitive, over-controlling, inconsistent, abusive or deficient, and will determine how small or large a range of possibility was conveyed and how much support and how much space for initiative seems to have been offered to the child. The values and procedures governing the sense of self and of others will be shaped and limited in these ways. Therapists need to work with their patients by identifying these restrictions and distortions by offering a different, respecting and accurate scaffolding in the patient's ZPPD.

The use of these metaphors of scaffolding and of the ZPPD offer crucial insights into the process of therapy and will recur through this book. They must be used with caution in one respect: the zone is not a place and the scaffolding is not a structure and neither is static; as development and therapy proceed both undergo continual revision. With change from therapy or other influences the extent of the zone may be extended and new forms of scaffolding may be called for.

DEVELOPMENTAL STUDIES OF ROLE ACQUISITION

The key importance of reciprocal roles in CAT theory was presented in Ryle (1985). It was derived from early work with the dyad grid and from clinical experience and involved in particular a restatement of ideas put forward by Ogden (1983). From a quite different background, the basic importance of reciprocal roles in early development are described by Oliviera (1997, p. 116) in her summing-up of a detailed and sensitive Vygotskian study of interactions between children in day care aged between one and six. She writes: 'From birth, the child is involved in social matrices in which meanings are constructed in each baby–caregiver dyad. Then, in the dynamic process of coordination of the roles that the partners assume in the here-and-now situation, a confrontation of needs, goals and senses is created. While playing roles ... the individual has to follow, not necessarily in a conscious manner, a way of acting that involves complex abilities, dealing with postures, gestures and emerging representation... Children become able to master several role relationships... while interacting with others with their own and maybe opposite intentions. The as-if atmosphere created in symbolic play and in other situations ... allows them to examine and modify some rules and images mediating their interactions'.

Oliviera's study traced the development of forms of collaboration from the one-year-old's use of expressive gestures and reciprocal imitation through the creation by two-to-four-year-olds of 'a collage of fragments of experiences' integrated by a range of signs or 'starters', including the use of language to take turns and reverse roles. Between four and six this 'memory in action' is increasingly replaced by speech and by rule-governed playing as the process of alternate imitation and reciprocation continues.

Oliviera's paper serves as a reminder of the extent to which other children are involved in the acquisition of reciprocal roles, but it is important to recognise the particular power of parents who may impose rather than negotiate their reciprocal role patterns and who have the power to define the agenda. The parents' personal restrictions and distortions may create idiosyncratic and confusing patterns and they may be unable to supply mediating concepts with which to make sense of some aspects of reality. This last point can be underlined by paraphrasing Vygotsky as follows: 'what the child does not do or say with the adult today she will not do or say on her own tomorrow'.

Further evidence for the powerful way in which observed and experienced role enactments are internalised and re-enacted by children comes from a fascinating projective test known as the 'the teddy bears' picnic' developed by

Mueller (1996). In this test, young children are asked to describe what would happen next during a story about a picnic, using teddy bears and props such as a cart and picnic basket. The range of responses to imaginary situations, such as the cart getting a puncture, is remarkable. In the case of 'daddy' teddy bear, for example, the child may describe a calm, reassuring and problem-solving response or, at the other extreme, an angry and abusive outburst directed towards 'mummy'. These results correlate well with the quality of the family background and with a child's psychopathology, much of which might have been undetected by conventional clinical interviewing. These descriptions clearly demonstrate the fundamental and pervasive effect the experience of such family role enactments has on the developing internal world of the child and on how they will be, for the most part unconsciously, re-enacted, in this case by proxy. Many other projective tests can be interpreted similarly in terms of reciprocal role enactments.

BAKHTINIAN CONTRIBUTIONS

Although Vygotsky and Bakhtin were contemporaries and worked in overlapping fields they did not collaborate and their perspectives were different in important ways. Leiman (1992) introduced the ideas of both into CAT thinking and has drawn on the latter to propose a 'dialogic' model of the self (1997). In a recent paper, Cheyne and Tarulli (1999) offer a further, illuminating discussion of the implications of the differences between Vygotsky and Bakhtin which, although at first reading apparently rather esoteric, in our view merits consideration. What follows here draws on and attempts to summarise their work.

Vygotsky was primarily concerned with the ways in which the skills and knowledge of the culture were acquired by the child. A narrow interpretation of his theory of the social formation of mind would define the parent or teacher as an agent or interpreter of the wider culture, aiming to transmit what the culture values and knows to the receptive child. For Bakhtin, on the other hand, the emphasis is different; for him, open-ended dialogue is seen as the essential and most valued basis of human consciousness: 'To live means to participate in dialogue: to ask questions, to heed, to respond, to agree and so forth. In this dialogue a person participates wholly and throughout his whole life: with eyes, lips, hands, soul, spirit, with his whole body and deeds.' (Bakhtin, 1984, p. 293). Dialogue is a fundamental human activity; every utterance will be directed to an addressee who may be 'an immediate participant-interlocuter in an everyday dialogue, a differentiated collective of specialists…, a more or less differentiated public, ethnic group, contemporaries, likeminded people, opponents and enemies, a subordinate, someone who is lower, higher (Bakhtin, 1986 p. 95).

To this model of dialogue Bakhtin adds a highly significant idea, that of the third voice or 'superaddressee'. In the address of the first (e.g. parent, teacher, therapist) voice to the second (child, pupil, patient) voice there is this implicit third voice, representing the wider culture or some part of it. The third voice (superaddressee) legitimises the first one who is in effect its conduit to the second voice. What is transmitted might be the current paradigm of a branch of science, the membership rules of a club, the articles of faith in a religion, the definition of gender roles, and so on. The social formation of mind, in this view, can be seen as a distillation of the whole range of human history and culture, while being inevitably focused and filtered by the particular time and place and family into which the child is born.

The discussion by Cheyne and Tarulli of the forms of dialogue employed as scaffolding sets the comments made above on the effect of different styles of parenting in a wider context. Drawing on Bakhtin's ideas they propose a spectrum of scaffolding styles from the authoritative 'Magistral' dialogue typical of religious training in the Middle Ages through the 'Socratic' questioning dialogue to the 'Menippean' upturnings and carnival. The voice of Menippean dialogue is described (Cheyne and Tarulli, 1999) as a mocking and cynical questioning after the Menippean satire which Bakhtin considered and associated closely with the notion of carnival. The 'Magistral' voice provides a restrictive scaffolding which imposes compliance on the pupil or initiate. In the 'Socratic' form of dialogue the scaffolding is less rigid; the first voice (parent, teacher etc.) will question the second (child, pupil) but may in turn be questioned. Through this, the child, pupil or patient not only receives a broader and more complex introduction to the conceptual tools of the culture but may actively enter into dialogue, using, modifying and elaborating the ideas provided by the other voices and not necessarily arriving at an agreed conclusion. This is clearly the preferred therapeutic mode, but Cheyne and Tarulli, in an interesting aside, point out that some psychotherapies, while supposedly 'Socratic', in reality impose a disguised form of the 'Magistral' approach in which clients are taught to ask the right questions. In a developing 'Socratic' dialogue the relation between teacher and pupil becomes decreasingly hierarchical and increasingly mutual. As a result, the assumptions of the third voice may also be questioned. From this often liberating scepticism of the child, pupil or patient (or citizen) more extreme refusals may emerge in the increasingly undermining, mocking, seemingly comic but also tragic and potentially violent and destructive 'Menippean' dialogue.

The internal dialogue of psychotherapy patients inevitably bears traces of their childhood scaffolding. Some bear signs of the childhood internalisation of harsh 'Magistral' scaffolding (or in more extreme cases of persecution and cruelty); others may convey the chaos and confusion of an essentially tragic 'Menippean' revolt against such harshness and others again show the lack of structure consequent upon the absence of adequate scaffolding. Psychotherapists need to provide a reparative scaffolding, explicitly 'Socratic', respecting and caring, creating descriptions of current procedures in words and diagrams which open for reflection the patterns which have operated automatically since their early formation.

It is of interest that whole cultures may be characterised by certain dominant modes and voices in this fashion. Protestant cultures, for example, would be partly characterised by harshly self-critical (or 'Magistral') voices and the task of therapy may in fact be at times to work explicitly with a patient to question internalised culturally derived voices.

MODELS OF INDIVIDUAL DEVELOPMENT AND THEIR RELATION TO CAT

Psychoanalytic models

In the early stages of CAT the model of development was based on the attempt to restate psychoanalytic object relations theories in accessible language (for an account see Ryle, 1982). Developments in the field since that time, introducing concepts such as 'internal working models' and 'implicit relational knowledge', have to some extent paralled the development of the CAT model, although these developments appear to have had little impact on psychoanalytic practice. Nonetheless, object relations theories made a considerable contribution by indicating the importance of early development in determining personality, by offering an account of how parental figures were 'internalised' to form a part of the personality and by recognising the parallel, linked features of intrapsychic and interpersonal processes and their emergence in transference relationships. Many psychoanalysts have, however, remained preoccupied with innate structures and processes, the detection and understanding of which has appeared to depend for the most part on theoretical invention. Historically, the only clinical confirmation sought for many psychoanalytic theories and practice was the assent given by analysands to interpretations based upon them. The resulting constructions offered infinite scope for in-house debate, but as a basis for understanding early development such theories are long overdue for radical dismantling.

The evolving CAT model aimed to offer an account which was compatible with the growing body of observational research, especially of infant–mother interactions, which over the last two decades has offered a major challenge to conventional psychoanalytic tenets, particularly those within the Kleinian tradition, concerning the qualities and capacities attributed to infants and the timetable of development. Stern (1985, p. 255) concludes his survey of the implications of observational research for a model of development by insisting on the primacy of experience over fantasy, as follows: 'It is the actual shape of interpersonal reality, specified by the interpersonal invariants that really exist, that helps determine the developmental course'. This assertion has major implications for certain forms of psychodynamic psychotherapy. In some of these, the traditional aim to construct, by interpretation, the unremembered past and the implicit requirement to find evidence for the effects of such entities as the

Oedipus complex or for a 'death instinct' have deflected attention from the indirect evidence for, or memories of, childhood experiences presented by patients. Even the increasing emphasis on 'here and now' interpretations of transference remained constrained by these theoretical requirements. There still appears to be a reluctance within the psychoanalytic tradition to discard old theories although to some extent these issues are now being reconsidered in ways more consistent with observational studies and convergent with developments in CAT.

The recognition of the importance of intersubjectivity has, in some quarters, altered the traditional interpretive stance and the description of 'implicit relational knowledge' and of its modification through the 'shared implicit relationship of therapy' by the Process of Change Study Group (Beebe, 1998; Lyons-Ruth, 1998; Stern et al., 1998; Tronick, 1998) has some parallels with the CAT model of reciprocal role procedures and their modification in therapy. Implicit relational knowledge is described by this group as procedural and is distinguished from what is conscious and from what is dynamically repressed. The recognition of this kind of knowledge in the development of CAT was first based on the experience of feeding back repertory grid analyses to patients (Ryle, 1975). Implicit relational knowledge is seen to create an intersubjective field which includes reasonably accurate sensings of each person's ways of being with others, a process described in CAT as the enactment of reciprocal role procedures (Ryle, 1985). Description of this process has, of course, become fundamental to CAT theory and practice. In the 'dyadic expansion of consciousness' hypothesis Tronick (1998), with reference to mother–child and therapist–patient interaction, suggests that each self-organising system can be expanded into more coherent and complex states in collaboration with another. These are described as 'moments of meeting' and are considered a crucial aspect of therapeutic change. Here too, some convergence with the dialogic model of CAT is apparent.

However, it is not clear from these accounts what modifications to traditional analytic practice are being suggested. This would be of considerable importance given that, in our view, many aspects of traditional psychoanalytic practice are actually antithetical to the joint recognition, acknowledgement and changing of procedures.

Attachment theory

Although Bowlby's development of attachment theory initially provoked considerable hostility from, and was neglected by, the psychoanalytic community, it has latterly been enthusiastically embraced by some. Many of the more implausible aspects of psychoanalytic theory were derived from the attempt to construct a model of personality based on drives embodied in conflicting structures or internal objects within the 'mental apparatus'. Bowlby offered a more acceptable biological basis in ethology, suggesting in particular that experiences and behaviours related to attachment and loss could be seen as examples of complex innate behaviour patterns found throughout much of the animal kingdom. This revision, easily linked with some versions of object relations theory and in his view constituting a version of it (Bowlby, 1988), drew attention to the profound importance of the quality of the infant's bond with the mother. This constituted a radical and humane revision of contemporary psychoanalytic theory although it was received with considerable hostility and misrepresentation at the time (Schwartz, 1999). The theory was developed using cognitive psychology concepts to describe the early formation of internal 'working models of relationships' responsible for the subsequent shaping of relationship patterns.

Workers in the attachment theory (AT) tradition have carried out research describing how the form and content of parents' recollections of childhood are linked to the patterns of attachment displayed by their children. These findings are of considerable interest and importance but ultimately appear to be limited by a number of features: (1) the exclusive focus on patterns of attachment to the exclusion of other aspects of the active infant's concerns; (2) the use of the one-way concept of bonding to describe the intense reciprocal activity of mother–infant pairs; (3) the heavy reliance on limited forms of experimental observation—the Adult Attachment Interview and the Strange Situations Test—which attend separately to child and parent and do not observe their interaction directly; (4) the relative neglect of the extensive observational research into caretaker–infant interaction of the past two decades; (5) the often loosely-used concept of the 'secure base'; (6) the reduction of the complexity of relationship patterns to a list of categories. Crittenden's (1990) theoretical developments of AT to take more account of pathological forms of attachment have multiplied these categories considerably (Jellema, 2000). It has been observed that they are now as numerous as the signs of the Zodiac! This, and the laborious processes involved in assembling the data on which this classification rests, means that these categories are only marginally useful clinically. (7) More fundamentally, in seeking a respectable scientific base in biology, AT has, it appears, largely ignored what is essentially human, namely the formative role of culture and, from Bowlby's 'working models of relationships' on, has adopted restricted, cognitivist assumptions. The creation and maintenance of self processes and the transmission of social values in the mother–child relationship are not explicitly considered.

It would appear that AT has been enthusiastically overextended in an attempt to account for all aspects of development (including the generation of 'theory of mind') and psychopathology. In our view, and that of many others (Gilbert, 1992; Leiman, 1995; Aitken and Trevarthen, 1997, Brown and Zinkin, 1994), this theory, although important, describes only some of the factors involved in healthy growth and development. Although the issues which attachment theorists stress are important, in particular loss and attachment throughout the life cycle (Bowlby, 1988), AT does not, in itself, appear to offer an adequate account of the complexity and subtlety of development or of psychopathology.

Cognitive psychology and cognitive therapy

One important early influence in the development of CAT was personal construct theory (Kelly, 1955), an approach which challenged both psychoanalytic and behavioural assumptions and which, especially if linked with social constructivism, goes some way towards acknowledging the specifically human, cultural influences on personality. The dominant cognitive theory of the last decades, however, influenced by artificial intelligence research and computer metaphors, has been concerned with information processing and storage. In our view this is still largely the case, although some authors show an increasing interest and awareness of the effects of early interpersonal experience and of the importance of (social) meaning in development and in therapy (see Brewin, 1988; Stiles, 1997; Salkovskis, 1996; Perris, 2000; Safran and McMain, 1992; Power and Brewin, 1997). An important contribution of these cognitive and behavioural theories to the CAT model was their demonstration of the value of analysing and describing sequences (for example, linking behaviours to outcomes, cognitions to emotions) and their demonstration that many problems can be understood without postulating unconscious forces. The cognitive component of CAT theory was derived initially from the work with repertory grids and, to a degree, from personal construct theory. Miller, Galanter and Pribram (1960) and Neisser (1967) were also significant influences. In Ryle (1982) the Procedural Sequence Model (PSM) was compared in some detail to Beck's model of cognitive therapy (Beck, 1976), to Roth's model of learned helplessness (Roth, 1980), to Rehm's model of depression (Rehm, 1977) to Rotter's model of generalised expectancies (Rotter, 1978), to Forstelling's attribution theory (Forstelling, 1980) and to Bandura's model of self-efficacy (Bandura, 1977). In terms of practice, the use of patient self-monitoring was derived from Beck and became one important aspect of the reformulation process, but in CAT the focus of attention was shifted as soon as possible from symptoms to procedures. Later developments in cognitive-behaviour therapy (CBT), for example the work of Guidano (1987) on the self and the development of schema-focused approaches (Young and Lindemann, 1992), have shown some convergences with CAT in shifting attention to higher level functions and more complex disorders but important differences remain, as will become clear in later chapters.

The early CAT model (PSM) therefore resembled cognitive ones, but differed essentially in that the unit of observation—the procedural sequence—involved linking environmental, mental and behavioural phenomena. The level of address in CAT is on self processes and structures understood in developmental terms, whereas CBT is still usually focused on particular beliefs, symptoms or behaviours and pays little attention to development or structure. Differences in the practice of CBT and CAT are further considered in Chapter 9.

ABNORMAL DEVELOPMENT AND THERAPEUTIC CHANGE

Adverse early experience may affect development of the self in three main ways, namely through the internalisation of negative or maladaptive reciprocal role procedures (RRPs), through the replacement of these by restrictive or symptomatic procedures and through the anxiety or trauma-induced dissociation of self processes. This damaging process is depicted diagrammatically in Figure 4.2 where all levels of potential damage are shown. A tendency to dissociate into different self states is indicated by broken lines. All three forms of damage are found in overt Borderline Personality Disorder (BPD) and to varying extents in other disorders, both neurotic and psychotic, where the

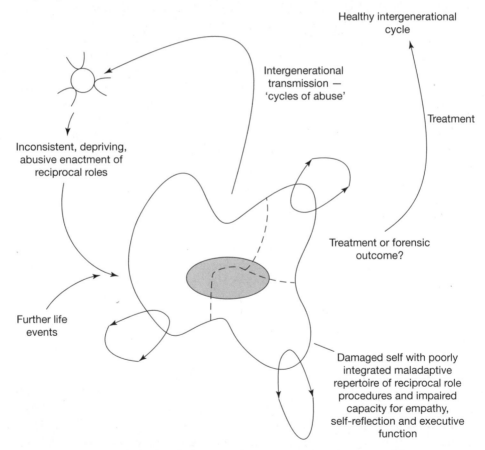

Figure 4.2 CAT-based diagrammatic sketch of abnormal develoment of the self

internalisation of abusive and neglecting role relationships is manifest in abuse and neglect of self and others. In addition, the metaprocedures, which normally link and mobilise appropriately the individual's reciprocal role repertoire, are disrupted or undeveloped with the result that separate, unconnected (partially dissociated) reciprocal role patterns persist. Furthermore, deficient parenting, marked by little or no concern with the child's experience (as opposed to obedience or appearance, for example), offers no source from which a self-caring role might be internalised. This, combined with the disruptions of self-reflection accompanying switches between states, results in an impaired capacity for self-reflection and hence an impaired ability to take responsibility for damaging behaviour or to learn from experience.

Persistent negative role patterns

In less severe disruptions, where the scaffolding provided by caretakers was authoritarian or neglectful, a wide range of individual problems may be created but the main legacy will be concerned with issues of control and care. Thus the child of a parent offering critical, conditional care may be critical of self and expecting criticism from others, manifest in perfectionist striving or placation and depression, and may also be critical of others. It is the overall pattern, not the detailed manifestations, that persists through to adult life. Such patterns persist because they are the only ones known and constitute identity and because apparently confirmatory reciprocations can usually be elicited from others. These patterns may be involved in various forms of disorder such as anxiety or depression as well as in psychotic disorders such as schizophrenia (see Chapters 9 and 10).

Avoidant, defensive and symptomatic role replacements or 'coping strategies'

Role procedures which are experienced by the child as dangerous or forbidden may be replaced by avoidant, restrictive or symptomatic procedures. Psychoanalytic theory emphasises the role of fantasy—for example the Oedipal castration threat—but in clinical practice the 'actual shape of interpersonal reality', as experienced in the preverbal and later phases, offers a more parsimonious explanation, although it remains true that such experience may be amplified, distorted or misinterpreted.

The actual shape of experience may reflect direct parental prohibitions on acts or feelings, the persistance of which may further provoke guilt. Or the consistent failure to name evident facts—for example sexuality—may mean that the child has no way of thinking about the area and may again feel unease or guilt. A depressed mother may be unable to offer the appropriate affirmations of the child's explorations and energy, an anxious parent may convey mistrust in the child's capacity and in the world, an emotionally needy parent may discourage independence in the child, an obsessional parent may inhibit all signs of spontaneity in the child, a parent deprived and abused in childhood may overprotect the child, may envy the care the child receives and may react abusively to the child's anger, which may be felt to be abusive. In all these cases the child may feel irrationally guilty, as if the abuse or deprivation was deserved. Symptoms (affecting mood or somatic functions) and avoidant procedures can be located on the role procedures governing self-management and relationships, serving either to replace, avoid or punish acts or feelings sensed as forbidden (primary gain, in psychoanalytic terms) or they may serve to control others (secondary gain). All role procedures are, in some sense, compromise formations between the desired, the possible and the culturally and parentally provided definitions of the permissible. The ego defences of classical psychoanalysis are conceptualised here as aspects of RRPs in which the avoidance of feeling and memory and the editing out of certain behaviours— usually linked to anger and sexuality—are linked to patterns of relating to others or managing the self.

Dissociation

A third legacy of negative childhood experience, one in which inherited vulnerability plays a large part, is the failure to achieve adequate integration of self processes. While everyone is aware of being made up of many component parts, most of us have a clear sense of a central identity, are able to acknowledge all aspects and can usually mobilise the aspect appropriate to the context. These features are absent or partial in borderline personality disorder (BPD) and also certain psychotic states. In severe personality disorder genetic predisposition and abuse and neglect have disrupted or impaired the development of an integrating central self. Much of the phenomenology of BPD is the result of the presence of a number of partially dissociated RRPs (self states) which are narrowly defined and often extreme and of rapid, confusing switches between states. Such patients put powerful pressures on therapists and others, seeking reciprocation to their extreme and unstable states.

Some psychoanalytic object relations theorists attribute many of these features to 'splitting' and projective identification, locating the pathology in the posited internal system of object relations and in 'ego weakness', innate destructive instinctual forces and unconscious fantasy. The phenomenon of projective identification, whereby others are powerfully induced to experience feelings or play roles which the person cannot tolerate, is not regarded as a defence in CAT; it is seen to represent an exaggerated example of the normal processes of reciprocal role relating. Self states (dissociated reciprocal roles) are precarious and this leads the person to induce powerful identifying responses in, or to forcefully seek reciprocations from others, even where these are harmful. While usually discussed in relation to destructive procedures, the same intense pressures can characterise the seeking for ideal care.

COMMON THERAPEUTIC FACTORS

Change in psychotherapy is in part the result of those factors common to the majority of approaches, namely the experience of a relationship with a recognised expert who offers close attention and respect and provides some new framework of understanding, features which serve to restore morale. The early negotiation of a definition of the problem in a language shared by patient and therapist is also helpful (Frank, 1961). CAT would aim to address all of these factors. As an individual therapy it also fulfils most of the criteria reviewed by Bateman and Fonagy (1999a) for effective treatments for very damaged patients with personality disorder. Such treatments should be well structured, have a clear focus, devote effort to enhancing compliance, be theoretically coherent to both therapist and patient, be longer term, encourage a powerful attachment relationship and be well integrated with other services.

CHILDHOOD DEVELOPMENT AND THE CAT MODEL OF THERAPEUTIC CHANGE

Many therapies, especially those derived from psychoanalysis, see parallels between the process of childhood learning and therapy. Whereas in psychoanalysis this has meant that 'deep' change is seen to depend upon a process of regression and recapitulation, in CAT the emphasis is on working with the adult prospectively to enlarge the capacity for conscious self-awareness, through the reformulation process. Reformulation makes recognition possible and recognition opens the way for revision. It is based on description rather than interpretation. Understanding and control are derived from this joint work of therapy in which the therapist offers a reparative scaffolding designed to allow the maximum opportunity for the patient's own initiative by working together to create and use carefully developed conceptual tools. In most cases direct attempts to modify defensive and symptomatic procedures are not needed; they fade from view as the agenda shifts to the revision of the associated or avoided role relationships determining self-care and interactions with others.

In the course of reformulation and with the help of symptom monitoring, most somatic and mood disorders can be identified as accompanying defined reciprocal role procedures, either those that are continuations of early damaging patterns or those that have replaced the more effective modes which were disallowed by others or by an internalised voice derived from others. An internal prohibition on anger, for example, is likely to be accompanied by submissive behaviour to others and by guilt and anxiety if anger is experienced; depression and somatic symptoms are common accompaniments. Reformulation will focus attention on the procedure rather than the symptom. As patients begin to apply their new understandings, as they experience the reality of the therapist's concern and as the expressions of their problematic procedures in the therapy relationship are described and not reciprocated, symptoms and negative moods usually fade without direct attention.

Practitioners who use both CBT and CAT usually use CBT with more cooperative and less disturbed patients. It is our impression, however, that even in such patients the CAT 'top down' focus on high level self processes (which can incorporate more focal attention to lower level issues if this is indicated) is as effective and quite possibly quicker than CBT in controlling symptoms, while also dealing with interpersonal and self-managing procedures and avoiding its possibly diminishing (Magistral) assumptions. Some therapists with a CBT background have a need to be busy and helpful and can find the less active, dialogic and reflective CAT mode difficult. Clearly a controlled trial comparing CBT and CAT in less disturbed patients would be helpful. With more disturbed patients the understanding and use made of the difficult therapeutic relationship in CAT is a boon to both patients and therapists and can be extended, in some situations, to other members of a treating team (Kerr, 1999, 2001).

It is of interest that Fonagy (1999), from within psychoanalysis, suggests that 'therapeutic work needs to focus on helping the individual identify regular patterns of behavour and phantasy' and says that 'there is good reason to believe that psychoanalysis works by modifying procedures [sic] rather than by creating new ideas'. However, this convergence with the ideas and language of CAT has not so far led to a convergence in respect of therapist activities.

WHO DOES THE THERAPIST SPEAK FOR?

Every family and every culture will determine and set some limit on what may or may not be said and done; the dominant range of social values and attitudes will be made evident by what is celebrated, what is acknowledged, what is discouraged and what is ignored and by how power and privilege are distributed. In this way every individual's internal regime (including the psychoanalytic 'unconscious') will contain the voices of the external social and political reality as refracted by parents and teachers. Therapists have themselves been formed in the same society as their patients, but, in many cases, are seeking to offer a different perspective in order to remedy the effects of harsh external social realities and of forms of control which have been internalised by their patients. So who is the 'superaddressee' in therapeutic dialogue? To what social agency or what value system does the therapist refer in his or her comments?

We seek to extend awareness, choice and control but we inevitably convey some more specific social values for, although procedural descriptions can be

understood in utilitarian terms as simply pointing out the unwanted consequences of current behaviours, most therapists do not conceal their ethical
concerns. Thus most, when considering damaging relationship patterns, will
favour revisions towards more mutual and respecting modes and all will vote
with varying force against murder, child abuse, wife beating and racism. In less
extreme ways, many personal restrictions or deformations, while socially
congruent and adaptive, seem to contradict the therapist's broader definitions
of human values and needs. In these circumstances the neutral therapist is a
myth; tacitly he or she is either challenging or identifying with current social
power. If a patient holds views which the therapist cannot stomach it may be
impossible to work effectively, but assuming or imposing normative ethical
values should be done with extreme caution. One should remember that many
therapists have argued (and some still do) that homosexuality should be 'cured'
and that working class patients cannot use therapy.

As psychotherapists, a heightened self-awareness of our tacit social assumptions is every bit as important as the forms of self-knowledge which may be
acquired through personal therapy. We do want to have influence in order to
help our patients change but we do not want to impose compliance to our
personal views. Whether we identify ourselves as agents or as critics of society,
we should be explicit when we voice or convey an opinion and should emphasise that our aim is to extend conscious choice not to impose solutions. To this
end, we should encourage a therapeutic relationship which is argumentative as
well as collaborative.

We need also to avoid too literal an understanding of the stories patients tell.
While the origins of the internal conversation may usually be directly linked to
historical experiences, it is of course the case that children may misjudge and
misremember their experience (Offer et al., 2000) and the extent of their own
responsibility and the meanings and intentions of others. The range of charac-
ters and behaviours described in fairy tales are often extreme in the degree of
their wickedness or their perfection; they still appeal to children whose life
experiences have been relatively benign and mild, serving as concrete representations of their fantasies and misinterpretations.

AVOIDING COLLUSION

Having a therapist whom one likes and respects is effective in assisting change
in patients with mild or moderate levels of disturbance and in these cases
psychotherapy 'technique' is of limited importance, provided it does not
damage the quality of the relationship. In more disordered patients, however,
the maintaining of a good relationship and the provision within it of useful
understandings is often problematic as patients disrupt or distort it, just as they
do their everyday relationships. In these cases the specific CAT techniques and
understandings play a key role in establishing and maintaining a working

relationship; without them, therapists are likely to be drawn into inadvertent collusion which will reinforce problem procedures or lead to the end of the therapy.

The most problematic collusions are those which are justified by the system belief guiding the therapist, especially when these prescribe withholding or controlling attitudes which commonly echo the patient's childhood experiences (although becoming over-involved and excessively sympathetic to a patient can be just as unhelpful). Only an accurate and sensitive awareness of the evolving therapy relationship can allow the establishment of a therapeutic relationship which is emotionally intense, honest and thoughtful and which generates well-focused mediating conceptual tools which can be internalised as a corrective to, or replacement of, the previous damaging and restricting patterns.

In summary, the CAT understanding of therapeutic change requires the following:

1. The creation and maintenance of a non-collusive and respecting relationship with the patient.
2. The collaborative creation of mediating tools (descriptions, diagrams) which make the patient's specific problematic procedures and structures available for conscious reflection. In most cases the ZPPD is seen to include the high level 'strategic' procedures operating in relationships with others and in self-management. More focal and limited issues may be addressed within this overall procedural understanding.
3. Movement through the stages of reformulation, practice in recognition and the process of revision or replacement of problematic procedures. The process is not a simple linear one as the safety established through reformulation may allow access to previously avoided affects and memories which need to be addressed and worked on. The time limit and the use of concrete, collaboratively constructed conceptual tools, including the goodbye letter, encourage the internalisation of what has been learned in therapy.

SELF-ESTEEM

Many descriptions of psychiatric syndromes refer to the level of self-esteem; it is, for example, low in depression and excessively high in hypomania. The term is used more often than it is defined and is sometimes taken to represent a stable character trait. It is important to assess not only the level of self-esteem but to work out what maintains it. Any maladaptive procedure as listed in the Psychotherapy File if persistently enacted might result in low self-esteem. Arguably one of the most fundamental and defining procedures contributing to low self-esteem would be one based on historical experience leading to an assumption that 'whatever one does, nothing will ever work out'. The result of this is that one gives up trying with the consequence that nothing changes or improves, so perpetuating the original assumption. Low 'levels' of self-esteem may reflect (1) external realities such as unemployment, poverty and social powerlessness; (2) restrictive procedures such as the traps listed in the Psychotherapy File, dilemmas such 'as if either a brutal success or a nice failure' or snags whereby success is felt to be undeserved or forbidden; (3) dominant patterns of reciprocal role relationship, for example having a *critical/conditionally accepting or loving* to *guilty/striving* pattern which is manifest in unreasonable, idiosyncratic and extreme conditions for self-acceptance and in the taking on of submissive or humiliating roles in relationships. Understood in these terms recognising low self-esteem is only the first step; the range of underlying maladaptive procedures must be identified and accurately described. The Personal Sources Questionnaire, described in Ryle (1990, pp. 249–252), can help the systematic exploration of individual sources of self-esteem.

THE 'FALSE SELF'

This somewhat loosely used term suggests a person whose sense of self is overdependent on the responses of others and in some sense out of touch with 'authentic' feelings. In CAT theory, where conscious experience is seen to be mediated by signs created with others, what is the basis for a distinction between a 'true' and a 'false' self? Both the development of the self and restrictions upon its development are determined by the form and content of the scaffolding provided or imposed by parents and society. While the shaping of personality in terms compatible with the society is a necessary and inevitable process, there are some societies, or some sections within societies, and some families, and maybe some therapies, in which compliance to social norms leaves little room for individual exploration. Their scaffolding imposes narrow solutions and fails to provide the materials for personal learning. Seen in this way the concept of the 'false self' implies a restricted sense of self and, given our quintessentially social character, a consequent sense of inauthenticity or not being 'in dialogue'. It suggests that the concept of the 'false self' may be seen as a shorthand for a certain group of RRPs which result in the features described above, including the critical feature of being 'out of dialogue' with self and others. This conception also implies an extensive ZPPD within which personal development might occur provided that therapy can offer a reparative, constructive scaffolding and a meaningful dialogue through which change may occur.

UNDERLYING PHILOSOPHICAL DIVERGENCES; DIALOGISM VERSUS CARTESIANISM

The divergences of CAT from psychoanalytic and cognitive theories are aspects of a more general difference in assumptions which can be illustrated by considering a recent proposal to link research into how children acquire a theory of mind with attachment theory (Fonagy and Target, 1997). According to Premack and Woodruff (1978) an individual has a theory of mind if he imputes mental states to himself and others. Research in this field measures a child's performance in two kinds of test, namely the change of location paradigm and the surprise paradigm (Jenkins and Astington, 1996). The child who answers the test questions correctly understands that people pursue their goals on the basis of beliefs and that these beliefs may be false. Povinelli and Preuss (1995) attribute the acquisition of a theory of mind to an 'evolutionary specialisation of human cognition'. This biological view is challenged by research findings which suggest that the achievement of a theory of mind is associated with general intellectual development, is correlated with verbal intelligence (Jenkins and Astington, 1996), with the presence of siblings (Perner et al., 1994), and with using tests which resemble the child's normal activities, all findings which support the view that learning in a social context provides a satisfactory explanation (Boyes et al., 1997).

Fonagy and Target (1997) seek to link theory of mind research with attachment theory. They properly question cognitive theories in which the child is seen as an isolated processor of information engaged in the construction of a theory of mind using biological mechanisms, and point to the fact that the child's central cognitive concern is with its emotional relationship with its parents. Their account of how attachment encourages mentalisation remains essentially a cognitive one, however, depending on 'representational mapping', which is defined as the process of coordinating representations of self and other. As an example, an anxious child, seen to be suffering a confusing mixture of physiological changes, ideas and behaviour, is helped by perceiving the mother's mirroring of the anxiety, a process described as follows: 'the mother's representation of the infant's affect is represented by the child and is mapped on to the representation of his self-state'. Representation is used confusedly here; presumably the mother's representation of the infant's affect refers to her expressive enactment or mirroring of it, not to her mental processes. They add that the mother's mirroring of the anxiety should not be exact for, if it is accompanied by the expression of other affects, the soothing effect on the child is greater because, it is claimed, infants recognise the reflected emotion as analogous to, but not isomorphic with, their experience and thus the process of symbol formation may begin. However, it is not clear how a perception (of the mother's enactment) is mapped onto a self-state representation, how a child determines whether mother's enactment and its own subjective state are analogous or isomorphic and what converts mother's added expressive elements into symbols.

This account describes the infant as a separate if immature entity, reflecting the Cartesian assumption of the centrality and independence of the thinking self (monadic cognitivism), an assumption which appears to be as hard to dispose of as was the belief that the world was the centre of the cosmos. An alternative view, which can be called dialogism, will now be presented.

Dialogism

As described in the last chapter, natural selection favoured individuals who were biologically endowed with the potential to be socially formed, who were therefore capable of living in groups and able to adjust flexibly to a wide variety of physical circumstances and social structures. The biological underpinnings on which these capacities rest are far more complex than can be explained by the persistence and modification of attachment behaviours. The newborn human infant is engaged from birth in activities with caretakers. Every infant in every culture enters into a particular world in which it finds the reciprocating activity and conversation of its caretakers. Rather than simply receiving impressions, storing representations and constructing theories, the child is engaged in an evolving joint enterprise through the experience and creation of which the self is shaped. In Bakhtin's words: 'Just as the body is formed initially in the mother's womb (body), a person's consciousness awakens wrapped in another's consciousness' (Bakhtin, 1986, p. 138). In a related understanding, Winnicott's 'there is no such thing as an infant' emphasised the need to make the unit of observation in understanding development this infant–caretaker dyadic system rather than the infant alone. In essence, the dialogic approach replaces the 'I think, therefore I am' of Descartes with 'We interact and communicate, therefore I become'. This dialogic model presents an unproblematic way of understanding the acquisition of a theory of mind. It differs crucially from that of Fonagy and Target and from cognitivist models in drawing on three Vygotskian assumptions, namely: (1) that a child's activity in the presence of (scaffolded by) a more experienced other will come to be repeated independently, (2) that the activity and the meanings related to it will involve the joint creation and use of signs, and (3) that internalisation occurs through this process of joint sign mediation rather than through representation and that external conversation is transformed into the internal conversation of the dialogic self.

CONCLUSION

At a minimum, to be doing CAT, a therapist must engage with the patient in a process of descriptive reformulation, itself a powerfully alliance-generating activity, and must aim to use the descriptions and the therapy relationship to modify the identified problematic procedures. This basic practice involves even unrepentant Cartesians in a form of dialogic understanding and exchange. However, the detailed application and the further development of the model require that practice is rooted in a dialogic theoretical understanding. Knowledge, memory, meaning, affect and action, although differently processed in the brain, are joined in life and are considered together in procedural descriptions. They are formed and maintained in relation to past and present others. This understanding involves the linking of a developmental history with current structures and current relationships (RRPs) and requires the description of (1) procedural sequences, (2) internal and enacted reciprocal patterns of relationship and dialogue, and (3) structure. The latter involves (a) hierarchy (how tactical procedures are determined by strategic ones) and (b) a system of metaprocedures which organise and mobilise procedures. Therapy represents the modification and development over time (which may often be much less than traditionally postulated) of the patient's self system by conscious sharing of these understandings and by the deeply felt, mutual experience which they make safe and possible.

FURTHER READING

The specific characteristics of the CAT model rest upon interpretations of observational data strongly influenced by the ideas of Vygotsky and Bakhtin. Accessible introductions to, and comments on, Vygotsky's ideas will be found in Wertsch (1985) and Wertsch and Tulviste (1992). Holquist (1990) provides a good introduction to Bakhtin. The paper by Leiman (1992) played the major part in introducing these ideas into CAT. The notion of the socially formed dialogic self presents difficulties to many. Burkitt (1991) presents an historical account paying particular attention to Mead and Vygotsky. Various contributions on the Vygotskian concept of internalisation, some of which describe fascinating empirical studies, are to be found in Cox and Lightfoot (1997). Bruner (1990) offers a thoughtful review of the importance of language and culture in the formation of mind which is highly critical of much current cognitive psychology. Psychoanalytic self psychology is described by Kohut (1977) and Mollon (1993). Guidano (1987, 1991) offers a cognitive model of self processes. Jellema (1999, 2000), writing from a CAT perspective, argues for a less critical evaluation of attachment theory than is offered in this chapter.

Chapter 5

SELECTION AND ASSESSMENT OF PATIENTS FOR INDIVIDUAL CAT

SUMMARY

CAT is applicable to a wide range of disorders of varying severity and in a range of contexts. It is important to undertake a thorough assessment with prospective patients in order to establish the nature of their problems, the presence of any risk factors, and their particular suitability or wish for this form of therapy. The experience of an assessment interview should give patients an impression of the style of CAT and contribute to their motivation and 'psychological mindedness'. In CAT these are not seen as 'all or nothing' phenomena nor prerequisites for therapy but rather as something which therapy may cultivate and expand. Some problems may require other or additional forms of treatment, including pharmacotherapy. There may be reasons not to undertake therapy at a given time due to, for example, active substance abuse, threat of violence or active psychotic disorder. Assessment may be amplified by use of questionnaires such as the Personality Structure Questionnaire (PSQ) as well as, increasingly in the UK, the 'CORE' questionnaire. These issues are illustrated by six brief case presentations.

REFERRAL

CAT offers a general model of psychotherapy applicable to a wide range of diagnoses and severity but each patient needs to be considered in relation to both their disorder and the treatment context. Patients reach psychotherapists by a number of routes and therapists work in a number of settings; the kinds of patients seen in forensic settings, in hospitals or community Mental Health

Centres or in general practice are likely to be of diminishing severity, but severe disturbance will be encountered in all. In some settings there may be a range of therapy options available, in others there will be little choice. In long-established outpatient departments the referrers will have learned which patients are suitable, but there will still be inappropriate referrals. Where psychotherapy is carried out in the more hostile environments offered by some psychiatric departments inappropriate referrals may represent the dumping of difficult cases, usually personality-disordered or somatising patients or examples of the 'treat that if you dare' referral of hopeless cases designed to demonstrate that therapy is useless. Whatever the referral route, therapists have to make their own decisions about which patients to accept for treatment. Therapists working privately and with essentially self-referred patients will need to be particularly alert to the presence of psychiatric illnesses and to the assessment of potential risk from more disturbed patients.

ASSESSMENT DATA

Certain cases may be unsuitable for psychotherapy, at least at the time of assessment. These include those with acute psychotic disorders, active and continuous substance abuse or serious, acute physical disorders. Those individuals who pose an active risk of violence based on either past history or present behaviour should be taken on only with due circumspection and regard for safety. Depending on the context and referral route, a proportion of patients will be unsuitable for psychotherapy and may need to be referred for psychiatric assessment. Therapists should be alert to, and able to identify or refer for a further opinion, conditions such as severe depression (particularly if an individual describes serious self-harm intentions), bipolar affective disorder (manic depression), schizophrenia and delusional/paranoid disorders, early dementia and other organic, especially neurological, disorders which may present as psychological impairment. Many of these disorders may still be amenable to and helped by psychological treatment, but will require particular consideration, caution and usually collaboration with other health professionals. In addition it is always wise for psychotherapists to enquire routinely about drug use, whether illicit or prescribed. Basic teaching on these topics should normally be offered on any psychotherapy training and these conditions are described in any student psychiatric textbook.

In cases suitable for therapy the following questions need to be answered: Is individual, as opposed to group or couple or family therapy, indicated? Are there contraindications (possibly amenable to prior treatment) in the form of psychiatric illness or substance abuse? Are the patient's current social and personal situations sufficiently stable to allow therapeutic work? Is there an unacceptable risk of violence (assessed in relation to the treatment context) or of suicide and if some such risk is evident are psychiatric facilities available if needed? In addition to these factors the assessor, when responding to the patient's story or commenting on the way the interview has been coped with, will propose explanations and links which will give some idea to the patient of what is being offered; the style of the interview should already provide an experience of a collaborative 'doing with' approach. How patients engage in this will provide some idea of their ability to make use of the treatment but this does not imply that CAT requires patients to be already 'psychologically minded'; it is their response to appropriately delivered interventions and explanations that determines treatability. Greater psychological mindedness can be one outcome of the assessment interview.

A further, useful discussion of the assessment process and of case formulation from a CAT perspective is offered by Denman (1995).

THE CONDUCT OF THE ASSESSMENT INTERVIEW

Before meeting with the patient the therapist should read the referral letter and any other clinical notes and psychometric test results. These may convey important information such as suicidal preoccupations or abuse histories about which patients are reluctant to speak. Patients should be told what information has been received but in general should be invited to retell the story in their own words; any reluctance to speak at this stage should be noted but accepted. The purpose and duration of the assessment meeting and the role of the assessor should be made explicit; thereafter the interview should be largely unstructured, because what the patient chooses to say and how it is said may convey as much as the content, but the therapist needs to be aware of his or her implicit agenda and may use prompts or direct questions to open important aspects which are not volunteered and to explore the feelings and meanings associated with reported facts.

Towards the end of the interview the assessor should rehearse the main 'headlines' of the story and propose possible links and patterns between reported events. He or she should offer provisional descriptions of the main issues and should seek the patient's comments; any ways in which the patient's problem procedures have been evident 'in the room' during the interview should be noted. This recapitulation and linking show the patient that the story has been attended to and provide a sample of what therapy can offer; it also allows the therapist to gauge how far the patient can make use of such comments. The patient's own understanding about the nature of his or her problems and expectations of therapy should be clarified and the response to the interview should be asked for. An outline of the CAT therapy model explaining the time limit, the reformulation process and the expectation of homework and indicating how the patient's particular problems might be helped should be given. The nature of the therapy relationship and the ways in which the patient's problem procedures might affect it are also explained.

Alternative treatments, if available, should be described so the patient can make an informed choice. Practical arrangements and an account of what is to happen next should be clarified at the end of the meeting.

Assessment interviews are not technical exercises; they call for the full range of therapy skills and for an ability to respond to individual patients in ways enabling them to reveal significant aspects of their lives and problems, even if they had no clear prior idea about what is expected. What is learned in the course of the interview needs to be related to the conceptual model and fed back to the patient in a way which contributes to the establishment of a shared language. Such comments need to be tentative and the patient's understanding and comments sought and considered, exemplifying the collaborative nature of the therapy. Areas where knowledge remained incomplete should be noted and occasionally a second assessment meeting may be needed.

In writing up assessment interviews it can be a valuable but time-consuming exercise for trainees to describe in detail the evolving process of the meeting. It is more accurate and more revealing to audiotape and replay the session. With experienced assessors it is enough to record the main content and themes, the feel and process of the meeting and the assessor's judgements and counter-transference. The account can then be re-cast in the order:

1. Referred by whom and reason for referral.
2. Process of session and impression or countertransference.
3. Main problems and why they have led to coming at this time.
4. Early history, other life events, current relationships and social situation. This should not take the form of a detailed biography, the need is to identify and describe key themes.
5. A diagnostic formulation covering (a) any psychiatric illnesses and (b) a provisional reformulation of how present problems are derived from procedures developed in coping with past events, and which notes how these procedures may influence how current life difficulties and underlying issues such as unresolved mourning are coped with.
6. The treatment plan. In team situations final decisions about the treatment plan will be made by the team meeting, a procedure which guards against the influence of unrecognised countertransference on decisions.

This formal account of assessment procedures fails to convey the density and complexity of a satisfactory meeting or how much powerful feeling may be evoked by the often horrific life experiences and often admirable efforts at survival reported by patients. A more live impression may be given by the following selection of vignettes of assessments carried out in an outpatient CAT clinic. As with all case material these will be modified to avoid recognition. The provisional identification of key reciprocal role procedures given in these summaries would suggest issues to pursue and clarify in therapy and would not be considered in any way final.

The cases will be summarised under the six headings suggested above and a brief retrospective comment on the issues illustrated by the case will be added.

Nora

1. A 28-year-old London West Indian referred by an experienced GP counsellor whom she had consulted on account of her inability to show affection and her increasingly aggressive feelings towards her daughter.
2. She appears as intelligent, articulate and insightful and her survival of a very difficult life is impressive.
3. She is increasingly concerned with how she treats, and sometimes beats, her nine-year-old child; she knows it is in part because she is like her father and in part because 'she is too much like me'. The child was by the first of three relationships, the last of which she has recently ended; in all three she was clearly dominant, refusing any hint of being controlled or abused but also intolerant of her partner's displays of affection and at times being 'vicious and revengeful'.
4. She was raised in a chaotic family, the only reliable figure being one older sister (out of a total of 'about 15' offspring of her mother, father and step-father). She indicated that there were experiences she did not feel ready to talk about at this interview. Despite this background she did well at school and attended a Further Education College until her first pregnancy. She is now working part-time and attending further education classes.
5. Apart from the older sister's care she seems to have derived from childhood a pattern of *defiant coping* in relation to *neglect and abuse*. To her distress, she enacts the abusing role to her daughter and expresses contempt for most others, especially men, although she has one intimate woman friend. Under her tough coping mode there is probably a degree of self-contempt.
6. Despite this history she was frank and open in the interview and I believe she will work hard in therapy to understand herself better but, as her main coping mode has been to avoid emotional exposure, she will find it difficult to risk contacting her childhood pain and may well be dismissive of the therapist.

Comment: Admiration for this woman's evident strength needed to be tempered with a realisation of how hurt and angry she was. Therapy, if she became involved, would mean contacting and expressing powerful feelings of anger and deprivation and losing the safety her emotional distancing provides. The therapist would need to be ready for a rough ride and should anticipate this in the reformulation; survival of this could be the most important aspect of non-collusion. The time limit may make risking this exposure tolerable to her, however. The GP and practice counsellor were aware of her anger with the child and at this time there seemed no need to involve Social Services.

David

1. David, aged 27, was seen at the request of his psychiatrist. He was an in-patient, detained under the Mental Health Act, having been brought in by the police after threatening to jump off a Thames bridge.
2. He struck me as a compliant, anxious young man, saying he wanted to have therapy, but it was difficult to get a strong impression of who he was.
3. He had been depressed since early adolecence, and had had two hospital admissions at the ages of 18 and 20. Since that time there had been phases during which he drank heavily and I gathered from the notes that he had also used a lot of cannabis. The recent depression was associated with the end of a three-year-long gay relationship, an ending provoked by his drinking. He had also recently lost his clerical job due to poor time keeping.
4. He described his father as a very authoritarian man; for much of his early life his maternal grandfather was his main support. This was especially the case after he was upset and felt rejected following the birth of his sister when he was aged six. His grandfather was also the only one in the family who accepted his announcement of his homosexuality.
5. A main thread in his life would seem to be his wish not to resemble his father in any way. He understands that this makes him over-placatory and that the ensuing resentment leads to depression and drinking. The basic role pattern derived from his relationship with father would be something like *resentful placation* in relation to *harsh control*. The suicidal acts seem to have followed sudden and extreme mood changes, perhaps better described as state shifts, representing a switch from depressed placation and resentment to angry defiance, and there remains some risk of this anger leading to an impulsive suicide. He is currently on antidepressants and will remain under psychiatric supervision.
6. Contraindications to therapy include my feeling that he was compliant rather than frank in the interview and the incompletely declared history of substance abuse. Therapy should be conditional on controlling this. It might be wise to offer a provisional 4–6 sessions before committing to a full course. On the positive side he has a reasonable work record and did sustain a relationship for three years and his grandfather provided some real care which he still remembers. If he can engage in therapy he might be best referred on to group therapy after 8–12 sessions of individual CAT.

Comment: There were a number of doubts about how far this patient could be engaged in therapy. It might have been wiser to have suggested a prior period of outpatient support to see if he could remain substance free. On the other hand, starting therapy at a moment of crisis can often promote rapid engagement at the level of underlying self processes and can allow fundamental change rather than the restoration of defensive or coping compromises. In this case it seemed important to offer treatment while accepting that there was an above average likelihood of him not completing the course.

Nick

1. Nick, a 31-year-old lecturer, was referred by his GP on account of a long-standing low-grade depression (with no biological features) and episodes of loss-of-control anger.
2. He was close to tears during the interview and seemed highly motivated to make better sense of his life.
3. He described an increasing sense of dissatisfaction with his life, feeling that others saw him as a resource but never remained as friends. His second marriage had recently been under strain when he felt ignored by his wife but they are now on better terms again. He gets unreasonably angry.
4. Nick is the eldest of two children from a working class family in Scotland. Following the birth of his sister when he was five his mother became psychiatrically ill and she remained unstable thereafter. Father was impatient with her and devoted himself to his daughter and Nick became his mother's main practical and emotional support. He did well academically and went to university where he met and married his first wife. She was described as clingingly dependent and he left after two years. His present wife, in contrast, is a strong, independent woman. He manages his working relationships and enjoys the performance of lecturing but feels others to be bewilderingly inconstant. He could agree with my suggestion that maybe he was inconstant in how he saw them. He described how, in addition to the performance mode, he had three distinct states, one the thoughtful one he was in today, one a state of maudlin self-pity and one a state of being out of control.
5. It seemed that his mother had been dependent on him and his father had been unavailable to him as a support or model (*neglected* in relation to *needy and unsupported*). His first marriage had been a repetition of his relationship with his mother, suggesting a pattern such as *needy, unsupported caretaking* in relation to *controlling dependency*. His second marriage avoided a repetition of this but he acknowledged that he sometimes resented his wife's admired strength and social ease. He was clearly anxious to understand better his own contribution to his difficulties. He gave a clear description of differentiated states and state shifts. He did not meet full borderline personality disorder diagnostic criteria.
6. He clearly has real strengths and should make good use of therapy. I suggested he should discuss with his wife whether a session together might be helpful at some stage.

Comment: This man made the decision to seek therapy on the basis of unhappiness and the realisation that he was at least in part the author of his misfortunes;

this suggests that he is likely to be a rewarding patient. Essentially he was someone who had been trapped in the caretaking role he had acquired in childhood and had repeated in his first marriage. No longer having to be the dutiful caretaker he is now, it seems, more aware of being the neglected one, and he elicited from me a concerned, fatherly countertransference. He is now suffering from the distance he creates between himself and most people and from intrusions of the unhappy and angry feelings he had never expressed in the family situation. Therapy can give him a chance to mourn what he never had in the way of care and to free himself from the historically rooted anger, while experiencing focused care and manageable disappointment.

Debby

1. Debby, aged 26, was referred from the Accident and Emergency (A&E) department where she had been psychiatrically assessed after overdosing on paracetamol.
2. She told her story with clarity and some urgency and made me anxious. This was mitigated to some extent by the use she had made of her recent meeting with the referring psychiatrist and which she seemed to make of this session.
3. Her overdose followed a row with her current boyfriend. They have lived together for a year and she recognises a negative spiral in which her possessiveness and threats provoke him to increasingly rejecting behaviours. She had recently opened a window and threatened to jump; he had pulled her back angrily and this had provoked the overdose.
4. Her father had shot himself when she was six. Since then until last year she had lived with her mother and older sister. Unlike her sister she said she had no clear memories or feelings about her father, knowing only what she was told by her mother, from which it seemed he had been unstable and quarrelsome. However, in telling me how her mother broke the news of his violent suicide to her and her sister, she cried. After a number of transient relationships Debby fell desperately in love at the age of 19. A year later her boyfriend confessed to an infidelity; her response was to threaten to jump from the window. He dragged her from the window sill and phoned her mother 'who came and took her away to cool things off'. Two days later she was contacted and told that he himself had jumped to his death from a high building. She was unable to face going to his funeral and had remained deeply obsessed with his memory for the next three years.
    She was quite aware of the spiral of possessiveness provoking rejection which had characterised that relationship and was evident in her current one, but she felt she really could not bear to be left. I tried to explore how one might understand her story, linking the history of two relationships with men marked by intense possessiveness and the terror at abandonment with

her apparent absence of memory or feeling about her father's death. This link with her father was something she seemed not to have thought of before.

5. Since the recent crisis she has stayed in close touch with her mother and is continuing to work in her civil service job. It did not seem that there was an immediate threat of suicide—a view shared by the psychiatrist who had interviewed her in the A&E department. The underlying dilemma could be simply summarised: 'it is as if, if I am deeply involved with a man, then he is bound to leave me'. A more explanatory description might be a reciprocal role pattern derived from the unmourned loss of her father, for instance *desperately seeking love but fearing abandonment and therefore quickly angry* in relation to *apparently loving but inevitably abandoning*.

6. I urged her not to have the means of self-harm to hand and to make use of the A and E department (in which she had confidence) if the impulse to self-harm returned. She would like therapy and it will be set up as soon as possible.

Comment: The history of at least toying with a violent means of suicide was certainly anxiety-provoking, particularly given that her first boyfriend and father had both chosen violent methods of killing themselves. It was as if the only safe relationship was one of fusion and the only coin available to deal with its loss was a lethal one. Despite the somewhat macabre feel to the story, there was no indication for compulsory treatment and I felt that she was relieved to have discussed the situation with the psychiatrist in the A&E department and to have committed herself to therapy in order to understand better the origins of her behaviour.

Evelyn

1. Evelyn was a graphics designer aged 32 referred by her GP. She had requested the referral following a year in which she had experienced many disturbing feelings and intrusive memories after taking 'ecstasy'. She had taken no drugs since that time.

2. She arrived breathless and late and for the first part of the session was speaking under great pressure and somewhat incoherently. By the end I felt I had built up a fairly clear but incomplete picture of what she was wanting from therapy.

3 and 4. The effects of the drug had been to open her to periods of intense feelings associated with childhood. These centred on her relationship with her mother who, she felt, 'had been overinvolved with me emotionally and unable to set any realistic boundaries'. Evelyn began to use alcohol and drugs in early adolescence, preferring cannabis because it calmed her. A brief unsatisfactory sexual relationship with a man at 17 was followed by an

intense but confusing relationship with a woman. Since that time she had had a number of short-term sexual relationships with men, 'preferably boring ones with whom she could avoid emotional closeness'; she also referred to elaborate forms of sexual fantasy which we did not discuss. In her work life she has set up and run successfully her own business. Two previous attempts at therapy (in early adolescence and in her mid-twenties) had not been helpful.

5. Her fear of emotional closeness can clearly be associated with her mother's overinvolvement and lack of boundaries and was probably reinforced by her intense, confusing lesbian relationship. This suggests a reciprocal role pattern something like *overwhelmed but with own needs neglected* in relation to *invasively overinvolved*. Men are still felt to be safer than women and she emphatically requested a male therapist. The possible advantage of therapy from a woman—the more feared gender—was discussed, but it seemed that initial engagement might be too difficult and her request was agreed to. Her main coping strategies have involved hyperactivity and the avoidance of closeness.

6. She now wants to know herself better and has clearly been flooded with memories of childhood which point to the source of her difficulties. Therapy will confront her right away with the urge to avoid feeling involved but I feel there is a real chance that she will be able to use it.

Comment: The success of therapy will depend on establishing a manageable working relationship which can be sustained as she faces the fears and angers associated with closeness. As these are clarified the nature and significance of her undisclosed sexual fantasies may become apparent. CAT is particularly appropriate because of the containing effect of reformulation and the clear time limit.

Diana

1. Diana, aged 33, was referred by a social worker attached to her GP's surgery with an eight-month history of nightmares, depression and fits of uncontrollable weeping.

2. She told her painful history in a way which was dignified and intensely moving.

3 and 4. She was clear that her present state dated back to her five-year-old adopted daughter starting at school. This had brought back intense recollections of how, at that age, her parents had separated and she had been put in care. She had stayed in a very large, harsh institution until she was 13. No emotional closeness between the children was permitted; she had had a brief relationship with an older caring girl which was forbidden. The dormitories were locked with no access to toilets and wetting the bed was punished by being paraded in the wet sheet.

Leaving there aged 13, she was rejected in turn by her mother and by her father and stepmother. From 15 she had managed on her own and trained in dressmaking. At the age of 24 she married an inarticulate but reliable man in whom she has little sexual or emotional interest, especially since she was found, after extensive investigations, to be infertile. She is intensely loving of her adopted daughter and expressed the fear that, from fear of hurting her, she may not set appropriate limits.

5. The story and its telling put me in mind of Winnicott's notion of how adults may need to have the breakdown that they could not experience in childhood; Diana's grief and nightmares were appropriate expressions of what she had been too unsupported to bear to experience fully as a child. Given that her early life could be summarised as involving little more than the pattern *lonely coping* in relation to *depriving, abandoning and hurting*, it was an achievement to have found her way to a job and a relationship and to have survived the disappointment of her infertility. Her adopted daughter's starting school was both a separation from her most loved other and a reminder of her own deprivation. She shows concern for the child in the middle of her own pain (and no evidence of the destructive envy certain object relations theorists might insist on interpreting).

6. I was moved and impressed by her ability to have survived a bleak life and by her ability now to experience and communicate her released feelings. I think she will make very good use of CAT and might be particularly helped by a mature female therapist, given the absence of any maternal figures in her past.

Comment: Diana exemplifies those patients who seem to have found the strength to survive with very little help from others and who can make very good use of what help they are given.

The six cases

No two stories are alike and no simple classificatory system can group patients in ways relevant to psychotherapy, but the six case vignettes together illustrate many of the issues which need to be considered in the assessment interview. All six were considered to have psychological problems potentially amenable to CAT. Only David had a significant, associated, psychiatric condition—depression and a history of alcohol dependency—for which he was receiving medication. None met the full criteria for borderline personality disorders but all had long-standing evidence of damaging patterns of self -management and of relating to others. Provisional reformulation of the underlying reciprocal role patterns suggested that current disturbed patterns often combined repetitions of childhood patterns (as in the uncontrolled anger in Nora and Nick and the uncontrolled mood variations in Evelyn) with enduring alternative procedures in the form of emotional distancing (in Nora, Nick and Evelyn) and of substance abuse (in the case of David and Evelyn). Possible contraindications to therapy included David's recent substance abuse and the risk of suicide in David and Debby. Evidence of at least one valued, emotionally significant relationship in childhood is usually taken to be a basis for a positive therapy relationship; in this respect Nora had her caring sister and one friend, David had his grandfather and one three-year relationship, Nick had his second marriage, which represented an escape from the childhood compulsive caring role, and Diane had one brief supportive relationship in the children's home. Evelyn was basically still avoiding repetition of the smothering closeness experienced with her mother. Debby seemed to have a reasonable relationship with her mother; she presented an unusually violent consequence of an unresolved mourning reaction, but early instability in the parents' marriage and the unremembered attachment to her father may have generated the reciprocal role pattern described above. The fact that all six had fairly stable work histories is a good prognostic sign in that those who can cope with employment are more likely to cope with the work of therapy.

OTHER CONSIDERATIONS

To complement the discussion of the six cases some issues which are relevant to making the diagnosis and assessing suitability for CAT in different clinical settings and with different diagnostic groups will now be discussed. In contrast to most brief therapy models, the use of CAT is not restricted to less severe disorders and change in central self processes (personality) is the common aim. Both clinical (mental) disorders (Axis I in DSM IV) (American Psychiatric Association, 1994) and personality disorders (Axis II in DSM IV) may be amenable. But there are important distinctions to be made, with implications for treatment, between the restrictions and distortions of Axis I disorders, usually regarded as departures from the longer-term characteristics of the patient and defined as clinical disorders (as if they are 'illnesses'), and the more enduring traits and structural problems of Axis II personality disorders (see also discussion in ICD 10, World Health Organisation, 1992). The 'state–trait' distinction is, in practice, not always clear; episodes of distress and dysfunction which occur in response to new situations often represent the 'de-compensation' of flawed but normally adequate ways of coping. It is also the case that the personality disorders identified by standard diagnostic criteria are hardly ever found in isolation; patients frequently meet criteria for more than one of them and they are virtually always accompanied by Axis I disorders. The concept of 'co-morbidity' is of little value; it seems better to think in terms of the range and intensity of symptoms (Axis I) and of the degree to which self processes are distorted and poorly integrated (Axis II), both of which result from genetic predisposition and adversity in childhood.

Psychotherapists will encounter many patients who could be diagnosed in Cluster B of the DSM classification; those with borderline personality disorder (BPD) are the most demanding and the treatment of these patients with CAT has been studied systematically. Establishing a working therapeutic relationship is difficult because they repeat their general tendency to mistrust, disrupt or idealise their relationships with their therapists and all too easily provoke collusive reciprocations, eliciting offers of ideal care or rejection. These interactive patterns, and abrupt switches between them, frequently occur during the assessment interview as the patient experiences the assessor as intrusive, unconcerned, critical or rescuing; such events need to be identified as early as possible, even to the extent of drawing provisional part diagrams during the assessment interview. The recognition of personality factors at a single assessment meeting is aided by noting the often powerful and confused countertransference feelings which they induce, but many have developed socially acceptable modes of self-presentation which can make them seem relatively integrated and for that reason the routine use of screening questionnaires, described later in the book, is recommended.

CAT is primarily directed at the understanding and modification of high level processes concerned with the management of self and most common behavioural and symptomatic problems are understood to be low level manifestations of more general patterns. In milder disturbances any respecting therapeutic input can be helpful, through the influences common to all approaches as discussed by Frank (1961), although the collaborative nature and high level focus of CAT may lead to more rapid change. In more difficult cases with borderline features the assessment and reformulation methods of CAT offer particular advantages, contributing to the quick establishment of a therapeutic, rather than a collusive or irrelevant or failed, relationship. Preliminary verbal or diagrammatic understandings suggested during the assessment session(s) can identify, anticipate and control those procedures which are otherwise likely to lead to dropping out.

The treatment of other, less common Axis II conditions with CAT has not so far been systematically studied but it appears that the basic approach, which allows considerable flexibility, is of value in the full range. In cases where there is doubt about the capacity of the patient to engage, a 3–4 session assessment, aiming to arrive at a provisional reformulation, will usually make it clear whether CAT or some other treatment is indicated.

COMBINING CAT WITH OTHER TREATMENT MODES

While many symptomatic disorders can be treated by the basic CAT approach, by identifying and modifying the problematic self-management and relationship procedural repertoire, there are some which require treatment in their own right, either because of their direct impact or because they may make patients inaccessible to psychological treatment. In these cases prior or concurrent treatment by other means may be indicated. Even where such treatments directed at symptoms are necessary, and even where there may be good evidence for the role of genetic predisposition in the symptomatic condition being treated, it is helpful to indicate the role of the treatment within a general procedural understanding. The predominant medical assumptions and the pressures of the pharmaceutical industry tend to mean that psychologically maintained problems are all too easily regarded as equivalent to somatic illnesses and their origins in problems of living ignored. One of the values of symptom monitoring during the early phases of treatment is that it helps patients become aware of the way situations, thoughts, behaviours and feelings are associated with the symptom and it is often appropriate to initiate such monitoring at the assessment interview.

The use of medication or other symptomatic treatments often needs to be considered at the assessment meeting, because some patients will already be taking prescribed medication and others will have symptoms which may be amenable to such treatment. Nearly all psychotherapy patients suffer from some degree of anxiety, depression and associated physical symptoms, as is witnessed by their scores on symptom inventories.

Depression

If depressive symptoms are severe enough to impair sleep and concentration or include other evidence of biological changes it is usually best to combine medication with the therapy; severely depressed patients are unable to participate in therapy. In marginal cases, especially if the patient is reluctant to accept medication, the response to the first few sessions of therapy will indicate whether or not medical treatment is needed.

Anxiety

Pharmacotherapy for anxiety symptoms is best avoided except in the short-term management of severe disturbance. It should otherwise be postponed, or if already in use should be slowly withdrawn; it is more useful to identify and control the sources of anxiety than to suppress the symptom. Dependency on anxiolytic drugs is easily established and once the procedural and situational associations of the symptoms have been worked out medication is usually unnecessary. In some cases behavioural approaches to control symptoms offer the quickest relief, for example in the treatment of phobic avoidance, after which the need for CAT for associated interpersonal problems can be assessed.

Obsessive-compulsive symptoms

The same considerations apply to much obsessive-compulsive symptomatology, but in long-established and severe cases the need for both behavioural and pharmacological treatments may need to be considered.

Somatisation

The common somatic accompaniments of anxiety and depression are usually relieved by the revision of self-management and relationship procedures but long-established psychosomatic disorders, where other factors such as allergy may play a part or where structural changes may have developed, may need parallel medical management. Psychological associations with physical symptoms need to be positively identified and demonstrated, not asserted.

It is important to bear in mind that any symptoms, whatever the underlying cause, may be associated with, or constitute the means of, interpersonal control. For this reason a procedural understanding and the possible involvement of psychologically significant others in CAT or systems theory therapy should always be considered. In this respect, CAT understandings are close to those of systems theory.

IMPLICATIONS OF SOME SPECIFIC DIAGNOSES AND BEHAVIOURS

Some diagnoses indicate the need for modifications of CAT methods or their integration into broader management systems. The treatment of personality disorders is reviewed in Chapter 10 and the CAT treatment of a number of specific conditions for which there is some accumulating experience and evidence, either published or in preparation, is reviewed in Chapter 9. These include eating disorders, substance abuse, psychotic illness, deliberate self-harm, poor self-management of diabetes and asthma and issues related to age and gender.

ASSESSING THE RISK OF SUICIDE

Many patients referred for psychotherapy will have a history of deliberate self-harm or attempted suicide, as did David and Debby described above. Such patients, especially where there have been multiple episodes, have an above average risk of successful suicide. Self-harm can involve a range of behaviours from superficial scratching to deep cutting and from taking a few extra tablets to potentially lethal overdosing. It always needs to be assessed in relation to a full understanding of the patient's procedures and current life situation. Unless the cause is an untreated major depression, psychotherapy is the only intervention likely to be of help.

Patients reporting an untreated, deepening depression with heightened self-blame and marked physiological symptoms affecting sleep, energy and concentration and patients reporting detailed plans for suicide need urgent psychiatric treatment and are not accessible to therapy. Excluding these cases, assessors may accept patients for CAT who have a history of attempted suicide or current suicidal preoccupations. In doing so they need to be clear in their own minds, and make it clear to their patients, the limits of the therapist's availability and of their tolerance for anxiety. Realistically, therapists cannot be continually available in person or by telephone and in any case to attempt to provide such care would feed idealisation (and in due course disillusion) and undermine the patient's autonomy.

The risk of suicide is greater in patients who have no close relationships or whose key relationships are deeply disturbed. If a patient is determined to die, nobody can stop them and making this clear establishes that therapists cannot be controlled by threats. Patients who fear that they cannot control self-harming impulses should be encouraged to keep a list of, and be prepared to use, available resources such as psychiatrists in local A&E departments, telephone contact with friends or with the Samaritans and any other sources they may have already identified. If, at assessment (or later during therapy) the threat of suicide seems active, and if the therapist is not working in a Community Mental Health Centre or other professional structure, it may be advisable to arrange to share management with psychiatric services from the beginning.

Despite the fact that therapy often involves accessing very painful memories and feelings, and despite the rapidity with which this may happen in time-limited CAT with deeply disturbed patients, serious suicidal incidents in the course of therapy are extremely rare. It is probably the case that reformulation and the early bonding of the therapy relationship which it encourages provide a safe containment and within this most patients will access feelings and memories only when they feel safe enough to do so.

ASSESSING THE POTENTIAL FOR VIOLENCE

The assessment of potential violence is not easy. The main predictor is the history of past violence, but episodes of uncontrolled anger (such as were reported by Nora and Nick) are common, especially in patients with borderline personality disorder, and in many patients these may have involved inflicting serious injury on others. In forensic practice there may well be a history of murder or the infliction of grievous bodily harm. Classical psychopathic individuals showing no remorse and professional killers are unlikely to seek or be referred for therapy, but many treatable borderline patients have escaped inflicting serious or lethal harm during outbursts of out of control rage more by luck than judgement.

Part of the decision about offering treatment to potentially violent patients must depend on the setting; such patients should only be seen in institutional settings with the agreement of the other staff members and appropriate safety arrangements. Therapists need to include a direct consideration of violence and its possible mobilisation in the reformulation letter and therapy will, of course, be conditional on the control of threatening behaviour. Accessing memories of victimisation in childhood in the course of therapy can sometimes mobilise dangerous anger in such patients, sometimes associated with switching into dissociated states in which the therapist is confused with past abusers. It is important to be aware that there is a death rate among therapists and others who are drawn into working intensively with violent patients.

Current disagreements about the treatability of personality disorders and about the respective roles of police and psychiatry, combined with the shortage of resources, means that many seriously disturbed patients end up in the care of clinical or custodial staff lacking appropriate training and facilities for any therapeutic approach. We are sceptical of the value of behavioural anger management in patients whose underlying pathology is one of fragmentation and dissociation and we believe that the scope of CAT in direct treatment and in supporting management, to be discussed later in the book, deserves wider evaluation.

ASSESSING MOTIVATION

It is not a CAT requirement that patients for therapy must have an already established ability to think about their own procedures. In many more disturbed and deprived patients there is little obvious capacity for this. However, the development of increased self-reflection through the joint work of developing and using the conceptual tools created during reformulation can be surprisingly rapid. This being so, there is no call for a separate programme of 'motivational enhancement'. Motivation is not a separate faculty, it does not depend on a motor being wound up and it is not something which can be simply taught; people will proceed to involve themselves in a task when the task makes sense to them. The early sessions of CAT are motivating because they induce or enlarge self-understanding and the capacity for self-reflection and have as their explicit aim the extension of awareness and control. The few patients who cannot be recruited to the work of therapy in the course of assessment and early exploratory sessions may be better served by more directive methods.

OTHER THERAPEUTIC MODES

Most patients referred and assessed for individual CAT are suitable for it and are happy to accept it, but there may be alternative approaches available, at least in some settings. Cognitive-behavioural therapists working alongside CAT therapists would probably define some cases as better served by CBT (panic and phobia, obsessive-compulsive disorders, some simple depressions, for example) and there are clearly many cases suitable for either approach, or for combinations of the two. Some patients may prefer and be suitable for group therapy as an initial treatment and others may benefit from it after individual CAT has helped to define the problem procedures but has not seen the patient through their revision. Involving partners at some point in an individual therapy may be valuable, especially when desirable changes in the individual may expose or provoke strains in the couple's relationship patterns. Where a relationship is the main arena for an individual's difficulties and where both accept it, joint work may be helpful either instead of, before or after individual CAT. In most settings the range of available alternatives is small, however, and systematic study of what is best, alone or in combination, remains to be done. In so far as there are choices, however, the patient should be involved in making them on the basis of a realistic consideration of what is involved, which may require some correction of the versions described in the media.

PAPER AND PENCIL DEVICES

Self-report inventories can be taken as approximate indications of patient pathology and there are strong arguments for including them as a part of the initial assessment. They provide baseline data on which to compare different patient samples and changes between pre- and post-therapy measures can contribute to the clinical audit of the performance of the service.

Of the many self-report tests available those which have been used over time in different populations and are relatively crude are the most suitable for routine use. Unfortunately many of these have now been patented and payment is demanded for their use, a practice which is contrary to the old humane assumptions in medicine whereby all findings of potential value and usefulness were regarded as in the public domain. Fortunately the recently developed 'Core Battery' (Barkham et al., 1998), which appears to have considerable clinical utility, has been explicitly not copyrighted (it is 'copyleft'). This offers, on the basis of some 30 questions, an overall score and scores on four subscales, and is suitable for repeated administration through the course of treatment. It is likely to become the standard instrument in the UK. The Personality Structure Questionnaire (Pollock et al., 2001) was designed on the basis of the CAT 'Multiple Self States Model' of borderline personality disorder (BPD) with the particular aim of identifying patients' awareness of having distinct self states. This is reproduced in Appendix 3 and its use is described in Chapter 10. It yields an overall score which correlates with the diagnosis of BPD and with measures of dissociation. Rather than defining a diagnostic cut-off point, patients scoring 28+ should be asked to elaborate on their experiences. If they describe distinct states and state shifts involving contrasting perceptions of self and others rather than just mood changes they will require reformulation and treatment methods developed for BPD. The Core Battery, the PSQ and any other tests administered should be scanned before the assessment session, as some patients acknowledge symptoms of importance which they do not easily report at interview.

TREATMENT CONTRACTS

If, when the assessment process is completed, the patient is accepted for CAT and chooses to pursue it, the offer made and the expectations from the patient may be summarised in a treatment contract. This can ensure that issues such as the proposed duration of sessions and of the therapy, the use of audiotaping, the limits of confidentiality and arrangements concerning absences and missed sessions are unambiguously spelled out. Failures to abide by the contract by either the patient or the therapist can only be used to explore therapy-related issues if a clear statement of this sort is available.

CONCLUSIONS

It will be clear that the assessment interview makes heavy demands on the interviewer. The main aims are to get to know enough about the patient to make sensible decisions about therapy and to give the patient an experience which provides some idea of what therapy would involve. The means whereby these aims may be achieved in a single interview should not include the use of a structured question-and-answer approach, however; as Balint famously said, 'if you ask questions all you get is answers'. If the ground has not been covered in the time allowed—and this may with advantage be 90 rather than 60 minutes— the choice is either to arrange a second meeting, which may be difficult under service conditions, or to note what has been left undone so that the therapist can supplement the assessment details.

Chapter 6

THE REFORMULATION SESSIONS

SUMMARY

The early sessions in CAT focus on the joint creation of written and diagrammatic descriptive reformulations of a patient's overall picture of distress and dysfunction and its developmental origins. These become central to the subsequent work of therapy. Reformulations focus principally on the acquisition and enactment of reciprocal role procedures. A written, narrative, reformulation letter is followed by a diagrammatic one, although in order to contain more disturbed patients it is helpful to attempt even a rudimentary diagrammatic reformulation as early as possible. These documents serve as 'tools' which promote a powerful therapeutic alliance by providing a means of understanding and mapping an integrated picture of often highly maladaptive role enactments, especially those which may constitute threats to the therapeutic alliance. Revision of these inevitably provisional documents may well be required during the subsequent course of therapy. Constructing a reformulation is a clinical skill which requires practice, supervision and an ability to remain empathic towards the patient whilst also thinking reciprocally. These principles are illustrated by case material.

This chapter describes the defining activity of the CAT therapist. To those unfamiliar with the approach it will repay careful reading, because the ideas and practical tasks are relatively complex.

CASE FORMULATION AND CAT REFORMULATION

Psychotherapists of all persuasions make case formulations of their patients, a process involving the selection and arranging of data according to their theoretical understanding of the issues to be addressed in therapy. In CAT the account will seek to identify the personal meanings accorded to their experience by patients and to describe the problem procedures and evidence of poor integration of the procedural system which are responsible for maintaining their dysfunction and distress. CAT practice differs from that of most other models in a number of respects:

1. Therapists work collaboratively with the patient from the start. This involves patients in activities such as self-monitoring and reading the Psychotherapy File and therapists in sharing their provisional understandings with their patients and inviting their ideas, comments and modifications.
2. Therapists make use of writing and diagrams to make their understandings explicit and 'portable', allowing patients time to test out their accuracy and usefulness and to contribute to their revision.
3. In order to demonstrate how problems have been formed and maintained, therapists offer both a 'narrative reconstruction' of the patient's story, in the form of a letter tracing the links between past experience and current procedures, and a verbal summary or diagrammatic model of the patient's current role procedures.
4. The reformulation, once agreed, is recorded in written and diagrammatic form. It provides a common agenda for the work of therapy and a conceptual tool of use to both patient and therapist. And it offers a global, 'top down' perspective, setting the range of symptoms and costly behaviours in the context of a preliminary understanding of the patient as a particular person living a life in particular life circumstances.

THE PROCESS OF REFORMULATION

Reformulation, which may have started in the assessment meeting, is usually completed at the fourth or fifth session. Therapists explain that the aim will be to achieve an agreed understanding which will be presented in writing at that session. The sessions leading up to the presentation of a provisional reformulation are devoted to largely unstructured interviewing combined with the use of the Psychotherapy File. Symptom monitoring, the construction of family trees and other tasks to be completed between the sessions may also be suggested. The File items identified by the patient will be discussed and examples asked for. For unreflective or emotionally disorganised patients (and for insecure therapists) these tasks introduce the practice of applying thought to feelings. Passively resistant patients will demonstrate their ways by non-completion of agreed tasks, thus alerting therapists to a procedure which is likely to have a considerable impact on therapy, while for patients who are more reserved or defended the need is to explore the felt meanings behind their more factual accounts. Possible procedural patterns recognised by the therapist should be presented in a tentative way for discussion. Throughout these sessions the therapist should be alert not only to the content of what is said but also to the form in which it is said and to attitudes or behaviours expressed directly or indirectly. It is important to distinguish idealisation from cooperation, cooperation from compliance, reasonable criticism from contemptuous dismissal, fear of exposure from control and so on. The aim through all this is to get to know the patient, to attempt to achieve an understanding of what this patient has experienced, done and learned in the course of his or her life, to demonstrate in these ways a genuine and accurate empathy, to engage the patient in active collaboration and to offer preliminary new ways of understanding and conducting life.

Everything that is discussed will be presented more formally at the designated reformulation session, usually the fourth. The understandings will be presented in two main forms, one a reformulation letter and the other a sequential diagram; these will be described in detail below. After discussion and, if necessary, modification, these written and drawn conceptual tools define the agreed agenda and shared understandings which are the basis of the therapy. As the process is primarily descriptive not interpretive and as patients are encouraged throughout to comment on, challenge or revise what is said or written out, the danger of imposing false understandings is slight. An adequate grasp of key issues is usually achieved, unless the patient is largely unavailable through a procedure such as passive resistance or emotional blankness. In those cases reformulation needs to focus on this therapy-undermining procedure, which will usually be an example of a more general one related to the presenting problems. If events arise later in the therapy which cannot be linked to the verbal descriptions of target problem procedures (TPPs) or cannot be located on the diagram, the reformulation should be revised. In most cases, but especially in more disturbed or poorly integrated patients, the formation of the diagram may involve a series of provisional or incomplete versions which will be corrected or clarified in discussion.

THE EFFECTS OF REFORMULATION

The impact of jointly fashioning and beginning to apply the conceptual tools described in the reformulation is complex and various. The experience of being attended to by a thoughtful other and the preliminary glimpse of how new understandings may be helpful is often unique and powerful, especially for deprived or abused patients, so in nearly every case the process serves to raise patient's morale and strengthen a working alliance. The understandings themselves, even before they are fully grasped and integrated, are containing, relieving confusions and uncertainties, reducing the need for anxiety- or guilt-avoiding procedures and hence allowing greater access to memories and increased awareness of emotion. Symptoms begin to be understood and become less preoccupying. The creation of a meaningful story out of incoherent accounts of distress contributes to the extension of personal meanings which is an essential element in the achievement of psychological well-being (Crits-Christoph, 1998). And for the therapist the understandings serve to make collusive reciprocations to problem procedures more avoidable or remediable.

The different elements of the reformulation are commonly carried out over the same time period. The reformulation letter is often presented first, serving to establish the therapist's grasp of what it has been and is like to be the patient, but in more disturbed patients recognising the damaging reciprocal roles needs to start in the first session if inadvertent collusion is to be avoided. These may be listed or represented in partial and provisional diagrams for discussion with the patient, an activity which may be the best way to demonstrate what therapy can offer.

For the purposes of this chapter the reformulation letter will be discussed first, followed by a description of sequential diagrammatic reformulation (SDR); the latter will include a preliminary consideration of the reformulation of partially dissociated borderline patients but a fuller consideration of this will be postponed to Chapter 10.

THE REFORMULATION LETTER

This section will begin with an example—another was given in Chapter 2—and will then summarise the principles on the basis of which letters are constructed.

Case example

Beatrice, aged 28, was referred by a psychiatrist after 14 months' treatment of depression; she was currently taking tricyclic antidepressant medication, which had improved her sleep to some degree. At the interview she gave a clear account of herself. She looked tired and unhappy and wept on three or four occasions but was also able to respond with smiles and even a laugh. Beatrice was the youngest by five years in a family of four children. Her father had left her mother when she was aged six months and there had been no contact since. She saw her mother as resenting her, describing her as cold and concerned only with appearances. She was sent to boarding school aged 9 where she became a rebel and was finally expelled aged 12. Nobody seemed concerned with the reasons for her behaviour. At the age of 16 she was sent to visit her oldest sister in Canada; a letter followed from her mother asking the sister to keep her, but she refused to stay. She left school and took a secretarial training and at 18 set off alone around world, paying her way by typing as she went. She finally settled for six years in Japan, learning the language and making friends. While there she started her first deeply passionate sexual relationship with an

Englishman; when he returned to the UK she followed him, but within a few months he backed off, leaving her desolate. This had led to her seeking help.

Beatrice completed the Psychotherapy File after the first session, identifying the following items as applying to her:

Traps: Depressed thinking; trying to please; avoidance.
Dilemmas: *Either* trying to be perfect and angry and depressed or not trying and being guilty and dissatisfied. *Either* I get what I want I feel childish and guilty, *or* I do not and I feel frustrated and angry. *Either* involoved and likely to get hurt *or* not involved, in control but lonely.
Snag: I sabotage good things as if I do not deserve them.

At the second session Beatrice discussed a number of painful details from her past and she reported a dream of seeing herself wrapped in plastic among the frozen chickens in a supermarket. At the third session the following draft reformulation letter was read out (comments on it are written in square brackets):

Dear Beatrice,
Here is the letter I promised you; it is my attempt to understand your past life and how it has affected you now. We will discuss it and you will be able to alter any aspects which are wrong or do not make sense.

[It is important to stress the provisional nature of the letter, to discourage passive acceptance and to ensure that the final version will be 'owned' by the patient.]

You had a very desolate early life. You were much younger than your sisters and were probably not a planned pregnancy, and your mother was faced with your father's desertion soon after your birth. Because of that (and perhaps for other reasons we have not discussed) you remember her as a remote and unaffectionate figure; you felt she was concerned with appearances but not with your feelings.

[This is a bald summary of what had been discussed, naming clearly what seemed to have been the impact of childhood events. While it is important to avoid accepting patients' accounts as objective history—hence 'you remember' and 'you felt'—it is also important to fully acknowledge their subjective experience.]

Boarding school provoked your first rebellion but your expulsion did not seem to make anybody concerned about how you were. At 18 you set off alone and ended up making a success of work in Japan and making two or three good woman friends.

[This is perhaps an inadequate acknowledgement of the patient's strengths, a risk due to the focus in CAT on problems and problem procedures.]

Your first powerful (almost overwhelming) attachment to a man was with Richard; for the first time ever you felt securely loved. When he returned to the UK you followed, only to be rejected after a few months, leaving you desperately unhappy. Your depression stems from that time; although recently you have struggled to return to work and go to your evening classes you find life exhausting and joyless.

[Having summarised the story the letter goes on to propose some ways of linking the past with her present state. These links will have been explored verbally but often they are more clearly described in the letter.]

I feel that very early on you learned to expect little from others; it was safer to manage on your own. But, as you indicated when completing the File, you still find yourself trying to please others in the hope of getting acceptance, only to be used by them, which makes you hate yourself. Richard was the first person with whom you experienced the depth of your need for affection. Maybe what you hoped for was unrealistic or maybe, meeting abroad, it was difficult to judge what was possible. Or perhaps he was just not ready for commitment. Whatever the reason, his leaving was a terrible blow, and since then you have experienced the abandoned and uncared feelings which, I feel, you had learned to put aside in your early life.

[The letter now considers what has been learned in the first sessions. The inclusion of the patient's own metaphors or images in the letter anchors the reformulation in personal experience while extending and making explicit the understandings which they contain.]

After our first meeting you had the distressing dream you told me about, seeing yourself wrapped in a plastic bag among the frozen chickens in a supermarket. This disturbing image seemed to me to stand for the feelings of the forlorn child you have always carried within you, despite your achievements and strengths. In therapy we will be trying to thaw the chicken, to go through and beyond your hopelessness and the negative feelings you have about yourself (the target problems). To do this we will need to work on the patterns of thinking and acting which continue to make you vulnerable.

[Descriptions of the target problem procedures will now be proposed, bringing the focus of therapy onto current patterns described as traps, dilemmas and snags.]

You recognised in the File how, feeling uncertain of your worth or your rights, you try to do what others want and as a result feel used and resentful and still more uncertain about yourself. I also think that your mother's seeming indifference to your emotional needs left you with the belief that you must either be totally self-sufficient or emotionally involved and doomed to be abandoned. Having managed your life without deep involvements, the experience with Richard seemed to brutally confirm the truth of this dilemma. I also wonder how far you may have felt you deserved the difficulties of your childhood and whether this and the brief rebellion at school may be the source of your irrational guilt. I certainly have the impression that you often act as if you were guilty and ought not to be happy so you sabotage things that do go well.

[The work of therapy is now described and the possible effects of the patient's procedures on the therapeutic relationship are spelled out.]

During therapy we will work on recognising and controlling these negative patterns as they recur in daily life. We will also need to be alert to how they may arise in your relationship with me. For example, you may feel you need to please me to be accepted — and hence you may feel angry with yourself and with me because of that. You may feel that being exposed and vulnerable is too dangerous to risk. The time limit means you will certainly be 'abandoned' at the end of our 12 further weeks; this may make you reluctant to be involved, although it will also protect you from feeling overwhelmed by dependency. And your irrational guilt may make it hard for you to accept the help that you need. We must try to face and resolve these feelings if they arise.

No therapy and no relationship can make up for the lacks you experienced as a child but I believe that working together for the next three months will give you enough support for you to revise the damaging ways you have relied on up to now. It can give new understandings and a manageable loss and by building on your strengths can free you to find the good that is available in others and in yourself.

General principles of writing reformulation letters

Most letters can follow the form of the above example, drawing upon (but often saying more clearly) what has been already discussed. The following points must be borne in mind:

1. Make it clear that the letter is a provisional one, open to revision by the patient.
2. Give an outline account of what brought the patient to therapy and a summary of the significant points in the life history. There is no point in rehearsing the whole story.
3. Show how the patterns evident in the present were derived from this past history, representing either repetitions or restrictive replacements of negative patterns.
4. Provide a summary account of the present problems (TPs) and a list of the current damaging procedures (TPPs), either in terms of traps, dilemmas and snags or of problematic reciprocal role procedures.
5. Consider how these may be manifest in the therapy.
6. Offer a realistic, not blandly optimistic, suggestion of what may be achieved.

It can be daunting to write such an account after only three or four hours' conversation, even when this has been supplemented by the patient's use of the File and self-monitoring. Trainees at first need to spend a lot of time on the task and supervision is essential.

The accounts of early life will nearly always provide a key to current issues; reciprocal role patterns from that time may still be evident and most symptoms or ineffective procedures may be understood as continuations or replacements of such patterns. Reading through the File with the patient in mind can help link, under a few general descriptions, a range of patterns presented in a variety of ways. From the first minute, the patient's reactions to the therapy arrangements or the therapist may well be illustrations of a problematic procedure. With experience, recognising countertransference feelings can become an immediate way of identifying the patient's expectation of reciprocating procedures or attempts to elicit them.

Despite the difficulty of the task, in the great majority of cases therapists produce moving and accurate letters which are received by the patient with relief and emotion, sometimes profound. Letters do not have to be exactly right for, by stating clearly what their understandings are, therapists offer their patients an opportunity to suggest changes where the account does not fit; in that sense being 'wrong' can serve to clarify the story and can provide the experience of collaboration. In practice, it is often best to read the letter out at one session and give a written copy to the patient to be studied and brought back with amendments at the following session. After any necessary changes the final version is copied and retained by both therapist and patient.

DIAGRAMMATIC REFORMULATION

The reformulation letter concludes its developmental, historical account with a verbal description of current problem procedures. These descriptions may focus on the unrevised sequences described as traps, dilemmas and snags and on key reciprocal role patterns, and in less disturbed patients these offer adequate working tools. There are, however, important limitations; verbal descriptions of sequences and of relationships can become too complicated to remember and the interrelations between different identified problem procedures may not be clear. This is where diagrams prove of particular value. Both written and diagrammatic reformulation greatly increase the ability of patients to recall subsequently understandings which are reached during sessions.

Simple flow diagrams

The sequences described as traps, dilemmas and snags can be expressed as flow diagrams: such part diagrams can be sketched roughly during sessions as a way of clarifying sequences and of gauging the patient's capacity to think diagrammatically; in the event, nearly all are capable and many are enthusiastic. Examples are given in Figure 6.1. Such provisional part diagrams may lead on to more detailed self-monitoring of sequences which are not fully understood. During the development of diagrams the listing of central subjective difficulties or the spelling out of individual procedural loops demonstrating the reinforcing consequences of maladaptive procedures generates an active and often moving working alliance and provides a basis for further correction or development. Partial diagrams remain, however, like the verbal descriptions, unable to demonstrate links between different problem procedures or to demonstrate clearly reciprocal role patterns. With the development of the Procedural Sequence Object Relations Model, a more complex and formal way of constructing diagrams evolved.

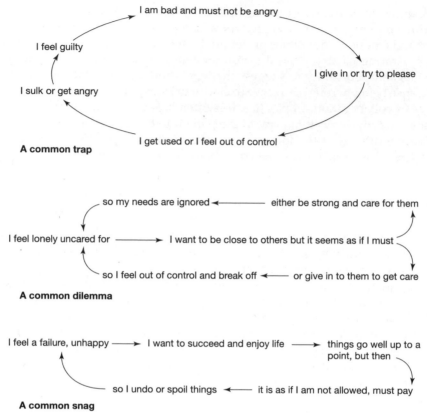

A common trap

A common dilemma

A common snag

Figure 6.1 Part diagrams: sequences illustrating traps, dilemmas and snags

The principles of sequential diagrammatic reformulation

Sequential diagrammatic reformulation (SDR) sets out to describe the core reciprocal role repertoire which was derived from the past and which is now repeated in current role procedures. This repertoire is deduced by the therapist from the direct and defensive procedures which patients report and manifest. It is a theoretical construct, not an account of experience. To avoid confusion it is best to confine the use of the word 'core' to this core of the diagram and to describe deep and postulated unaccessed feelings and memories as 'unmanageable' or 'hard to reach'; in time, these can usually be identified as concerned with unmet need or deep pain or rage. The description 'core pain', which is equivalent to James Mann's (1973) concept of 'chronically endured pain', as well as being liable to be confused with the core of the diagram, is often accompanied by an under-emphasis on the reciprocal role of, for example, hurting or abandoning, which the patient may perceive in the therapist and also enact.

The diagram's core is essentially an explanatory, theoretical device. The descriptions of the central repertoire of reciprocal roles are generalisations deduced from the range of reported and manifest procedures. Describing these patterns in general terms provides a basis for identifying the same patterns as they present (differing in detail) in later reports or enactments. In the diagram, enacted and experienced procedures are drawn as loops generated from the hypothesised central repertoire of role procedures and are traced out so as to demonstrate their outcomes—outcomes which in the case of problematic procedures will often reinforce the basic role repertoire, a fact indicated by drawing the loop as returning to the core of the diagram where this is described. For example, a pattern of *critical* to *striving* may be reinforced by hypersensitivity to any hint of criticism from others, or may generate perfectionist efforts which may lead to exhaustion and real or perceived failure, which in turn mobilises the self-critical voice. Or a *controlling* to *guilty submissive* pattern may generate placation with accompanying resentment. This in turn may lead to ineffective outbursts which serve to increase the guilt and reinforce the pattern of guilty submission to self and others.

In constructing a full SDR the procedures in relation to both self and others which are (or might be) generated from both poles of each reciprocal role pattern should be considered.

Diagrams constructed in this way embody clinically important basic theoretical concepts by (1) emphasising the reciprocal nature of procedures, (2) showing how each role is implicitly or explicitly directed to its reciprocal, (3) showing how the reciprocal may be a part of the self or another, and (4) demonstrating how a given reciprocal role pattern may be manifest in procedures described in either pole.

Sequential diagrammatic reformulation; practical procedures

In constructing SDRs therapists are called upon to remain empathically 'in tune' with the patient while thinking developmentally, sequentially, reciprocally and structurally. Here, as in the whole of CAT practice, feeling and thinking are supportive of each other. Patients will be involved in tracing particular sequences or patterns, but constructing the final integrated diagram requires experience and will have to be done by the therapist. Its use and accuracy will, however, be tested jointly and may lead to revisions or to the construction of simplified versions highlighting key therapy issues.

The construction of the diagram can start in different ways. One approach is to 'think reciprocally' from the start, seeking to identify key reciprocal patterns from the experiences which were described as significant in childhood, from current patterns of self-management or of relationships with others, from the patient's responses to the Psychotherapy File and from early transference–countertransference manifestations. It may be helpful to consult the list of common reciprocal patterns in Table 6.1 with the particular patient in mind. Once the reciprocal role repertoire is listed the key procedures generated from

Table 6.1 Common childhood-derived reciprocal role patterns

Parent-derived roles	Child-derived roles
Ideal care-giver	Ideally cared for/fused dependency
Over-involved	Over-dependent, suffocated
'Good enough'	Appropriate autonomy and trust
Incomplete, unreliable	Premature autonomy, fragile, needy
Conditional accepting or loving	Striving, performing
Dependent/uncaring	'Parental child'
Dependent/controlling	'Parental child'
Rejecting/controlling	Deprived/guilty or rebellious
Abusive/exploitive	Crushed or angry

it will then be drawn as procedural loops which trace the consequences of the enactment. For some patients it may be best to start with listing their key self-descriptions, possibly in the form of an invitation to describe their inner 'subjective self', and then to work out the reciprocal roles they relate to. All the experiences, actions, expectations, memories and symptoms described by the patient can be considered in terms of their roles and of the corresponding reciprocals as played by others or by aspects of the self. Symptoms will be located in the diagram either as accompaniments of particular roles, as when *striving* in relation to *perceived critical demand* generates anxiety, or as substitutions, as when situations where assertion or anger might be appropriate are dealt with by submissive behaviour accompanied by somatic symptoms and depression.

Procedural loops should aim to show the expected, perceived or experienced consequences of enacting a role, including the elicited reciprocations. The underlying role pattern will be described in a box (the core of the diagram) from which enacted procedures will be described on sequential loops; maladaptive, unrevised procedural loops will be drawn as returning to this core, indicating how the basic role repertoire has remained unmodified or has been reinforced. If there are also positive outcomes to some procedures they should be recorded; for example, *guilty perfectionist striving* in relation to *critical demand* could lead to exhaustion but also to achievement.

Patients find that descriptions of 'inner parent–inner child' reciprocal role patterns, based on recollections of childhood, are accessible, acceptable and often helpful, but simple equivalences between these and current procedures should not be assumed. Other significant sources, misinterpretations of experience and fantasy may all contribute to the final repertoire. It is a mistake to tie role descriptions in diagrams to the particular individuals in relation to whom they may have been formed as this may limit generalisation to other relationships and to self-management.

With experience, reformulation becomes a manageable task because key interpersonal and self-management procedures involve variations on a small number of themes, largely concerned with giving and receiving care, with lack or a loss of acknowledgement or care, with closeness or distance, with control and submission or with abuse and victimisation. These overall patterns will be repeated in a wide range of detailed interactions.

To illustrate the process the construction of the diagram in the case of Beatrice (see above) will now be described.

Case example (continued)

The information from Beatrice's history and the reformulation letter given above were developed into a diagrammatic form. The final SDR is reproduced in Figure 6.2. It was developed with the aim of illustrating the sources of her current deep unhappiness and previous long-standing avoidance of emotional involvement.

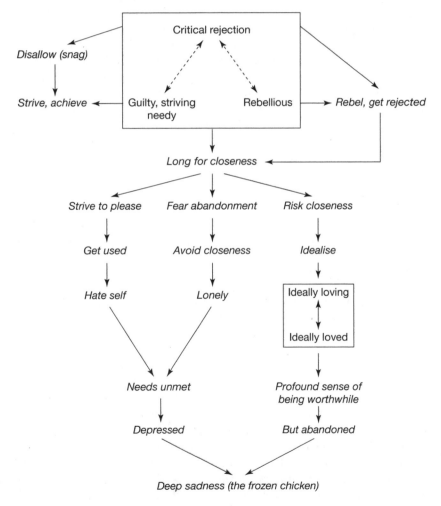

Figure 6.2 Beatrice—self states sequential diagram

The dominant reciprocal role pattern which stood out from the account of her early years was described initially as *'critical rejection* in relation to *guilty, striving and needy'*. This pattern was placed in the core at the centre of the diagram. The mother-derived critically rejecting role was seen to operate in relation to herself in self-blame (manifest in the snag identified from the File). The child-derived guilty, striving and needy role was seen to generate two main problematic procedures: (1) feeling needy and undeserving, so trying to please, leading to feeling used and to self-hate (i.e. feeling critical and rejecting of herself) and so reinforcing the core pattern; (2) striving (trying to avert anticipated critical rejection). This led to achievement, but left her deprived and emotionally uncared for, maintaining the core needy role. However, this description failed to incorporate her rebellious assertions at school and her refusing to stay in Canada, so the child-derived core reciprocal role was re-described as a dilemma between two possible responses to critical rejection, namely: either *guilty, striving, needy* or *rebellious*. Neither achieving nor rebelling did anything to satisfy her unmet emotional needs, nor did avoiding closeness. One other powerful reciprocal role pattern (RRP) was exemplified uniquely by the relationship with Richard. Put simply, this was an example of a relationship seeming to offer all that was missing in childhood; it was described as ideally loved to ideally loving. The contrast between this relationship and all past experence and the fact that it was unique and only mobilised with Richard was described by placing this pattern in a separate core box. The link between the two cores was then traced; a longing for closeness linked with a fear of abandonment had led to placation followed by self-hate (critical rejection) or to the avoidance of emotional closeness (prior to meeting Richard). Taking the risk of involvement and his subsequent withdrawal had repeated the experience of being rejected, reinforcing the first core pattern and leaving her desolate.

The final SDR of Beatrice showed how her seeking closeness had been constrained by her narrow range of options, as summarised in the procedural repertoire, and how the experience of finding and then losing a deeply felt relationship had led to her current extreme unhappiness.

Single or multiple cores in diagrams

In the example of Beatrice the problematic childhood pattern was condensed into a single RRP description. In many cases a range of associated reciprocal roles, derived from one or both parents and possibly also involving rivalry with, or care for or from, siblings, can be described within a single core box in the diagram, indicating that the roles are compatible and that transitions between them are smooth and appropriate. In the case of Beatrice, the ideal role pattern was described in a different core box because it referred to procedures enacted in different phases of life and with only one person. In patients with borderline personality structure, however, there may be a range of alternative, partially dissociated reciprocal role repertoires ('self states'), only one of which is operating at a given time; a similar pattern may be evident in psychotic disorders. This is manifest in markedly discontinuous behaviours and variations in self-awareness which provoke powerful but confusing and contradictory countertransference feelings in the therapist. (The term 'self state' refers to the CAT Multiple Self State Model of BPD.) These patients, because of their discontinuities, present their stories in a jumbled manner, showing what Holmes (1998b) called 'narrative incompetence'; for such patients the reformulation letter, even if incomplete, has a powerful impact in that it offers a preliminary sequential account in place of this confusion.

Contrary to a widespread assumption about the role of 'the unconscious', many patients can give clear and informative accounts of their shifting between states, although these are often not volunteered as they may be felt to indicate 'madness'. The use of screening questionnaires, as described in Chapter 10, is therefore helpful. When the presence of dissociated states is suspected, patients should be asked to record what they know about their states of mind and should monitor switches between them. Once states of mind are reliably identified, the reciprocal patterns need to be recognised. The therapist should help the patient to describe not only the dominant mood or behaviour of each state but also the sense of self and of others, the degree to which feelings are accessed or cut off and the accompanying symptoms. Finally, the therapist will need to assemble these data, locating each state as an aspect of a role and identifying the reciprocal. It is often the case that both poles of the reciprocal role pattern will be described as subjectively experienced states, as when both an abuser and a victim state are recognised, but in other cases only one pole will have been recognised as experienced subjectively, perhaps because the reciprocal is always perceived in, or elicited from (or in psychoanalytic terms 'projected into'), others.

Diagrammatic reformulation in these cases requires the recognition and characterisation of these separate 'self states', for each of which separate core boxes need to be drawn. This can be aided by discussion of the patient's replies to the Personality Structure Questionnaire (see Appendix 3) or to the last section of the Psychotherapy File, followed by self-monitoring by the patient. Partial dissociation between RRPs is indicated diagrammatically by locating core repertoires in separate boxes which define the separate self states. 'Self state', it must be emphasised, is a theoretical construct and should be clearly distinguished from the terms 'state' or 'state of mind 'or 'state of being' which describe the subjective experiences associated with playing a particular role in relation to others or to an aspect of self.

When in a given self state characterised by a particular reciprocal role pattern the patient may enact either of the roles, perceiving or eliciting the reciprocal in others. Abrupt state switches are a common feature of BPD, reflecting three types of instability which may be differentiated in the diagram:

1. Response shifts in relation to the same reciprocal, as in Beatrice's switch from trying to please to rebellious in response to critical rejection.
2. Role reversals while in a given self state, for example from victim to abuser.
3. Self state switches, for example Beatrice's switch from the self state *ideally loved* to *ideally loving'* to the self state in which once more she felt critically rejected.

A full consideration of reformulation in BPD will be presented in Chapter 10.

Sequential diagrams and self state sequential diagrams—a recapitulation

Diagrams offer an abstraction, setting out reciprocal role repertoire(s) in one or more boxes. This repertoire is a heuristic, a theoretical construct, it does not refer to a bit of the brain or to experience. It is derived from, and is designed to make sense of, what is manifest in experience and behaviour. Listed in this way the repertoire is placed in the core of the diagram from which procedures can be seen to be generated. As argued above, descriptions of the profound feelings, which are often described as 'core pain' and which are related to Mann's description of 'chronically endured pain', should use words like profound or unmanageable so as to avoid confusion with the diagram's core. Descriptions of behaviours, symptoms and experiences should be located on the procedural loops.

Patients will describe their states largely in terms of moods and behaviours; such states are the subjective accompaniments of enacting or being drawn into a given role. The therapist's job is to explore and describe the feelings, acts and perceptions associated with each role and to define the implicit or explicit reciprocals.

How many cores in a diagram?

There are various degrees of complexity in constructing the core or cores of diagrams. The aim is to describe all major problematic role procedures in general terms. The decision about whether to list reciprocal role patterns in one, two or several cores is a clinical and a practical one. Everybody has a range of ways of being; in that sense the self is a confederacy of states rather than a single nation. The pragmatic issue is to decide how best to describe the level of their integration. The patterns illustrated in Figure 6.3, demonstrate ways in which the integration of the core repertoire may be displayed. The procedural loops are not described.

BASIC: single RRP

'FRENCH LOAF': RRPs co-exist, mobilised appropriately, smooth transitions

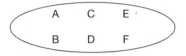

'SPLIT EGG' AND SSSD: abrupt transitions, often inappropriate, some roles extreme

'Split egg'   'Self state sequential diagram'

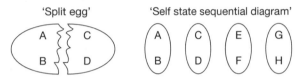

DIALOGIC SEQUENCE ANALYSIS: traces rapid shifts between roles and RRPs

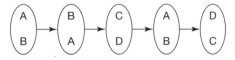

Figure 6.3 Types of cores in sequential diagrams

Basic: A single reciprocal role pattern offers adequate understanding.
The 'French loaf' diagram: A number of reciprocal role procedures are listed
within the core; these may be mobilised separately or together.
Self states sequential diagrams (SSSD): One form is the 'split egg' diagram,
which was the first version of divided diagrams used in CAT. There is a division into two clear self states. In BPD the common pattern is of *abuse and
neglect* in relation to either *abused, deprived and guilty* or *revengeful anger* in one
part. The other dissociated role pattern is commonly some version of *ideal care*
in relation to *ideally cared for*. In narcissistic personality disorder (NPD) the
'split egg' patterns are more in the form of *grandiose contemptuous dismissal* in
relation to *humiliation and envy* in one self state and *seeking special care and admiration* in relation to *being special and admired* in the other. These patterns are
evident as alternations between grandiosity and shame. In many cases
borderline and narcissistic patterns are combined. Examples will be found in
Chapter 10.

'Split egg' diagrams may be satisfactory but in most cases a more complete way
of mapping borderline structures is needed. In these, the early *abusing–abused*

pattern is shown to lead to some direct re-enactments or experiences and to some defensive, coping procedures involving symptoms, avoidance and so on; in either case the outcome may be to confront the individual with unmanageable levels of unmet need, sadness or anger. These may be experienced as echoes or repetitions of the original abusive experiences which led to dissociation. This 'flashpoint' or 'crossroads' may be indicated on the diagram (as in the diagram of Rita (Figure 7.1) near the end of Chapter 7), as the point at which switches to other self states occur. At times this leads to the expression of primitive rage, leading to violence or self-harm, and at times to dissociative symptoms such as perceptual distortions, depersonalisation and derealisation. Most frequently it provokes a rapid switch to an established more manageable alternative self state. This may be a 'zombie' state, in which perceived threat or abandonment are responded to by emotional blankness (*emotional withdrawal* in relation to *abandoning or threatening*), to a state characterised by *frenetic, highly focused but emotionally blank activity* in relation to *anxiety-provoking threat*, or to the search for an *ideally caring* to *safely cared* for state.

An important, overall distinction may be made between the processes (described as 'ego' defences in classical psychoanalysis) where emotional restriction is one aspect of limited role procedures, derived from the internalisation of critical, controlling relationship patterns and self-organisation marked by disorganisation and discontinuities where no continuous, central or coherent pattern exists. Flexibility in making and revising diagrams is important and the above styles are not exclusive or mandatory. The diagram made of Beatrice, described above, does not exactly match the examples for, while there were two distinct self states, these did not show the typical borderline features of frequent and abrupt alternations, being activated at different times in her life.

THE ORDER OF REFORMULATION

In the early practice of CAT the use of the File and the listing of TPs and TPPs was carried out initially, followed by writing the letter and then, as RRPs were recognised, by the construction of diagrams. This meant that the descriptions of dilemmas, traps and snags were linked later to diagrammatic descriptions of the underlying reciprocal roles. This linking often shows how a single role pattern underlies a number of TPPs; in this way diagrams offer a more succinct and general understanding. For example, the RRP *critical* in relation to *guilty* could be at the root of a placation trap or a depressed thinking trap, a perfectionist dilemma, a dilemma such as 'either blaming others or blaming myself' or of a snag whereby any success is undermined. In our opinion there are many advantages in thinking in terms of reciprocal role patterns from the start, noting (1) descriptions of past and present relationships, (2) how the self is cared for, managed and judged, and (3) the emerging relationship with the therapist. This may be apparent from overt statements and behaviour and from the therapist's 'educated countertransference' (see Sheard et al., 2000). General patterns deduced from these sources can be suggested and described provisionally, perhaps in preliminary diagrams, from the earliest sessions. Further discussion with the patient, detailed procedural monitoring and the integration of information from the File allows the final diagram to be constructed in this way, in most cases by around session 6. While there are no absolute rules in this, except to find what works best for the patient, it is our conviction that thinking reciprocally from the start and incorporating this understanding in the reformulation process offers the best preparation for the work of therapy. Because of the dominance of monadic, individualistic assumptions in our culture some therapists have to work very hard to acquire a reciprocal perspective.

THE IMPACT OF REFORMULATION

Patients respond to their completed diagrams in three main ways. Some are relieved to have a new understanding of why it has been so hard to change. Others feel sad or appalled to realise how they have boxed themselves in and fear there will be no way out; this is a common enough response in any therapy at the point at which patients realise their own contribution to their problems. For them, it is important to emphasise that these are maps of problematic procedures and not of the whole person, and important to emphasise that description is the first step, to be followed by recognition and change. A third, less common, response may be confusion. Therapists need to be careful not to impose over-complex diagrams on their patients, even if they may need them themselves. Simplified maps describing the most damaging sequences are of more use than are brilliant reconstructions of the whole psychopathology, and leaving out many connections in the pursuit of readability is preferable to the creation of interlocking mazes resembling a street map of Birmingham.

EXITS

In general, it is best to leave the drawing in of alternative, more effective procedures ('exits') until the use of the map for a few weeks has made it familiar and well understood; recognition is the first task and only when it is reliably achieved can patients begin to explore alternatives on their own. The exception to this is where symptoms or other procedures threaten the patient's staying in therapy or where serious self-harm is a possibility; in these cases working on provisional exits located on incomplete diagrams is the priority.

In CAT, individuals are understood to be inherently motivated and socially formed rather than being rational information processors or at the mercy of unconscious and conflictual forces. The role of reformulation is to illustrate and challenge the negative consequences of the individual's particular social formation and to support the patient in the recognition and revision of what has not gone well but was previously not recognised. Diagrams indicate in a non-judge-mental way both how restrictions were maintained and how they may now be overcome and, by extending awareness of different aspects of the self, contribute to integration and control.

FURTHER READING

Case formulation methods used in a range of therapies, including CAT, are presented in Eells (1997). Examples of CAT letters and diagrams, some demon-strating earlier forms, will be found in Ryle (1990, 1995a), Ryle, Spencer and Yawetz (1992), Mitzman and Duignan (1993) and Cowmeadow (1994). Dunn (1994) describes the use of pictures in a sequential diagram made with a very disturbed patient. The diagrammatic reformulation of borderline patients is presented in Ryle and Beard (1993), Ryle and Marlowe (1995), Pollock (1996) and Ryle (1997a) and of an offender in Pollock and Belshaw (1998). The thera-peutic impact of CAT reformulation is discussed in Ryle (1994). Schacht and Henry (1994) and Luborsky and Crits-Cristoph (1990) describe research-oriented ways of modelling relationship patterns.

Chapter 7

THE THERAPY RELATIONSHIP: WORKING AT CHANGING

SUMMARY

The tools of reformulation are used to guide subsequent work during which a range of other specific techniques may be used. However, the fundamental work of CAT involves continual reference back to and focus on these reformulations, which should describe and illuminate enactments of key RRPs both out of and in session. Therapists need, above all, to avoid reinforcing (colluding with) dysfunctional RRPs and must be alert to the state switches which occur in more disturbed patients. Monitoring and working on revising the enactment of such roles continues to demand high levels of concentration and intense work from both therapist and patient. This work is assisted by use of aids such as rating sheets and, possibly, other forms of 'homework', and may involve other techniques such as graded exposure or writing of 'no send' letters. Therapist responses to the patient are described in CAT in terms of personal *and* elicited *countertransference. The latter is further divided into* identifying *and* reciprocating *varieties. Awareness of these enactments is critical in avoiding collusion, particularly in working with difficult or personality-disordered patients. Sequences of patient RRPs and their associated dialogic 'voices' may also be mapped by the technique of* dialogical sequence analysis *developed by Leiman, an example of which is given. Finally, further enactments and difficulties are to be anticipated towards termination and these are explicitly considered by both patient and therapist through the writing of 'goodbye letters'.*

With the creation and revision of the written reformulation and diagram the first phase of therapy is complete; the therapist has acknowledged and explored the patient's experience and together a new way of understanding has been negotiated and agreed. At this point there is a change of gear; the descriptive tools which have been created and recorded must now be applied actively to the task of change. This change involves two overlapping phases; the first involves the deliberate use of the tools to recognise each time the problematic patterns of behaviour or thinking recur, the second is devoted to their control or replacement.

In this chapter the main issues and techniques involved in this phase will be considered; a more fine-grained consideration of therapist interventions will be provided in the next chapter. It is important to recognise that, in all but the simplest problems, the work of therapy involves much more than the use of the reformulation tools under the didactic guidance of the therapist; it requires the skilful continuing development of the therapeutic relationship. The therapist's focused attention and concerned curiosity have been, for many patients, a new experience generating a new optimism but change is not easy and old patterns reassert themselves. Wider issues concerning the sense of self and meanings of others will be brought to the therapy relationship and will be addressed by the formal tasks but also and crucially by the human quality of the relationship as it evolves and is thought about. The early clarifications offered by reformulation encourage patients to think about changing but also serve to create an opportunity for mourning of past experience of losses and reflection on missed opportunities and unfulfilled potential. Here therapists need to be capable of attuned silences and of active exploratory methods such as empty chair techniques and responding to and exploring the patient's painting or imaginative writing. In these ways, while focusing on the recognition and revision of maladaptive procedures, therapists also convey a trust in the patient's capacity for further growth and individuation in the ways emphasised by humanistic and Jungian approaches (Samuels, 1985; McCormick, 1990).

THE WORKING ALLIANCE IN THE ZPPD

Vygotsky was describing the teaching of intellectual skills when he defined the the zone of proximal development (ZPD) as the gap between current ability and the level of learning which the individual has the capacity to attain if provided with the support of a more competent other. As discussed in Chapter 4, good teaching aims to operate in this zone and, by analogy, good therapy should aim to address the zone of proximal personality development (ZPPD). Because the idea of self-reflection, in the sense of thinking about one's own thought processes, is an unfamiliar activity for many people, one task of therapists is to provide concepts and experiences supporting the development of this capacity. Using the Psychotherapy File and taking part in the collaborative process of reformulation are ways in which CAT therapists are active in their patients' ZPPD, and many so-called 'pre-contemplative' patients (Prochaska et al., 1994) are able to rapidly extend the scope of their self-reflection. However, the wish to undertake therapy and change one's life in some way does undoubtedly depend in some measure on an individual's experience of a sense of personal crisis, whether focal or at an existential level. Motivation, in CAT, is not seen to represent an innate quality of the patient but is rather seen to be the result of experiencing a helpful and meaningful relationship in which an understanding of unhelpful role procedures is generated.

As discussed earlier, the therapist is not a teacher in the ordinary sense of the word. Wood et al. (1976) described the teacher's role as the provision of a 'scaffolding' of necessary concepts which become the intellectual tools used by the pupil. This metaphor is transferable to therapy and reformulation exemplifies it, but the emphasis is different. The creation and transfer of the conceptual tools needed for self-reflection represents only one aspect of therapeutic learning. The child's learning about the self and others is conveyed by the mode in which his or her explorations of the world are supported by parents and other caretakers. Earlier learning may have been conveyed by constricting, authoritarian ('Magistral') straitjackets rather than by scaffolding, or the individual may have been left largely unsupported. Where the assumptions about the values and meanings accorded to self and others are concerned, the levels of respect, acceptance, acknowledgement and control provided by caretakers is more important than any direct instructions about values or behaviours. For example, an authoritarian parent may proclaim benign beliefs and liberal values but will be present in the child's mind as a source of instructions to be obeyed. It is important that therapists do not convey their understandings in a similar style. Nor will the child of emotionally unavailable or mystifying parents get help from a therapist who offers silence or incomprehensible interpretations. Forceful therapists may succeed in shouting the parental voice down, sending the patient away obeying a better set of internal instructions; in other cases, given world enough and time, patients may finally discover something useful from obscure or baffling therapists. The aim in CAT is to offer a more equal, exploratory, explicitly collaborative (Socratic) relationship which can generate a thoughtful, accurate, accepting and generous internal conversation. Understood in this way the creation and maintenance of a good working alliance requires the full range of sensitivities and skills. The tools and techniques of CAT are intended to support the therapist in maintaining such a generative relationship even in the face of all the ways in which patients may withhold trust and undermine change.

The working alliance of therapy is therefore a special and unfamiliar form of relationship, combining teaching and learning with the provision of an arena for the manifestation of the patient's procedures. Observing the relationship as it evolves in this arena allows a different kind of learning: the capacity to sustain relationships is developed by the therapist's recognising and not reciprocating destructive patterns and encouraging the patient to participate in a new form. Therapeutic 'technique' is aimed at generating and living through an intense, reconstructive relationship.

TRANSFERENCE AND COUNTERTRANSFERENCE

In every relationship people bring their own repertoire of reciprocal role proce-dures and expect or attempt to engage with others in terms of one or other of their familiar patterns. They (we) will usually seek out others who have, or whom they believe to have, a matching repertoire, with shared or reciprocal features. If they do not get the expected and desired reciprocations they may attempt to extract them forcibly or they may give up. In close, emotionally significant relationships the reciprocal roles will usually repeat patterns evolved in early personality development and reflecting basic assumptions about trust, acknowledgement, care and power.

PSYCHOANALYTIC UNDERSTANDINGS

A major contribution of Freud's early work was his recognition that, when his patients demonstrated feelings and behaviours which he felt were inappropri-ate to the situation, they were manifesting assumptions originating in child-hood. This 'transference', first thought of as an obstacle, was soon seen to present a direct opportunity to address the patient's problems by recognising, interpreting and not responding in the ways expected or wished for by the patient. The origins of psychoanalysis in hypnosis, with the patient recumbent and (in Freud's case) with the analyst being out of sight, combined with the classical analyst's principled denial of ordinary conversational responses, means that a particular form of transference is liable to be elicited, typically one in which initial dependent idealisation is followed by anger and a regression to more childish modes. This supposedly neutral stance of the analyst was claimed to be the necessary way of achieving an understanding of unconscious processes and over the course of the last century many influential schools of psychoanalytic practice have proposed an increasingly exclusive and intensive attention to the regressed relationship evoked by the technique. However, the traditional assertion that cure may be effected through interpretation alone of such a transference neurosis has not been substantiated. Indeed there is evidence that therapeutic outcome may be inversely related to frequency of transference interpretations (Piper et al., 1991). Recently, however, more atten-tion has been paid to the limits of this approach and the focus has shifted to addressing what Stern et al. (1998) describe as 'implicit relational knowledge'.

A related understanding concerns the responses of the analyst; this 'counter-transference' was seen initially as the contamination of the analytic stance by the analyst's neurotic reactions (an idea leading to increasingly prolonged train-ing analyses, the value of which has never been demonstrated) but emerging from this was a realisation that countertransference was also a specific response to what the patient was conveying. With this understanding the trained aware-ness of countertransference became an important source of information about the patient and greater attention is now paid to the intersubjective nature of the analytic relationship.

CAT UNDERSTANDINGS OF TRANSFERENCE AND COUNTERTRANSFERENCE

In linking transference and countertransference, psychoanalysis, especially in object relations theories, developed a more interactional model of therapy. But it remained largely concerned with the particular form of unequal, regressed relationship generated by the rules governing psychoanalytic practice. In CAT, transference and countertransference are seen to be one particular example of the general model of relating through the meshing of reciprocal role procedures. To focus exclusively on this is, from the CAT perspective, curious and unhelpful. Freud's original observation that what patients bring into the relationship with the therapist is news about them and offers a therapeutic possibility is fully accepted in CAT, but the belief that change can only be achieved by means of deliberately inducing regression is not. The conventional analytic reciprocal role pattern locates power in the analyst and could be summarised (or perhaps caricatured) as *'unself-revealing omniscient interpreter* in relation to *recumbent, regressed, interpreted object of interpretation'*. CAT, being a time-limited therapy, has not time to reduce patients in this way but, more importantly, there is no need to. The use of information about the patient's past and present relationships and evident sense of self on the one hand, and the therapist's cultivated sensitivity to what the patient is imposing or seeking on the other, allow a reformulation of the central problematic role procedures to be arrived at in a few sessions in most cases. This can both account for the problems for which therapy is sought and predict what is likely to emerge in the therapy relationship.

Patients can use this understanding to recognise and change their everyday relationships and self-management procedures, and many do so, but learning is more immediate in the therapy relationship, where recognition can be linked to non-reciprocation and the exploration of alternatives. Failure to recognise negative procedures operating in the therapy relationship, whether hostile, avoidant or idealising, will inevitably block progress. Conversely, the use in CAT of the same concepts to consider the therapy relationship and the relationships of daily life aids generalisation of what is learned from the lived understanding of transference and countertransference to daily life.

The therapy relationship is not characterised by one single transference–countertransference relationship; many changes may occur in the course of a therapy or indeed of a session as different RRPs are mobilised. Early listing and mapping of the repertoire of reciprocal role procedures and continuing use of the diagram to trace what is happening during sessions is one of the major contributions of CAT technique; it enables therapists to become skilled at recognising the meanings of the range of feelings evoked during their time with each patient. Reformulation indicates the patient's likely pressures and invitations to collude; it can be a useful exercise to trace how countertransference varies according to where the patient is located on the sequential diagram. In the case of borderline patients which events or remarks from the therapist provoke state switches and which states are signalled by symptoms can only be identified and clarified by meticulous use of the diagram.

PERSONAL AND ELICITED COUNTERTRANSFERENCE

It is useful to distinguish two sources of countertransference. One, which may be called personal countertransference, will reflect the therapist's particular range of role procedures. These are bound to be idiosyncratic even after, and perhaps partly because of, years on the couch! They may include unhelpful vulnerabilities such as an undue wish to be depended on or to control or a tendency to avoid anger or trivial personal quirks like a dislike of fat people. Whatever they are, patients will seem to be remarkably skilled at eliciting them; trainee therapists need to use supervision to become aware of their particular tendencies; in due course one can learn to recognise the 'temptation' to collude and use it as evidence about the patient's procedures. Such personal countertransference is not totally distinct from the specific reactions evoked by the particular patient, which can be called the elicited countertransference, for the individual threshold for different feelings and behaviours is bound to vary.

IDENTIFYING AND RECIPROCATING COUNTERTRANSFERENCE

Within elicited countertransference reactions there is another useful distinction to bear in mind, that between identifying countertransference and reciprocating countertransference. This distinction bears some similarity to the historic concepts of concordant and complementary countertransferences described by Racker (1968). This distinction in CAT stems logically from the model of the dialogic self. A person enacting one pole of a RRP may either (1) convey the feelings associated with the role to others, in whom corresponding empathic feelings may be elicited, or (2) seek to elicit the reciprocating response of the other. These processes may involve direct speech and action but are often powerfully conveyed non-verbally by tone, posture and expression.

In the course of therapy, therapists can use their identifying countertransference to explore feelings which the patient is conveying non-verbally but does not acknowledge or experience consciously. This does not need to be done mysteriously or omnipotently; it is enough to say something like: 'in the last few minutes, while you have been talking, I have felt an undercurrent of anger (or sadness, or pain etc.); maybe it is your tone of voice or the way you are sitting. Am I picking something up from you?' Silences are often occasions when such indirect communications can be identified.

As regards reciprocating countertransference, the need is to recognise the pressures and to avoid reinforcing (collusive) responses. Here too quite straightforward comments can be made, such as: 'As this is the third week you have not brought the diary you and I had agreed it would be helpful for you to keep, I feel you are needing to show me that you are in control or are angry in some way. What do you think?' Or: 'Could your telling me how much help you had from your herbalist, your neighbour and from the article in the colour supplement and your dismissal of the Psychotherapy File as being too elementary to be of use be your way of telling me that you do not think much of this therapy and of me?' When negative feelings or intentions are picked up, especially when they are directed at an actual vulnerability, it is important that therapists avoid (or admit to) covert expressions of countertransference hostility in the comments they make. It is also important to know and acknowledge the possibility that the patient is reacting to an actual deficiency or error on the part of the therapist.

Either identifying or reciprocating countertransference may indicate feelings in the patient which contradict what is overtly said or done and may express feelings which the patient has not been able to acknowledge; naming and exploring these makes them available to the patient for reflection. To further add to the complexity of the therapist's task, different forms of countertransference may co-exist as, for example, when one feels distress on seeing or hearing of a patient's self-harm or self-deprivation (empathic identification with the victim) and at the same time feels angry in response to what they have done to themselves (reciprocating anger evoked by their undermining of their lives and of the therapy). The most confusing patients are those with borderline personality disorder (BPD), because of their abrupt switches between states. This is particularly the case when anxiety provoked by touching on feared subjects leads to 'whirlpooling', a continuous process of rapid switching between states. When this happens, therapists need to impose a pause for thought which may be linked with getting the patient to try physical relaxation. The therapist then needs to examine one segment of the patient's behaviour or narrative at a time. A clearer understanding can be achieved by using dialogic sequence analysis (Leiman, 1997), of which the following is an example.

DIALOGIC SEQUENCE ANALYSIS

Case example: Alistair

Alistair was a 52-year-old solicitor who had recently been asked to resign from his firm after he had been involved in some shady financial dealings and had narrowly escaped prosecution. His self states sequential diagram described two dissociated reciprocal role patterns, one 'arrogant contempt A in relation to scum B' and the other 'admiring C in relation to admired D'. This represents a typical narcissistic personality disorder pattern. This notation is used to trace the role reversals and self state shifts as follows:

Alistair arrived 10 minutes late for his sixth session, a little out of breath, and explained he had stopped to chat with an acquaintance near the hospital (Alistair A to therapist B) and adding that he had run up the stairs, which showed how superbly fit he was despite smoking and drinking too much (Alistair C to self D). He launched into an account of his holiday abroad; he had angered his wife by his arrogance (Alistair A to wife B) which he attributed to her failure to show concern for him (wife's failure to be C to Alistair D) when he had been infuriated at the airport by the incompetent airline (Alistair A to airline B) and by the rude, idiotic French fellow passengers (Alistair A to French passengers B). Where they stayed the other English guests had been a dreary lot (Alistair A to the English B) but there were two charming Irishmen (the therapist was Irish; Alistair C to therapist D). They were very free in their behaviour; doubtless the therapist had had numerous affaires? (Alistair A and C to therapist B and D).

TRANSFERENCE, COUNTERTRANSFERENCE AND THE WORKING RELATIONSHIP OF THERAPY

A therapist's response to a patient is, of course, evoked by the full range of the patient's characteristics, communications and behaviours, not all of which are transference manifestations derived from childhood and not all of which are problematic. Some are evoked by the unfamiliar way therapists behave and this points to the need for therapists to be explicit about their role and to invite and respond accurately to questions and arguments about it. There is no reason to believe that opaque, vague or emotionally blank therapists have a particular access to transference, for patients, like all of us, repeat their patterns wherever they go. Therapists doing CAT should be open about how they understand their role, preserving the right to limit their availability and to maintain their own privacy but able also, within the clear boundaries established through reformulation, to offer direct human responses. Therapist and patient roles are not symmetrical but they are of equal value and the aim should be to base them on openness and mutual respect.

CAT is a demanding model for therapists and patients. Because it involves a high level of participation from patients a common transference response is one of initial commitment followed by withholding or disappointment; the successful holding on to the working relationship through these threats to the alliance is a key therapeutic task. Because it is intense and brief, dealing with loss and disappointment is a necessity, but one which, with the support of the reformulation tools and goodbye letter, allows the internalisation of the work done together.

In the discussion of technique which follows it is assumed that every kind of activity occurs in the context of, and has implications for, the developing therapy relationship. The working alliance is an alliance between the therapist and the patient which depends on the rapid extension of the patient's ability to experience and feel and to think and reflect on the self. Jellema (2000), from an attachment theory perspective, suggests that patients whose tendency is to avoid accessing feeling need a different approach from those who have difficulty in thinking about themselves. But in many, if not most, patients both kinds of difficulty are met with, and the therapeutic response needs to address both, bearing in mind that it is often the 'cognitive' aspects of CAT which provide the safety within which feelings can be accessed. Where patients have little faith in their capacity to reflect it may be important, once the scaffolding of the basic reformulation tools has been constructed, for therapists to avoid being too busy, so as to allow space for initiative and experimentation, and to remember that silence may be the appropriate form of activity at times, even in time-limited therapy.

TECHNICAL PROCEDURES

Following the completion of the reformulation phase the first ('honeymoon') sessions are usually characterised by the patients' active involvement, buoyed up by a new optimism and a developing understanding of the sources of their problems. This mood may include an element of magical hope or of idealisation of the therapist who has brought them to this point, or may be expressed in compliant or placatory participation in the work. In the very short run these attitudes may serve to collect information and initiate new forms of diary keeping, but the procedures and their predictable, ultimately negative, outcomes should always be noted.

RATING PROGRESS

When verbal descriptions of target problems and procedures are employed, change can be rated on visual analogue scales the mid-point of which represents the state at the point that therapy starts (see Chapter 2 for an example). In the case of target problem procedures ratings may initially be made of recognition rates and only when recognition is reliably present should ratings of change be made. Where diagrams are the main reformulation tool used, ratings can be made of the frequency or intensity with which particular procedural loops are enacted; in BPD the frequency with which problem procedures and switches into negative self states occur can be noted.

The use of rating scales is disliked by a few patients and by rather more therapists and may have to be replaced by alternative methods. Regular review is, however, important. It has two functions: one is to build up the patient's capacity for realistic self-evaluation, the other is to ensure that both patient and therapist keep in mind the whole array of problem procedures and confront those in which no change has occurred.

RECOGNISING PROCEDURES AS THEY OCCUR

By the end of the reformulation phase, diary keeping and work in the sessions has usually located the place of symptoms, mood switches and unwanted behaviours in the procedural structure. The patient's attention has usually shifted from these once-automatic and apparently spontaneous experiences to the recognition of the newly identified problem procedures with which they are associated. In the case of borderline patients, the recognition of states and state switches will be the priority. Diagrams are the best basis for this monitoring and many patients keep them in their handbags or wallets or pinned over the bathroom mirror for ready consultation. The diagrams need to be as simple as possible and memorising them is helped if the core patterns and procedures are colour-coded. Borderline patients commonly choose predictable colours for their states and procedural loops, such as pink for idealising, black for depression and red for rage. Simple diaries of significant events can be kept for each day and colour coded by the patient; not infrequently the colour becomes the mnemonic device; so, for example, a patient may report 'I was feeling she was really wonderful—the kind of girl I had always hoped to meet. But then I realised that I hardly knew her ... so I saw that yet again I was off into my pink state'. Such colour coded 'maps' are best left on the table between the patient and therapist during sessions and during supervision so that both events occurring during the session and the reports of the previous week can be located and placed in the context of the whole picture.

RECAPITULATING AND REVIEWING THE SESSION

It is a good idea, especially in the first half of therapy as a common understanding is being established, to set time aside at the end of each session to go over the main themes and feelings and to repeat (or now notice for the first time) their meanings. Often, the content may have dominated the discussion and the mood and important aspects of the process with transference implications may not have been noted. At this recapitulation, both reports and transference enactments need to be located in the procedural system by reference to the diagram, a process which establishes the diagram as part of the shared language and understanding. This review leads on naturally to the rating of change; this should be done by the patient but commented on by the therapist, especially where there are discrepancies between the rating and what has been reported in the session. This review also serves as the basis for the negotiation of homework. Where audiotaping of sessions is carried out by trainees this re-capitulation provides a useful focus for supervision.

HOMEWORK

The term homework, taken over from cognitive-behavioural practice, has echoes of schooldays which are liable to induce delinquency. But the idea of doing work between sessions must be established in any brief therapy. The crucial thing is to devise with the patient an activity related to the themes and current preoccupations of the therapy. Learning to recognise problem proce-dures as they are mobilised is the essential task, as discussed above, but apart from this a variety of detailed homework tasks linked to the reformulation may be useful. Common examples would be:

1. Clarifying past history by constructing a life chart, completing family trees or writing brief self-descriptions.
2. Writing assertive 'no send' letters to hated past or present, dead or alive, people.
3. Writing to, or carrying out some ritual acts on behalf of, incompletely mourned loved ones.
4. Following simple behavioural programmes such as graded exposure to feared situations or practising alternatives to identified procedures, for example practising assertion in place of placation or passive anger.
5. Rehearsing ways of managing difficult emotional states. This may involve identifying misinterpretations of external events or getting their scale wrong through 'catastrophising' and overpersonalising.
6. Rehearsing alternative thoughts and forms of self-talk.
7. Practising physical relaxation or forms of meditation.
8. Identifying and amplifying whatever forms of control the patient may have developed.

This last may be particularly valuable where episodes of self-harm have occurred. Making a list of ways of coping, such as writing a letter to the thera-pist, contacting friends or telephone counselling services or following some form of distraction, provides a readily available repertoire of active alternatives to self-harm.

All these activities should be linked to the diagram so that when the patient recognises a negative procedure beginning to operate, an immediate rehearsed alternative is available. If homework is negotiated and agreed, then failure to carry it out is an example of a negative procedure in action which needs to be discussed and linked to the reformulation. Equally, therapists are responsible for following up and discussing what homework was done.

ACCESSING PAINFUL MEMORIES AND FEELINGS

In a therapy which is going well it will be a matter of only a few weeks before patients can locate themselves reliably on the map and at this point they usually report less anxiety and more control. But this stage may also be marked by the emergence of painful feelings and memories which will amplify, but do not usually contradict, the understandings summarised in the diagram. The pace at which these are contacted and their assimilation depends upon the safety offered by the therapy relationship; it should not be imposed by the therapist. Procedural changes are initially dependent on deliberate conscious control; the automatic mobilisation of positive or at least less harmful procedures may take a long time to become established. Once the use of the reformulation is reliably established, the need to refer to the reformulation tools diminishes but patients are advised to keep them to consult if the need arises. A common comment at post-therapy follow-up is that 'well of course I still get the old impulses and may even begin to go down the old road. But now I can stop and think'.

NOT RECOGNISING PROCEDURES AS THEY OCCUR

Not all patients get off to a flying start, however, and some who do go on to stagnate after a few sessions. Where clearly recognised procedures are responsible, such as the one summarised in the Psychotherapy File as 'If I must then I won't', they will need to be repeatedly identified and challenged. Stagnation in mid-therapy is often the result of therapists being drawn into unrecognised collusive reciprocal role patterns. Experience with audiotape supervising suggests that such unrecognised collusions may originate in inadequate diagrams in which the therapist and patient seem to have agreed to omit an important procedure. This points to the need to take careful note whenever an event occurs which cannot be located on the current diagram. It also indicates one of the limitations of normal modes of supervision and the value of audio-taping; therapists cannot report and may not convey phenomena, or the absence of phenomena, which they have not identified.

With or without audiotape supervision, if a therapy seems to be drifting into stagnation it may be helpful for the therapist to write a 'midway letter' to the patient reviewing what has and has not been discussed and suggesting what may be happening in the therapy relationship to account for the absence of movement. The most common explanation is that the patient's unexpressed but indirectly communicated anger has elicited in the therapist a placatory, avoidant, passively resistant or emotionally cut-off response. If such stalemates are not challenged the patient may go on to miss sessions and may drop out, whereas, if they are, the experience of having negative feelings acknowledged and allowed and understood in this context has a major therapeutic impact. As part of the challenge therapists should 'shake the transference–countertransference tree', that is to say they should identify and name what they are feeling and consider how far it is a reciprocation to what the patient is conveying and how far an empathic echoing of what the patient cannot express. Discussing these issues in supervision is helpful; not infrequently the stalemate and emotional flatness is reflected in the way the session is reported, which creates an inert, non-productive therapist–supervisor relationship and a bored, yawning supervision group. This is less a case of 'parallel process' than of serial role induction.

If the patient consents intellectually to the new understandings but remains unengaged emotionally in therapy and in daily life, more active methods may be called for, such as empty chair conversations, role play exercises with the therapist, directly confronting the patient with descriptions of countertransference feelings or the use of drawing, painting or writing. Work through parallel therapeutic modalities, such as music therapy or psychodrama if available, may also be very productive at this level. All of these should be planned and carried out with reference to the reformulation descriptions of the key procedures involved in maintaining emotional disengagement.

THE CAT MODEL OF RESISTANCE

In many models of therapy the failure of patients to engage constructively in the work of therapy is labelled resistance. This term implies an (unconsciously) motivated refusal to get better which overrides the consciously expressed wish for change. The word smacks a little of blaming the victim and it seems better to define the phenomenon as a manifestation of, and the therapist's failure to achieve change in, one of the patient's negative procedures. In CAT the likelihood of problem procedures operating within the therapy relationship will have been noted in the reformulation letter. As the therapy-blocking procedure will almost certainly have been manifest in other aspects of life it will have been described in the reformulation, so the phenomenon of non-cooperation can be made use of to illustrate and challenge a procedure of general importance. The work of therapy may need to be focused entirely on the manifestation of this procedure in the therapy relationship until it has been modified. A more general source of resistance is derived from the fact that the sense of identity is sustained by the enactments of individual procedures and is undermined by relinquishing any of these, even if they are harmful, an idea close to Fairbairn's concept of 'adhesion to the bad object' (Fairbairn, 1952).

DROPPING OUT OF THERAPY

One group of patients who drop out of therapy are those acting on particular role procedures concerned with resisting demands; the fact that CAT requires activity from the patient may mean that it is particularly prone to mobilise this reaction. In such patients all demands from others—but also their own plans and intentions—are experienced as oppressive; it is as if the only freedom lies in refusal. The underlying reciprocal role procedure is something like *exigent demand* in relation to either *surrender* or *passive refusal*. Such patients can be very difficult to move, despite the hollowness of their victories. Excellent fictional portraits of this are provided in Herman Melville's 'Bartleby the scrivener' and in 'Oblomov' by Goncharev. A similar but more tragic pattern is found where childhood has imposed a universal sense of guilt and non-entitlement (a pervasive snag) so that any dawn of pleasure or achievement is sabotaged.

Another group of patients with a high drop-out rate are patients with borderline characteristics. There are many reasons for this. Most have had seriously abused childhoods and have little basic trust in others and many have sought unrealistic ideal care only to be disillusioned. The response to these patients must be based on an early, accurate reformulation, often involving successive provisional diagrams, of their range of self states and of switches between them, with an acknowledgement of their past pain and with a particular focus on the procedures which threaten the therapy relationship. Without the self states sequential diagram to guide them therapists are almost bound to end up confused and 'back on the patient's map' in a collusive role. This may be based on accepting idealisation and then not managing the ensuing disillusion or may result from being provoked into some form of counterhostility. A more subtle collusion can take the form of focusing on only one self state by working hard on one of the more innocuous roles such as coping or placation or being emotionally cut off while leaving the other, more threatening aspects of the patient out of the room and off the map. Where patients are in the care of several individuals or agencies, maladaptive role relationships may be set up with different workers with negative effects on staff relations and on the patient. Containment under these circumstances requires a shared conceptualisation, which may be achievable through contextual reformulation as described in Chapter 11 (see also Dunn and Parry, 1997, and Kerr, 1999).

Borderline patients easily experience the therapist as intrusive and critical on the one hand and as unconcerned on the other and a therapist consigned to this knife edge should discuss it explicitly with the patient and try to work jointly on keeping the precarious balance. As far as possible, ways in which the patient can retain control of the pace of the therapy should be devised as otherwise, and often anyway, patients will do it by missing sessions.

In many borderline patients this 'knife edge' phenomenon reflects the fact that the safety and understanding offered by the early sessions, perhaps combined with the requirement to reduce substance abuse, leads to more direct access to memories of the original trauma and this can be a source of increasing distress. Therapists need to be concerned and supportive as the patients experience what they have spent their lives avoiding, and no pressure should be applied to pursue memories or to go faster or further than is manageable. It is as important to be able to control feelings as it is to access them. And it is important to recognise that some memories and feelings are too disruptive to face and are best left unaccessed.

RECOGNISING PROCEDURES AT TERMINATION; GOODBYE LETTERS

During the last phase of therapy the formal use of reformulation tools and rating of progress may become less important as the more turbulent relationship is lived through and understood, using the shared language established in the earlier sessions. In this phase, as termination is approached, the absence of anxiety and disappointment would suggest that the reality of the end is not yet felt by the patient, even if sessions have been carefully counted and the likely feelings around ending explored. Some therapists may be drawn into collusive responses which serve to avoid painful feelings and maybe sustain a degree of idealisation while others find it difficult to accept how important they have become to the patient. As termination approaches, indirect expressions of fear and anger often take the form of a recurrence of the initial symptoms; these need to be accepted calmly and further fluctuations predicted; even quite distressed patients will nearly always be able to regain the ground in the period before the follow-up meeting. Termination of therapy can also be seen as an opportunity, albeit usually a very anxiety-provoking one, particularly for very damaged patients, to enact a new role, namely that of *ending well*. This involves owning and communicating painful feelings of loss and uncertainty about the future and such a role enactment will be difficult but may also be highly therapeutic, especially when mourning for past losses has been incomplete. Discussing this final piece of work in these terms can be helpful in itself, since it will not be clear to the patient why ending is so difficult for them or why it may be important to attempt to do it well.

In CAT these issues are recorded in a 'goodbye letter' from the therapist which is read and discussed in the last or next to last session. The therapist will briefly rehearse the original list of problems and problem procedures and will consider with the patient how far these have been resolved, indicating where further work needs to be done. Both disappointment and gratitude need to be acknowledged but the main emphasis will be on assessing realistically what the patient has managed to go through and achieve, including noting how the patient has been able to be open and accept help and how what has been of value can be retained. Patients are also invited to write letters if they wish, and are encouraged to make these as realistic and frank as possible.

THE COURSE OF THERAPY

The last two chapters have provided an overview of the work of therapy, in which a sequence of activities occurs, namely:

1. The therapist listens actively to the patient's story and acknowledges the meanings of the experiences described in it, initially verbally in the sessions and then in the reformulation letter.
2. The therapist works with the patient to detect links and patterns in the experiences described in the story and evident in the developing working alliance and a summary reformulation describing these is agreed.
3. Further memories or reports of daily life and enactments of the patterns in the therapy relationship are linked with these general descriptions. This may include the patient contacting hitherto avoided memories and affects.
4. Once the patient's recognition of problem procedures is secure, alternatives are explored.

This sequence is paralleled by the individual exchanges around each new report or episode; this detailed model of good therapeutic practice will be presented in the next chapter. Meanwhile, the following excerpts from the therapy of a patient with a diagnosis of BPD illustrates many of the issues discussed above.

CASE HISTORY: RITA (Therapist Kim Sutherby)

Rita was aged 26 when referred for CAT. She had been brought up as the eldest in a large family but she herself had been largely cared for by her aunt. She gave an appalling history of early and persistent, childhood sexual abuse from her uncle and others and at the age of 13 had become pregnant. She was taken into care and the pregnancy was terminated (against her wishes). For the next four years she was intermittently in care or in hospital and was involved in heavy alcohol and drug abuse. At 16 she became pregnant again and since then had lived independently and cared for her daughter, now aged 10, while working part-time and continuing her education, obtaining 3 A-levels. Throughout that time she had used cannabis every day. She was currently living with a partner who had been with her for two years; he had been intermittently violent but she said he was currently making a big effort to control his temper and it seemed he was able to offer some support. Her daughter had recently been excluded from school on a number of occasions for disruptive behaviour.

During her first three sessions Rita gave a detailed history, showing little emotion and saying explicitly that she was not ready to discuss some of her memories. The therapist was impressed by her evident capacity in rearing a child and pursuing education and by the fact that she had been economically independent through various forms of part-time work. Rita marked ++ for all the descriptions of unstable states of mind in the Psychotherapy File. She did not complete the agreed homework task of monitoring her mood changes but went on to work cooperatively on the construction of her diagram, identifying three main reciprocal role patterns from her childhood. These were labelled as follows: *unsupported* (B) in relation to *neglect* (A) (derived from self in relation to parents); *scared and guilty* (D) in relation to *abusive* (C) (derived from self in relation to both parents and aunt); *submissive and placatory* (F) in relation to *cruel criticism* (E) (derived from self to aunt). She was distressed to describe how she often saw herself being cruelly critical (E) to her daughter just as her aunt had been to her; this often led to a guilty switch into placatory expiation (F).

These three patterns were clearly differentiated. They are described as three self states in the diagram (Figure 7.1). When Rita experienced others as repeating the patterns of rejection, abuse or criticism she could be overcome with unmanageable feelings of loss and rage; these acted as a trigger (marked as X on the diagram) which led either to a state of rage (G) or to an emotionally cut off, zombie state (H). She had managed her life for the past ten years by maintaining this emotionally cut-off state through regular cannabis use. This trigger point probably represents the point at which dissociation was initiated in childhood.

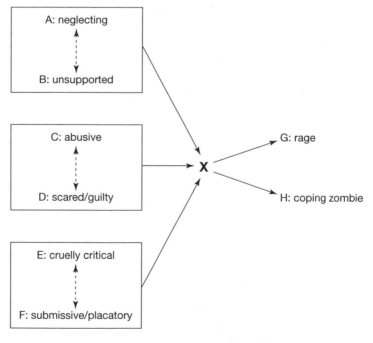

Figure 7.1 Self states sequential diagram for Rita showing reciprocal roles. B, D and F respresent childhood-derived roles which, when activated by experiences, perceptions or memories of A, C or E, lead to flashpoint X followed by either rage or the dissociated alternative coping zombie state

Rita missed two out of her first six appointments but cooperated actively in the construction of her diagram. During these sessions she was increasingly emotionally upset and her missed sessions were probably because of this. They were not deducted from her planned 24 sessions; to have done so before a collaborative relationship had been established would undoubtedly have been experienced as punitive. The therapist was moved by Rita's courage and pained by her story and by the continuing events in her life.

Nearly all the interactions with other people which Rita reported during her therapy were examples of her interpreting others' behaviour or her own behaviour in terms of the reciprocal role patterns identified on the diagram. Thus, over the 12 sessions following the completion of the diagram, 14 events or memories were linked to the A–B self state, seven to C–D, six to E–F, and five each to G and H.

The following is an excerpt from the sixth session. Rita had described being hit by her partner Derek (Derek C to Rita D) and she herself had hit her daughter Alice (Rita C to Alice D), following which her aunt had been very critical of her (Aunt E to Rita F). The following is verbatim:

Rita: She says to Derek that she is 'so concerned that I hit my daughter' … well she's never shown an ounce of concern before. If she was, why did it never occur to her that I was strung out and needed a break occasionally … . (*Rita B to Aunt A*). Anyway one thing about Derek—he doesn't hurt my daughter; I'm the horrible one (*Rita E to self F*).

Therapist: Can we just slow down a minute. You're furious today about a whole lot of things. Can we look more carefully at some of them. What it seems to me is that you are more aware of what you need from other people and that means you're more aware of what you don't get …

Rita: So what did I do? I took drugs. (*Rita C to self D or H*) I'm fucking out of my head and I just cannot cope all the time.

Therapist: I wonder how that switch from things seeming OK to suddenly becoming overwhelming happened?

Rita: I've not been sleeping and my eating is all over the place … everything is going wrong …

Therapist: I was wondering if this is to do with being angry with me? Coming here has made you open up so many painful feelings. (Therapist suggests *Rita D to therapist C*)

Rita: I thought about that and I thought I can't take it out on you because it's not your fault. I know I don't want to come here but that's not you it's me. I don't want to look at things that are painful and loads of things are getting stirred up. No, I'm not angry with you at all … (? *Rita F to therapist E*).

Therapist: You know it can be OK to be angry.

Rita: (shouts) I don't often get angry … because if I do I can't control it (G) and the next moment I've hurt Alice … I never meant that to happen.

At the next session Rita described her increasingly clear memories of her aunt sexually abusing her when she was aged three (*Aunt C to Rita D*). (Involving the insertion of plastic toys into her vagina.)

Rita: She is totally off her head. She and my mum had terrible childhoods and they have just shoved all that shit into me … I hate her. I think I should go home now.
Therapist: It's really hard to think about these things that make you so angry.
Rita: Not angry, sick.

Later in the session Rita spoke movingly about her sense of not having ever been cared for (*Rita B to others A*):

Rita: When you sit down and think about your life you realise that there's been thousands of people—social workers, care workers in children's homes—you know there's always been somebody, but there hasn't, if you know what I mean, been anybody. (*Rita B to everyone A*)

Some sessions later, at the therapist's suggestion, Rita wrote a 'no send' letter to her aunt. It was at once bitter and forgiving and ended by expressing the wish never to see her again. Reading the letter provoked a fit of weeping and then the following:

Rita: I hate that woman so much but I don't hate her as well you know. I haven't cried like that for ages.
Therapist: You managed to keep it all inside didn't you … Do you want me to keep the letter?
Rita: I don't want it. It's said now. I mean, I hate that woman; she'll never regret what she's done—she'll just never know …
Therapist: It doesn't really come across as a hateful letter.
Rita: Because I don't hate her … I don't … I forgive her … I forgive her for everything …
Therapist: It all comes across as very, very sad what you've been through, what you've had to face up to …
Rita: It is sad … the saddest thing is she'll never know, she'll never read it, she'll never get her head around it to see what she has done. She could read the letter and it would have no impact on her at all, not until she can admit to herself, you know … what she did.

Rita broke all contact with her aunt at this point, having meanwhile discovered that one of her siblings had also been abused by her.

With Rita's history it was inevitable that termination would be a very painful time. Two sessions before the end the therapist raised the coming end (not for the first time, of course).

Therapist: I don't want you to miss out on the chance of saying a goodbye that is not a rejection.

Rita, after listing her most painful losses, commented:

Rita: That's the only goodbyes I've had in my life ... well, not goodbyes but byes ... there was nothing good about them ...

Rita wrote a goodbye letter which included the following:

> *It takes so long to trust someone and they have to go through the mill to prove their love and loyalty and sometimes it goes terribly wrong. I feel like I have betrayed you and never really given you a chance—well not in the beginning anyway ... I do feel sad but not abandoned'* ...

In the event, Rita did not attend her final (six-month) follow-up and did not reply to subsequent letters. This was likely to be a sign of her anger at the pain she had experienced or of her choice of the abandoning role (A) rather than of the sadness of once more being left (B). It is unlikely that she would have committed herself initially to open-ended therapy (from which BPD patients have a very high drop-out rate) had it been available, but it is possible that a continuing supportive contact based on what was learned in this therapy would have been acceptable; unfortunately it could not be offered.

FURTHER READING

The CAT understanding of transference and countertransference is described in Ryle (1997c). An introduction to psychoanalytic models of therapeutic change is provided by Bateman et al. (2000) and by Bateman and Holmes (1995). Beck (1976) and Davidson (2000) give clear introductions to cognitive therapy and recent advances are reviewed in the volume edited by Salkovskis (1996).

Chapter 8

THE DETAILED CAT MODEL OF THERAPIST INTERVENTIONS AND ITS USE IN SUPERVISION

SUMMARY

CAT differs significantly from traditional psychoanalytic therapy in its focus on description (as opposed to interpretation) of current maladaptive RRPs. It differs from CBT in its understanding of the social and interpersonal origins of dysfunctional RRPs and in the emphasis placed on recognising and not reciprocating these. Process research has confirmed the validity of the technique of reformulation and has demonstrated the importance of therapist competence in developing and using reformulation tools. An empirically refined model of the resolution of RRP enactments in therapy has been developed involving acknowledgement, exploration, explanation, linking, negotiation, consensus, further explanation, contacting hitherto unassimilated feelings, discussion of aims and exits. The successful use of this approach, even with a psychologically unsophisticated patient, is illustrated. This model provides a basis for accurate supervision, in particular when sessions are audiotaped.

An alternative title for this chapter might be 'Does it matter what we do?'. Frank (1961) argued that many different kinds of influence, including that of various therapies, could be explained as the result of common persuasive elements, notably the effect on morale of being attended to by a recognised expert offering new perspectives. Luborsky et al. (1975), referring to the Dodo race in 'Alice', made a similar point in their paper entitled 'Comparative studies of psychotherapies, Is it true that everyone has won and all must have prizes?'. This 'equivalence paradox'—the embarrassing failure of research to establish clearly that any one model of therapy works better than any other—remains far from resolved despite the further 25 years of research reviewed by Roth and Fonagy (1996).

However, this should not be taken to indicate that therapy has no effect, nor that specific techniques are necessarily without value. Patients are smart enough to make use of a whole range of interventions. The Dodo phenomenon can be understood in terms of CAT theory; thus (1) procedures are related hierarchically, so that changes in a low level tactical procedure such as stopping smoking can both influence and be influenced by a change in assumptions about the value of the self; the former might be achieved by a behavioural programme, the latter by existential psychotherapy; (2) in terms of the procedural sequence model the continual cycle means that change in any one phase (involving either perception, appraisal, choice of action, enactment, consequences or the consideration of consequences) may lead to a revision of the whole sequence. Thus different therapies, focusing on different levels and on different phases, may achieve equivalent results.

In time, and given the present emphasis on the need for evidence-based practice, it may become possible to distinguish between the elements common to different approaches and the specific effects of detailed techniques on particular conditions, but it remains both important and difficult to measure clinically and humanly significant phenomena and to identify the factors relevant to service providers such as case selection and treatment costs. In the case of CAT, the model is a general one which can be applied with some modifications to a wide range of conditions and in different modalities. These include couple therapy, group therapy and work in contexts such as mental health centres (Dunn and Parry, 1997) and in therapeutic communities (Kerr, 2000); it may also have a role in coordinating treatment plans involving other kinds of treatment. Research evidence for its clinical effectiveness will accumulate from studies of different patient groups and in different settings rather than from a definitive demonstration that 'CAT works'. On the basis of the present, very incomplete, evidence it can be said that relatively well-integrated patients, suffering from disturbances of mood related to difficulties in work or personal relationships, who can benefit to some extent from any therapy offering the common factors within a respecting human relationship, respond well and rapidly to CAT. When we consider more damaged and disturbed patients, however, the particular value of CAT methods in establishing and maintaining therapeutic relationships is becoming well established.

CAT, PSYCHODYNAMIC PSYCHOTHERAPY AND COGNITIVE-BEHAVIOUR THERAPY (CBT): A COMPARISON OF PRACTICE

Good practice in both dynamic therapy and in CAT depends first of all on the therapist applying an exploratory, non-directive approach to the patient's reports and enactments. The agenda is set by what the patient brings and by the therapist's initial comments being open-ended and designed to evoke further details and associated feelings. This active empathic listening is usually well done, being part of the prior training of most CAT therapists. But what is learned from these exploratory conversations must, in CAT, be used from the beginning to identify and describe the recurrent patterns of problematic reciprocal role procedures and subsequently to link new material to these patterns. The essential act is *description* and is quite different from the interpretive interventions of traditional psychodynamic psychotherapy which may propose underlying, unconscious conflicts, memories or fantasies as the source of current problems. Insight, in CAT, seeks to answer the question 'what am I doing and what are the consequences?', not 'why am I doing this?'. Once established, this insight leads on to considering 'what else might I do?'. In practice, answering this will usually only be considered after the necessary prior stages of description and recognition have been completed.

In many cases the collaborative creation and application of the revised descriptive understandings are enough to allow the patient to explore alternatives. Some particularly entrenched maladaptive beliefs or behaviours may be challenged through the use of specific cognitive or behavioural techniques, but the premature or exclusive use of these can place the therapist in the expert teacher role, as described in Chapter 4, which assumes that patients are rational and requires them to be compliant and which can reinforce existing internalised critical or controlling voices. The traditional assumptions and structure of CBT can, in these ways, block the more fundamental work of exploring and changing underlying beliefs and values about the self. An example of this negative effect will be found in the description of a case (Susan) of obsessive-compulsive and panic disorder in Chapter 9.

The radical difference between CAT and traditional CBT can be described in terms of the kind of scaffolding provided. In CAT the emphasis is always on the place and meaning of symptomatic, mood, behavioural and relationship problems within the context of the individual's overall meanings, values and self-organisation. A premature or exclusive focus on individual symptoms, behaviours or beliefs can block the wider exploration of these central issues. Modifications in CBT involving links with interpersonal theory (Safran and McMain, 1992) or attachment theory (Perris, 1994, 2000) go some way to meeting these reservations.

EVIDENCE FOR THE SPECIFIC EFFECTS OF CAT TECHNIQUES

Early research into the impact of the developing CAT model provided some evidence for the specific effects of its methods. Ratings of change in the jointly specified goals of therapy were paralleled by related changes in measures derived from repertory grids (Ryle, 1979, 1980) and such grid changes, predicted at the start of therapy, were significantly greater in patients receiving CAT compared to controls receiving a psychodynamic intervention (Brockman et al., 1987). More recently, a series of studies of psychotherapy process, carried out by Dawn Bennett, has provided firm support for our belief that central aspects of CAT practice are of importance. These studies will now be summarised:

1. Bennett and Parry (1998) demonstrated that a CAT therapist and a patient with BPD created a diagram which contained all the main themes identified by two separate analyses of audiotapes of the early sessions using well-validated methods, namely the CCRT (Luborsky and Crits-Christoph, 1990) and the SASBY-CMP (Schacht and Henry, 1994). Bennett subsequently replicated this on three further cases (Bennett, personal communication).

2. The method of microanalysing transcribed excerpts of therapy sessions, of which early examples were given in Ryle (1997a), had relied upon a 'Therapist Intervention Coding' (TIC) based on a preliminary model of competent practice. In further work, Bennett (1998) refined this model of practice on the basis of a 'Task Analysis' of good outcome cases to produce an 'empirically refined model of RRP enactment resolution'. This research focused on how threats to the therapeutic alliance were resolved. Its refinement involved the serial revision of a provisional, staged model, based on analysing audiotaped records of good outcome cases, using independent raters to judge how far identified threats to the therapy alliance had been resolved. The model was revised accordingly and applied to further cases until no further revisions were called for.

3. Revised versions of the TIC were then applied to the supervision of therapists, using transcribed excerpts, and were also used by the therapists themselves, and Bennett then modified and quantified the TIC for use by observers (the TIC-O). This was shown to have good inter-rater reliability when applied to either transcribed excerpts or to the rating of whole session audiotapes. This yielded a measure of therapist competence which was shown to be correlated with an independent measure of the therapy working alliance. Using this method, Bennett demonstrated that therapists in good outcome therapies had recognised 80% of in-session enactments of problem procedures and had linked most of these to the diagram, whereas in poor outcome cases the rate was 30%. She also showed that experienced therapists received significantly higher ratings on the TIC-O than did trainees and that the ratings of trainees in supervision improved in the course of a therapy. Bennett's original and meticulous research is reported in documents submitted to the Mental Health Foundation and in a number of papers currently in preparation.

THERAPIST INTERVENTIONS IN CAT

Drawing on the research summarised above it is now possible to propose some overall guidelines. It should be emphasised that these should not be regarded as a prescriptive practice 'Manual'. Microsupervision has demonstrated clearly that therapists having a wide range of personal styles can apply the model and that each patient–therapist pair develops a shared language which manualisation could distort. Supervision using the TIC involves the retrospective application of general rules and principles to recorded material and its main aim is to heighten the awareness of therapists to what they are and are not doing; in this way it strengthens their capacity for self-reflection, acting much as reformulation does for patients.

The TIC, based on Bennet's 'empirically refined model of reciprocal role procedure enactment resolution', can be applied to any discrete episode in the course of therapy. It describes an overall sequence but may involve repetitions and tangents, ultimately going through the following stages:

1. *Acknowledgement.* To have others know and validate one's existence and experience is a primary human need without which any help offered may be irrelevant and is likely to be experienced as having something done to one rather than with one. Full acknowledgement involves an authentic and empathic acknowledgement of the experience of the other and will involve
2. *Exploration* on the basis of which,
3. *Explanation* and *linking* may be worked at. This needs to be engaged in with each new reported or enacted event, using the tools of reformulation. For this to be of meaning to the patient a process of,
4. *Negotiation* leading on to,
5. *Consensus* is necessary. The aim will be to relate the particular issue to the underlying general procedural patterns, usually by locating it on the diagram. This linking becomes real to the extent that the understanding is not imposed on the patient and is associated with emotion.
6. *Further explanation* can show how this linking can be understood. This may involve rehearsing the individual's history and how it contributed to the formation of the procedural repertoire. The difficulty in revising established patterns can be explained in a non-blaming way and the opportunity to reconsider these patterns can be emphasised.

The sense of being heard and understood and the repeated consideration of issues in these ways can lead on to:

7. *Contacting hitherto unassimilated feelings.* Supported by the new understandings and the safety of the therapy relationship, repressed and dissociated memories and feelings may be accessed and assimilated. This stage often follows the achievement of a shared understanding when, in Bennett's words, there is a 'lull in the engagement' and patient and therapist recognise what they have been through and that they remain connected. Once recognition is established, alternative procedures can be explored.
   Thus,

8. *Exits/aims* will be discussed in terms of procedural control and revision and by exploring alternative roles involving new ways of experiencing, judging and acting, both in the therapy relationship and in daily life.

These stages will now be illustrated in more detail.

Acknowledgement, exploration and linking

A therapist's possible interventions may be illustrated in relation to an example: The patient has just given a bald, factual account of a friend's grief over the terminal illness of her mother. Possible therapist explorations might include:

1. An expectant silence.
2. Direct questioning; for example: 'When your friend was crying when she told you about her mother what did you feel?'
3. Parallel linking: a reference to a possibly similar episode already discussed, for example 'Do you think the way you could not respond to her sadness was connected with the way you yourself cut off from your feelings after your father's death?'
4. Naming empathic countertransference: 'You gave a very matter-of-fact account of your friend's grief but I found myself feeling sad. Do you think I was picking up something you find it hard to allow yourself to feel?'
5. Linking to the reformulation. Early on in a therapy this might take the form: 'This seems to me to be another example of the dilemma we identified; how you move away from strong feelings as if you fear being overwhelmed'. (This could be summarised as *either* cut off *or* overwhelmed.) Do you think that is so? At a later stage, when reformulation is complete, the patient would be invited to make the link unaided.
6. Suggesting a transference link: 'Do you think that the fact that we have only three more sessions makes you wish to avoid thinking about anything to do with endings? Looking at your diagram where might we be?'

Any of the responses described above may lead on to further explorations involving the following stages.

Negotiation, seeking consensus, explanation and contacting unassimilated feelings

In the example above, the third response of making a provisional link to another reported experience, could, in the early sessions, be an important step in the process of descriptive reformulation, as it will introduce the idea of seeking for common patterns. It may also allow important differentiations to be made. For example in this case, the patient might go on to explain how he could now feel grief for his father but was aware of having been angry with his mother for her depending on him in ways which had allowed him too little space or support for his own feelings. This understanding could lead on to the exploration of his evident role in relation to his mother; this might be one of his basic role procedures identified, for example, as *'submissively but resentfully caring'*. If the patient recognised this, other examples might follow, for example, 'I was always the one left in charge of my little sister'. The next step would be to explore the reciprocal to the caring role. This might be *'weak'* or *'weak but controlling'* or *'selfish'*. Further exploration and explanation could serve at this point both to reach a clear consensual understanding of the particular procedural pattern which determined the patient's relationship patterns and management of emotions and to convey a wider understanding of how reciprocal role patterns are formed and sustained. This understanding could be enlarged and its emotional significance brought home by the therapist's account of being made to feel sad (countertransference); feelings which the patient's resentment had blocked might now be experienced and this in turn could initiate an 'exit' from the old procedural system.

Moves of this sort over the first half or more of therapy are frequently the source of a general mood of sadness which is painful but valued, representing mourning for what is now seen to have been missing in the past. In this case, a recognition of the loss of access to emotion and its maintenance by the established procedural pattern, combined with the shared 'in the room' feelings, would open the way for revision which could lead to changes in current relationships. Termination (whether in brief or long-term therapy) is an opportunity to experience a loss directly, neither denying sadness nor protecting the therapist from anger and disappointment; for many patients this is the enactment of a new role and can represent the most powerful transforming moment.

APPARENTLY PSYCHOLOGICALLY UNSOPHISTICATED PATIENTS

Not all patients are able to embark on self-reflection right away; they may need more educational approaches and the early exploration or modelling of alternative ways of proceeding ('exits'), but this does not mean that procedural understanding and change are not achievable, as the following case shows.

Case example: Grace (Therapist Michelle Fitzsimmons)

Grace's childhood had involved degradation and neglect; as an adult she had experienced violent sexual and physical abuse from two different partners; she had more recently terminated her relationship with a third partner who had been relatively kind. She was currently allowing herself to be used exploitively by two of her adult children who lived with her but gave her no practical help and stole from her; one was drug addicted and criminal and one had been diagnosed as schizophrenic.

In her early sessions Grace spoke in an uninterruptible monologue, cataloguing alternately her blaming anger with others and her dismissive contempt for herself as having 'bad blood'. She described how, when walking down the street, if anyone acknowledged her, she felt 'honoured'.

The audiotape of the seventh session was listened to by the supervisor. When the therapist managed to speak, her comments were emphatically positive (and not exactly in the formal negotiating CAT manner!) and they included proposing a description of a cycle of placation followed by explosive rage. This was drawn in a preliminary diagram. The therapist offered a consistent rebuttal of the patient's self-denigration and a consistent encouragement and celebration of change. The upper part of the final diagram (Figure 8.1), which was drawn in red, spelt out the origins of the 'bad blood' and traced how a snag and trap originating in this sense of self left her either sabotaging herself or placating others, in both cases leaving her needs unmet. Alternatives to these patterns were later

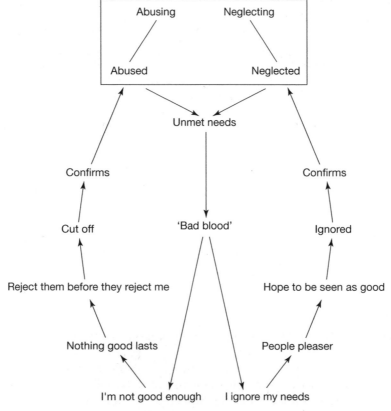

Figure 8.1 Sequential diagram for Grace

spelled out (in green) in the form of rehearsed self-statements. She repeated these to herself and soon began to revise her behaviour in current situations.

At session 12 her diagram was reviewed as follows:

Therapist: Do you understand this? These exits are all the things you told me in your own words.

Grace: Oh yes. It's getting better. It sounds terrible when you read all that (the trap and snag). I'm really doing well on these (the green). My son is out on bail at present. What he's doing is blaming everyone apart from himself for what he does—he says it's because he came from a broken home. I said that was a poor excuse because no matter what my parents have done, if I do wrong it's my doing.

Grace's therapy was interrupted and shortened because of her therapist's illness. She coped in a way which demonstrated that, despite her initial apparent impenetrability, Grace had learned to see and manage herself in a new way, and to recover when she relapsed in any way. Her weekly self-ratings showed consistent improvement.

Grace's goodbye letter read:

> 'I have really found our therapy sessions helpful in making me the much stronger person that I am today. I am at last enjoying my life and I'm no longer worried about upsetting people. If I think they are not doing their job properly I will confront them with it as now I know I am as good as anyone else …'

At follow-up, Grace reported an example of this in her successfully getting herself a long-delayed outpatient appointment in relation to some long-term physical symptoms.

The therapist's goodbye letter was accompanied by an elegant plastic card on one side of which the diagram was reproduced, in red and green, with an additional quotation from Grace: 'I am a snake which has shed its skin—I'm in control.' The reverse side of the card read as follows: 'If I have a day when I lapse I know it won't ruin things for me. I have broken the cycle of long and hard patterns of behaviour. I can recognise and stop things from affecting me like they used to in the past by: *Stop as soon as I recognise the old pattern. *Look at the problem. Think about the situation causing it (the trigger). *Listen to what I am saying to myself. Then ask myself: Is this what I want? Am I behaving in the way I want? If not, then ask myself: Where did it start to go wrong? When did it start to go wrong? Why did it start to go wrong? and How did it start to go wrong?' The card concluded, in green: 'Then think about how to break the pattern. Remember what I have learnt—in my own words! I can control it before it gets out of hand. Remember I am good enough.'

This example of unconventional CAT, in which rehearsed self-talk was applied to the understanding and control of specific interpersonal and intrapersonal procedures, produced significant change. This also reflected the therapist's genuine and warmly communicated respect for the patient, her explicit refusal to collude with the patient's largely self-directed destructiveness, her capacity to match the patient's verbal flow and her ability to build on the patient's own descriptions to make an accurate and user-friendly diagram. An originally unpsychologically-minded, uneducated and damaged woman was able to make remarkable use of the help she was given; at follow-up six months after termination she reported that her gains were maintained and in some respects extended. There had been one episode of uncontrolled drinking.

SUPERVISION OF THERAPISTS IN CAT

Therapy is aimed at the patient's ZPPD and the developed model of interventions described above can be understood as defining the appropriate scaffolding for CAT. There are many parallels between the therapist–patient and supervisor–supervisee relationship. The scaffolding role of the supervisor in training CAT therapists can be considered in the light of the same theory as that considered earlier in relation to therapists. Supervisors are working in the supervisee's zone of proximal development (ZPD) in their transmission of the methods and values of the model and, given that the relevant skills involve the formation and management of a personal relationship, they are also to some extent working in the zone of proximal personality development (ZPPD) – both the supervisee's and their own.

The discussion in Chapter 4 of the different styles of scaffolding is of some relevance here. The 'superaddressee' of this supervision dialogue is clearly the psychotherapy community and its official institutions and the particular features and structures of CAT. A trainee seeking recognition as a CAT therapist must follow the procedures and understand the principles of the model. Where conformity to these requirements and values is in question, the supervisor may correctly adopt the 'Magistral' voice, being the officially designated conduit of the organisation. However, given the variety and complexity of both patients and supervisees, the Socratic mode is generally preferred, in which rules and assumptions may be questioned and in which increasingly joint explorations of the detailed meanings of particular events can take place. In dislodging obstacles to understanding or failures to grasp the point, in challenging rigid adherence to inadequate versions of the model or in confronting limits and errors in the model itself, either supervisor or supervisee may indulge in 'Mennipean' humour—with a serious core.

Supervisors are simultaneously alert to adherence to the model and to the nature of the therapy relationship, where transference–countertransference manifestations may have been missed or where forms of collusion with negative procedures may have gone unnoticed. Provided supervisees have understood the model, failure to follow it is usually a manifestation of countertransference.

AUDIOTAPE SUPERVISION

Detection of these unrecognised processes, especially where collusion takes the form of not addressing certain topics or of settling into an inert truce, is far more likely to be recognised if audiotaping of sessions is employed. In such cases it may be the case that the significant procedure, commonly involving passive resistance in some form, has not been clearly identified in the diagram. The report of any significant event which cannot be located on a diagram points to the need to revise it. Listening to audiotapes of whole sessions or even of parts of sessions through the whole course of therapy is too time-consuming under normal NHS pressures; as a workable compromise therapist in training may be encouraged or required to audiotape all sessions and listen to them before supervision and to transcribe or play selected passages.

Experience is being accumulated of a less time-consuming form of audiotape supervision, based upon the rating of excerpts on a short version of Bennett's Therapist Intervention Coding (TIC-O). Listening to a number of taped sessions had shown that failures to intervene according to the model were common in respect of two key elements, namely linking new material to the reformulation and noting and linking transference manifestations. In an ongoing exploratory project, trainee therapists are required to listen to the audiotapes of their sessions before supervision. They are required to devote the last few minutes of the session to a recapitulation of the main themes. In this recapitulation, links to the diagram of reports of transference enactments should be made or repeated. These sections are transcribed and brought to supervision where they are discussed and coded. Despite the clear focus (and despite the unapologetically Magistral scaffolding being imposed by the supervisor), a proportion of therapists continued to omit these key interventions for several sessions. Therapists found the method exposing but usually reported that it had served to improve their practice. A study of the relation of these ratings to TIC-O analyses of whole sessions and to outcome is currently under way.

GROUP SUPERVISION

Most CAT supervision of trainee therapists takes place in groups of three or four supervisees and the ideal is to allow 30 minutes of supervision time weekly for each patient. There are many advantages in the group format, both in terms of learning from the work of others and because the authority of the supervisor is more likely to be challenged. Different previous trainings, cultural perspectives and life experiences among the supervisees enrich discussions and benefit all, including the supervisor.

'PARALLEL PROCESS'

The emergence in supervision of feelings and role patterns originating in the patient or the therapist–patient relationship is understood in CAT as the manifestation of transmitted reciprocal role procedures (RRPs). Thus, the therapist's identifying and reciprocal countertransferences, which, whether acknowledged and recognised or not, reflect the patient's RRPs, may be re-enacted in the supervisee–supervisor relationship. In group supervision, different members may respond to different aspects. In these ways unvoiced feelings and unrecognised RRPs may be recognised or at least considered. However, it should be noted that the traditional psychoanalytic concept of 'parallel process' is complex and poorly validated (Carroll, 1996), and such phenomena should be treated as a prompt to enquiry rather than as representing any exact mirroring or re-enactment.

DISTANCE SUPERVISION

An expanding interest in CAT training from people in remote areas of the UK and in other countries around the world has been met in part by developing fax and e-mail supervision, sometimes supplemented by telephone contact. Unless there has been some face-to-face contact the arrangements should be provisional until both supervisor and supervisee are satisfied that it works. Supervisees must have clinical experience and must be prepared to study the main CAT texts and supervisors must discover how far the potential trainee is able to convey the feel and content of sessions. If the trial is satisfactory then a weekly exchange may be set up, the sessions being reported and drafts of letters and diagrams being sent for comment. This arrangement has been surprisingly successful in a number of cases and reading the supervision records can contribute to the formal accreditation of the supervisee. In a current instance, three experienced and diligent Australian therapists supervised in this way also meet weekly for an hour's shared phone supervision. The addition of e-mailed voice recordings of the five-minute recapitulation at the end of sessions further strengthens the supervision. In time, the group will rely increasingly on peer group support. With further developments in technology more elaborate links may be available but these basic methods have proved effective and supervisors are able to take up transference–countertransference issues as well as issues to do with technique to a surprising extent.

(Information about distance learning and supervision can be obtained from the ACAT Office, Division of Psychiatry, Third Floor, South Wing, St Thomas' Hospital, London SE1 7EH, or via the website: www.acat.org.uk.)

Chapter 9

CAT IN VARIOUS CONDITIONS AND CONTEXTS

SUMMARY

CAT offers a general model of development and psychopathology which cuts across current, often unhelpful, diagnostic distinctions. A central feature of its practice is an emphasis on identifying and working with higher level self processes. The use of self-monitoring includes its use in investigating symptoms, as in CBT, but CAT focuses much more on the recognition of dysfunctional procedures and of state switches. The use of CAT for a variety of patient problems in various settings is reviewed along with theoretical developments associated with them. These include anxiety-related disorders, PTSD, depression, somatisation, deliberate self-harm, eating disorders, complications of medical conditions, substance abuse, gender-related issues, childhood sexual abuse, bereavement, primary care, old age, psychosis, learning difficulties, groups and organisations.

In this book so far we have presented CAT as a general psychotherapy model. In this and the next chapter we shall describe some particular applications of this model to different diagnostic groups and to work in various settings. Many of these are the focus of 'Special Interest Groups' and interested readers may find out more about these by consulting the ACAT website at www.acat.org.uk.

THE PROBLEM OF DIAGNOSIS

The word diagnosis comes from the Greek to discern or distinguish. It is a process well established in general medicine as the necessary basis for rational treatment and research, but its application to psychiatry raises a number of problems (Kendell, 1993; American Psychiatric Association, 1994; World Health Organisation, 1992; Roth and Fonagy, 1996; McGuire and Troisi, 1998). While we use diagnostic terms it is important to recognise their limitations. The discriminations made between psychiatric conditions are more arbitrary and less reliable than those made in general medicine and, in the case of psychotherapy, the emphasis is upon treating disturbed or depressed people, not on treating 'personality disorder' or 'depression'.

Categorical diagnosis involves fitting cases into defined groups. Such labelling can be arbitrary and reductive, but for some patients it is a relief to know that they have a recognisable and potentially treatable condition. Whereas in general medicine such categories are often based on clear understandings of the causes of the disorder, in psychiatry they have to rely upon a combination of features such as the presence of particular clusters of symptoms, the course through time and the response to treatment. This reflects the fact that there is no general and agreed understanding of the underlying psychopathological processes.

Dimensional classifications seek to remedy the arbitrariness of categorisation by relying upon measures of the extent to which certain features are present; these could be symptoms, personality traits or behaviours and for some purposes are more satisfactory. However, in the absence of a shared model of pathology, the choice of which dimensions to measure is equally arbitrary. Such contributory causes as are identified are of variable and partial importance. Genetic causes in psychological disorders, except in rare conditions such as Huntington's disease which is due to the presence of a specific gene and is really a neurological disorder, do not account for psychological illness by themselves. In identical twins with schizophrenia or bipolar affective disorder, for example, about half of twins remain unaffected. Other factors play their part in psychiatric illness and interact with each other, including biological damage, developmental distortions and past and present patterns of relationships, traumatic events and the current social context.

Competing paradigms

Apart from the innate difficulties involved in psychiatric diagnosis, much confusion can stem from the fact that there are competing or contradictory paradigms applied to understanding disorder, and in many cases people committed to a particular perspective may over-extend its applications. A fully adequate understanding of an individual patient may need to take account of genetic and biological factors, including the areas described in evolutionary psychology (McGuire and Troisi, 1998; Stevens and Price, 1996) and of the effects of early experiences on development as described in Chapter 3, which may currently be explained within psychodynamic, attachment or cognitive theories. In addition, although this is often neglected, the current life circumstances and their impact on the individual's sense of self and his or her ability to act needs to be considered. A disorder resulting from all these factors may meet a particular categorical diagnosis, and such diagnoses may be of value in predicting response to treatment and in comparing different treatments and for these reasons are a necessary aspect of understanding, but in our view their utility to the psychotherapist is restricted. For psychotherapists, once diagnoses are made, the main task is to relate them to a fuller picture constructed in the form of a case formulation. As Kendell (1993) observes, diagnosis and case formulation have different, complementary functions.

Case formulation in CAT, as has been shown earlier, is a collaborative enterprise aiming to set patients' problems and distresses in the context of an understanding of their lives. This may include acknowledging both biological and social realities which have to be dealt with but the emphasis will be on life experience and the conclusions drawn from it—conclusions which have seldom been fully reflected on and which are manifest in the values and procedures guiding behaviour and shaping experience. Whatever the diagnosis, case formulation will aim to provide a new perspective on, and a heightened awareness of, the problems which therapy will seek to remedy. It also cuts across the misleading notion that patients may suffer from several 'separate' conditions simultaneously. These are frequently and unhelpfully described as being 'co-morbid'. In reality, different levels of damage affecting different aspects of development and self structure are found. We suggest that a comprehensive, individualised, biopsychosocial formulation, such as that offered by a CAT reformulation, should be a minimum prerequisite for working with any patient or client within mental health services. Unfortunately patients are very often treated or simply managed on the basis of much lesser understandings. Before considering and illustrating how this process may vary according to diagnoses and contexts, it is necessary to consider how symptomatic disturbances may be understood and treated.

THE SCOPE OF CAT

The scope of psychotherapy is broad; feelings of unfulfilment in life, general unhappiness, disabling emotional distress, disorders of bodily functioning, damaging and unsatisfying social and personal relationships, negative self-attitudes and poor self-organisation may all fall within its scope. It may also have a part to play in the treatment of physical disorders which are complicated by psychological factors or which require careful self-management. These different problems often co-exist. Cultural beliefs and the theoretical model of the psychotherapy offered will determine which level of disturbance is considered to indicate a need for intervention.

The model of CAT presented in the previous chapters is a general one; CAT is not a diagnosis-specific intervention, it is a general model of psychological disorder and its treatment. In practice, it is primarily concerned with problems at the level of interpersonal and self processes and these are, of course, the central issues in treating patients with personality disorders. Leaving those aside, the problems which bring patients to therapy are commonly accompanied by physical symptoms and negative moods which can be understood at a number of levels from the biological to the sociological. At the present time they tend to be classified in ways parallel to the systems used in medicine and to be seen by both patients and clinicians as equivalent to organically determined illness. The pharmaceutical industry's eagerness to find a biologically focused treatment for every newly defined syndrome further reinforces such definitions. Behavioural and cognitive therapies could be said to address intermediate levels of disturbance. Thus the psychological understandings and interventions offered by behaviourists are largely based on simple animal models of nervous system functioning and learning and in cognitive therapy the main focus has been on associations between beliefs and moods and behaviours and on the extensive use of computer and cybernetic metaphors. Such treatments have their uses but also their dangers; to the extent that problems of living are defined as illness and to the extent that treatments are based on reductive versions of human activity and experience, and are delivered in didactic or authoritarian rather than collaborative ways, attention may be diverted from what are more fundamental, human and existential issues.

In CAT, the therapeutic aim is to understand symptoms in relation to the higher order processes derived from and continuously enacted in the relation between self and others. This emphasis does not deny the fact that these psychological issues may have important physiological determinants and expressions and that drug and psychological treatments addressing lower levels may have an important part to play. But the CAT therapist's concern is with anxious or depressed or somatising *people*, not with anxiety, depression and somatisation, and intervention will be concerned with how their symptoms are linked with their history, current context, sense of self and procedural repertoire as it affects their self-management and their interpersonal and social processes. Particular attention is paid to how the therapeutic relationship may reflect, reinforce or revise damaging patterns.

PRACTICAL METHODS—SYMPTOM MONITORING

The distressing mood changes, symptoms and unwanted behaviours for which patients consult are usually experienced by them as happening to them, that is to say as occurring without, or despite, their wishes or understanding. To understand how they relate to life issues, both CBT and CAT therapists seek to obtain an account of what internal and external processes and events precede and accompany their occurrence or variations in their intensity. These associations may be evident from careful history taking but in most cases instructing the patient in self-monitoring provides more detailed evidence and has the added advantage that this activity frequently leads to a rapid reduction in the symptom.

Patients keeping self-monitoring diaries of problems in the form of moods, symptoms or unwanted behaviours should be asked to note in detail the events, situations, thoughts and feelings preceding and accompanying the problem. These recorded sequences may be interpreted in two ways. Cognitive therapists will concentrate on identifying and challenging the associated 'faulty' beliefs about, and irrational interpretations of, the events and situations identified. In CAT, these cognitive methods may be employed but particular attention will be paid to three additional questions:

1. With what perceived, enacted or anticipated reciprocal role procedure is the symptom associated? For example, in response to feeling abandoned an individual might feel anxious and empty and binge on food.
2. How far might the symptom be understood as an alternative to feared or forbidden feelings or acts? (This represents the 'primary gain' described in psychoanalysis.) For example, in a depressed patient, being guiltily angry in relation to perceived criticism and domination might have been replaced by depressed, relatively guilt-free, resentful compliance.
3. How far does this symptom serve to maintain control in interpersonal relationships or represent self-punishment serving to alleviate guilt. ('secondary gain')? For example, illness, or playing the 'sick role', may elicit a reciprocal caring relationship (*controlling dependency* in *relation to submissive care-giving*) or guilt at failure to achieve perfectionist goals may be followed (relieved or punished) by a severe headache, the pattern *inexorably demanding in relation to desperate striving* being replaced by *caretaking in relation to needy sufferer.*

PROCEDURAL MONITORING

Thus, as well as linking symptoms with immediately accessible beliefs and cognitions, the CAT therapist will aim to locate them in the procedural system identified and described during the reformulation sessions. Once these associations are understood, attention can be diverted from the symptom to the revision of the relevant role procedures. This calls for a new form of self-monitoring; rather than noting the appearances of symptoms and what provokes them patients will now learn to recognise their newly described procedures as they are manifest in their impulses, behaviour or interpretations of events. Recognition is usually achieved over a relatively brief period of time; thereafter very little direct attention needs to be paid to the symptoms, except that they may serve as signals indicating that a negative procedure is being followed. If symptoms persist or cannot be clearly linked to the procedural system and if the possible cost (snag) of losing the symptom has been explored without effect, more direct treatments aimed at the symptom may be needed.

In this way the CAT approach extends the CBT method of monitoring. It also introduces, in a revised language, psychoanalytic understandings of the relation of symptoms to (conflicted) relationships with self and other. But rather than relying on speculative interpretations of unconscious determinants of these links it is based on locating symptoms in terms of the jointly-created descriptive reformulation.

STRATEGIC ISSUES: WHEN TO ADDRESS SYMPTOMS DIRECTLY

Most psychotherapy patients score high on general symptom inventories, recording their experience of a mixture of anxiety, depression and physical symptoms. As stated above, such general symptoms nearly always fade in the course of CAT without direct attention being paid to them. However, notwithstanding what has been said above, some symptoms appear to have little association with deeper issues. Some may resolve with simple direct interventions and some may need direct treatment on account of their severity (which may undermine an individual's ability to work psychologically) or because of their persistence, despite therapy addressed to higher level procedures. Other symptoms seem to have become self-perpetuating, and may only respond to medication or to symptom-focused approaches.

From a CAT perspective it can be seen that focusing on symptoms, as in standard CBT, or on transference interpretations of presumed, related, underlying unconscious intrapsychic conflict, as in analytic therapy, may actually enact and reinforce a particular patient reciprocal role procedure (RRP). These could include, for example, *helpless, needy symptomatic patient* in relation to *powerful, knowledgeable therapeutic other*. Reinforcing this or other maladaptive RRPs may in turn perpetuate or exacerbate the entrenched symptoms, such as panic attacks or bowel dysfunction, with which the patient may have presented and which may represent maladaptive attempts to communicate to or control others. For this reason, approaches such as standard CBT which simply attempt to work with overt symptoms would be predicted to fail because there is no incentive for the patient to abandon them unless the underlying RRPs are addressed. These various issues will now be considered in relation to a range of diagnostic groups.

PANIC AND PHOBIA

Phobic avoidance of situations or panic evoked by cues such as spiders or feathers and more general avoidance behaviours such as agoraphobia can often be understood in terms of conditioning and can be treated by supported graded exposure or by other basic behavioural techniques (see Marks, 1987). It has been suggested that our liability to simple phobias is due to predispositions to be afraid of certain stereotyped dangerous stimuli which have been highly conserved in evolution (McGuire and Troisi, 1998) and which would explain their relative independence of developmental and interpersonal issues. Symptom monitoring can identify the antecedent and accompanying thoughts, and cognitive rehearsal of alternatives may offer some control. Secondary worries about the accompanying symptoms, notably rapid beating of the heart or the fear of losing control, can usually be relieved by explanation. Instruction in symptom monitoring may be accompanied by the paradoxical injunction to have the symptom as thoroughly as possible as this often abolishes the symptom, presumably because you cannot deliberately lose control. In these self-reinforcing conditions it is appropriate to use CBT methods first but where such direct methods fail the wider issues of context and procedural systems must be addressed, in particular by attending to the interpersonal (usually controlling) role of the symptom. The use of medication to control symptoms may be effective and a satisfactory short-term response but its use should not leave unexamined the wider issues.

GENERALISED ANXIETY DISORDER

Generalised anxiety disorder (GAD) is described as a syndrome marked by excessive and widespread worry. Because of its poor response to conventional cognitive therapy Wells (1999) proposes a cognitive model in which the therapist, having identified the situational and cognitive antecedents of worry, explores the 'metacognitions' which serve to maintain 'negative feedback loops'. This metacognitive therapy model seeks to address higher order beliefs but, whilst this clearly represents an important advance on a focus confined to symptoms themselves, it shares with basic CBT a focus largely confined to individual mental processes, paying little attention to the formation and maintenance of self-managing procedures in interaction with others. Moreover, as is also true of psychiatric models of anxiety, it shows surprisingly little interest in the content and meaning of the worry or in the life circumstances with which the patient is coping. Whether or not these circumstances are objectively threatening, the fact is that they are beyond the patient's ability to evaluate and manage using their current procedures. The connection between threatening life events and circumstances and a vulnerability to anxiety disorders has been clearly demonstrated by many workers (Finlay-Jones and Brown, 1981).

In the CAT view, understanding generalised anxiety on the basis of enumerating faulty cognitions and metacognitions and deficient coping skills remains essentially impersonal and superficial. CAT would see it as being fundamentally important to seek to understand, acknowledge and work with the person's experience that their sense of self and their grasp of, and ability to influence, reality are inadequate and, in severe cases, that the whole of existence rests on shaky foundations. In such cases the individual will usually feel essentially isolated and without social support and will thus be effectively 'out of dialogue', which has destabilising consequences. Therapy based on the exploration of both historical meaning and current circumstances recorded in the narrative and structural reformulation of CAT can offer such patients new ways of describing and controlling their life in the world. It can also provide a new basis for reflecting on their own processes and as such offers a more fundamental intervention than CBT. We would anticipate that the majority of patients in whom symptoms represent the outcome of complex developmental and interpersonal reciprocal role enactments would be amenable to treatment with CAT whilst frequently remaining refractory to CBT-based approaches. It is increasingly recognised that trials reporting efficacy of CBT for circumscribed symptoms in highly selected populations do not generalise well, probably for the reasons we have outlined. Clearly this hypothesis requires formal evaluation in the context of comparative, controlled trials.

OBSESSIVE-COMPULSIVE DISORDERS

Most people (and many animals) show some tendency towards ritualisation and social life relies heavily on symbolic rituals, notably in the areas of religious authority and the assertions of military and political power. In this way they induce the sense of a shared meaning and also provide a means of coping with the pervasive anxiety inherent in the human condition, arguably especially in the contemporary 'post-modern' one. The underlying procedural patterns found in people suffering from obsessive-compulsive symptoms can be seen as pathological exaggerations of these general tendencies, often expressed in the dilemma 'as if *either* absolute order *or* dangerous chaos', or in the perfectionist dilemma where, in reciprocating critical conditional acceptance, the choices are seen to be *either* shameful failure *or* absolute success. Pseudo-moral preoccupations with questions of sin and dirt are often part of the story. Issues of control originating in everyday activities and relationships may generate apparently forbidden or frightening intentions or affects and the perceived dangers of these may be managed by repetitive 'magical' rituals involving completing arbitrary or symbolically related acts (as hand washing was for Lady Macbeth) or the use of mental exercises such as counting. In full-blown obsessive-compulsive disorders these magical ritualised attempts to control feared feelings become largely controlling of the patient's life and often of those involved with the patient. Assessment must take account of the full procedural repertoire and of how the obsessive-compulsive symptoms operate in current relationships; in some cases partners or families reinforce the rituals and may need to be involved in treatment.

Genetic factors may also play a part in predisposing to severe anxiety or obsessionality and contribute to obsessive-compulsive disorder and by implication determine what therapy can aim at or achieve. There is evidence from neuro-imaging studies of abnormalities of brain function, although it is not yet clear whether this is cause or consequence of the condition. It is of interest that these changes resolve following treatment whether with drugs or cognitive-behavioural therapy (Baxter et al., 1992).

In individual CAT, where the interference of the symptoms with life is moderate, self-monitoring can indicate how their frequency and intensity vary in relation to the context or the current procedures. Revising these procedures and challenging irrational guilt often allows the obsessiveness to recede. Where the pattern is established more thoroughly and where the reinforcement of the rituals by the short-term relief experienced when they are repeated has become dominant, behavioural methods, notably response prevention, may be helpful whereby, in a way analogous to graded exposure in phobic avoidance, patients are supported to resist repetitions for increasing periods of time. In severe cases medication may also have a part to play.

Case example: Susan (Therapist IK)

Susan was a young woman in her early thirties who had been referred by the local department of child psychiatry where the family had been seen because of the emotional and behavioural difficulties of her seven-year-old son. The team had been concerned about her and had referred her for an assessment for psychotherapy. Her difficulties centred largely around chronic feelings of panic and anxiety which related partly to her irritable bowel syndrome and her worry about whether she might lose control whilst far away from a toilet. She also suffered a continual worry that she might vomit although this had not happened since one episode 15 years previously. These anxieties were severely disabling and prevented her going far from home, for example to pick up her child from school or to eat in a restaurant. In addition, she had marked obsessive-compulsive symptoms, needing for example to rearrange clothes in her wardrobe before leaving her bedroom in the morning, a process which could easily take up to 20 minutes. She was also so anxious about untidiness in the kitchen that she could not go in to cook, leaving this to her husband instead. Interestingly, she found the Psychotherapy File disturbing to take home because there was no 'place' for it there, which caused her to bring it back very promptly! Because of her chronic panicky feelings she sometimes 'had' to call her husband back from work where he was a freelance IT consultant, as well as sometimes needing her mother to stay to help out. These anxieties had been clearly having a detrimental effect on her children (aged seven and three years) with whom she found it hard to engage. Frequently she would enlist her mother or husband to help out. She felt the need all the time to have a system around her which made her feel safe.

Susan had been the youngest of several children and she had always been, she thought, shy and anxious. She mentioned a photo of her bedroom taken when she was about seven which was meticulously tidy and ordered. Her father was 'lovely but absent'. Her mother suffered herself from severe anxiety and obsessional difficulties and had had eating problems, which had clearly got in the way of being a good mother. Susan had always kept her worries to herself and had always felt a pressure to do 'wonderfully well'. She had, in fact, done well academically at school and had been expected to go to university. However, she failed her A levels unexpectedly. Just prior to taking these exams she had suffered an episode of vomiting after an allegedly suspect meal and this had left her with her resultant fear.

She had done various administrative jobs and at the time of referral was working temporarily as manager in a clothes shop although she gave this up shortly afterwards because of her symptoms. The only serious boyfriend she had had was her husband whom she had met as a teenager. She described him as devoted and loving and a 'great support' although the sexual side of her relationship was described as 'fine' but 'not important'. He continued to worry about her and was anxious for her to receive treatment and would have been prepared to come along as well.

Susan had previously had experience of brief counselling through her GP, of an anxiety-management group and of a trial of cognitive-behaviour therapy with a psychologist. She had dropped out of all of these. During her work on anxiety, for example, she related that the more they tried to help her to let go and relax the more grimly she had 'held on'. At assessment it was felt that she was not a good candidate for analytic psychotherapy and was referred for a trial with CAT.

During her first few sessions of therapy her explicit agenda was focused around her 'symptoms' as she described them and she was very anxious to know if and how this therapy could help deal with them. It proved extremely difficult to divert her towards any reflection on their meaning or origins or indeed about her early life. It was clear that she was very distressed by the symptoms and the difficult feelings associated with them, which she was able to acknowledge explicitly. Apart from her obvious distress, however, she was recurrently obviously irritated by the lack of progress in sorting out and curing her symptoms. The therapist felt throughout the first few sessions that she was determinedly attending as if going through the motions to make a point of how difficult things were and to prove that things could never really change. This hopeless feeling was also induced in the therapist, as was a recurrent irritation that she would not act as a cooperative patient who would be willing to work. It seemed that this might have been a partial replay of what had happened during her previous failed 'attempts' at therapy and might be illustrating some of the roles which were enacted at home.

The reformulation phase

When going through the Psychotherapy File (see Appendix 2) the procedures she had identified strongly as applying to her were the trap of 'trying to please others and being anxious not to upset them, as a result of which we end up being taken advantage of which makes us angry, depressed or guilty' and the dilemma of '*either* trying to be perfect and feeling depressed and guilty, *or* not trying and feeling guilty, angry and dissatisfied'. She also identified the typical obsessional dilemma of '*either* keeping things in perfect order *or* fearing a terrible mess'. She also identified the dilemma of '*either* being sustained by the admiration of others *or* feeling exposed and contemptible'. She recognised the snag, of feeling limited in life by something inside herself, and of 'having to sabotage things as if she didn't deserve them'. She noted, interestingly, that she had tended to do this at school also. Finally, she noted most of the difficult states of mind as applying to herself to some extent at various times and also some of the different states. These included 'feeling bad but soldiering on and coping', 'being in control of self and other people', 'provoking and winding up others' (which she would do with her son), 'feeling agitated, confused and anxious', 'vulnerable and needy', 'resentfully submitting to demands' and 'intensely critical of self and others'.

The first intimation that something might change came during the drafting of the initial sequential diagrammatic reformation (SDR) (Figure 9.1) when, having jointly sketched a rough core 'subjective' self which seemed acceptable to her, the subsequent implications of her role enactments, both outside and in sessions, were persistently explored by the therapist. At this point she became for the first time overtly very angry and tearful, saying that she did not want to open up her 'messy' side and that it was 'none of his business'.

The initial, rough SDR centred around a 'core subjective self' is shown in Figure 9.1 and the subsequent simplified version showing one key reciprocal role procedure in Figure 9.2. What emerged powerfully from the work around the initial version was her intense and desperate inner feelings and the consequences of her attempts to cope with them by enacting various role procedures. These appeared to have in common the attempt to keep things under control (either her own emotions or other people's behaviour). It seemed important to acknowledge what a struggle this was and also her frustration and irritation when people would, for example at church, 'jolly her on' without understanding just how bad things were. She was also able, with reluctance, to describe bursting out angrily at times when she could no longer contain her feelings, mostly with her husband who could, as she put it, 'cop it'. She also described a 'keeping busy' coping mechanism which, however, never seemed to help for long. The therapist noted on the SDR those procedures which she might be enacting with the therapist in the room (shown as '*? in here*' or '*? with me*'; Figure 9.1). With persistence, this focus of the work was reluctantly accepted. It continued to be difficult for her, however, to own the '*controlling–controlled*' role

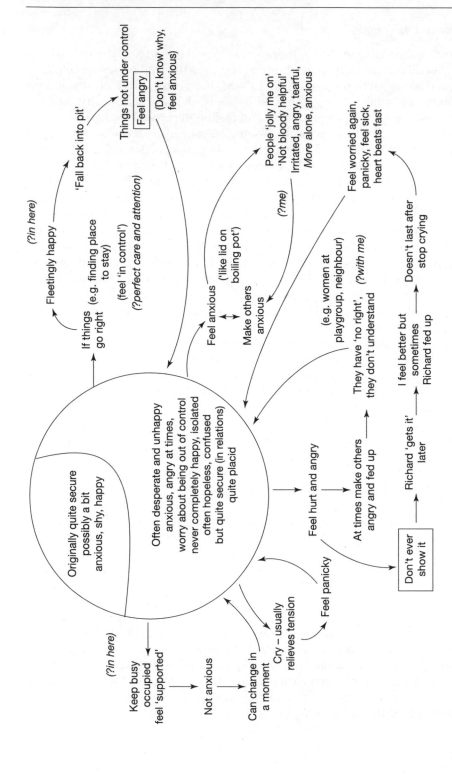

Figure 9.1 Initial version of SDR for Susan constructed around a core 'subjective self' showing mainly childhood-derived role enactments. The therapist's challenges on the enactment of these in session are in italics

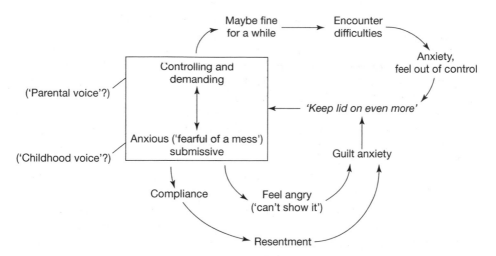

Figure 9.2 Simplified SDR for Susan showing the enactments of her key RRP

pattern which was subsequently highlighted on the simplified diagram (Figure 9.2).

Target problem procedures (TPPs) were described as follows:

1. Trying to keep to yourself worries about your imagined inadequacies, your anxieties and your angry feelings for fear of terrible consequences if they came out, but as a result feeling isolated, exhausted and desperate about how you can carry on. *Aim 1*: Try gradually to express some of your worries and emotions to people in all settings, and see what the consequences really are.
2. Dealing with your worries and your 'messy' side by keeping busy and keeping in control of things and of people (like me in therapy), which has the result that no-one gets 'let in' and that nothing ever changes. *Aim 2*: Try to consider that keeping in control of everything all the time may actually make things worse and try out the effect of letting people (like me) in.

Rating progress

For TPP 1 there was little recorded change on her rating sheet during therapy for either recognition or revision. Interestingly she wrote on her rating sheet for TPP 2 that *'I like being in control!'*. For this procedure her ratings showed increasingly good recognition but little apparent change. In therapy she continued intermittently to be angry at the therapist for apparently ignoring her symptoms and not curing them and for focusing on her feelings and role enactments. Similarly, she continued to insist until the end of therapy, despite seeming at times more relaxed and able to discuss her feelings and the consequences of her role enactments, that this would never really help. She insisted that she was only going through with it in case she ever needed further help so that it would not be held against her that she had yet again dropped out. She repeatedly accused her therapist of being unempathic and not really understanding her difficulties or helping with them and this was very much the tone of her farewell letter, although she did say that she had found therapy 'challenging'.

Nonetheless, her therapist did feel that by the end of therapy Susan was noticeably more open about discussing her feelings and difficulties and more able to be 'in dialogue' and that she was possibly also surprised that this could happen. Parallel to this she reported that her irritable bowel symptoms had curiously diminished. In addition to clinical impressions that her symptoms had diminished, her scores on routine psychometric measures ('CORE' (see Barkham et al., 1998) and a standard anxiety questionnaire) also reduced considerably. The 'CORE' reduced from 76 at the start of therapy to 46 at the end with subscale ratings related to anxiety showing a parallel decrease from 36 to 23. At six-month follow-up these scores had diminished even further ('CORE' overall reducing to 34, with the anxiety-related subscale ratings reducing to 14, with parallel shifts in standard anxiety measures). She wrote a letter six months post therapy saying that things had improved considerably in her life and stated that:

> I originally came to you with one set of anxieties and insecurities; these seem to no longer play a large part in my life and, although lonely and isolated at present, I feel there is hope for the future.

It seems clear that for this patient the symptoms with which she presented were aspects of one key reciprocal role pattern around a *controlling–controlled* axis. What is of particular interest is that the enactment of this key RRP had undoubtedly prevented her from simply and cooperatively working on her symptoms as had been previously attempted by symptom-focused approaches. Indeed, such approaches could have been seen to be examples of colluding with this RRP, hence intensifying her 'resistance'. This case illustrates the point that, unless these role enactments in the therapy relationship are identified and worked on as a principal focus, the work will be sabotaged and the patient will acquire the epithet of being 'difficult' and elicit all the unhelpful reactions which go with it.

Formal research evaluation of CAT with 'difficult' patients with anxiety-related symptoms clearly needs to be undertaken. This could be either in the form of a controlled trial against CBT-based approaches or, alternatively, in treating those who, as in the case of this patient, have 'failed' to engage with previous treatments.

POST-TRAUMATIC STRESS DISORDER

Post-traumatic stress disorder (PTSD) usually develops weeks or longer after experiencing or witnessing very threatening events. Individual susceptibility clearly plays a part; according to a recent review by Adshead (2000) between 20% and 30% of individuals exposed to major disasters go on to develop PTSD. In theory this vulnerability could reflect both biological and psychological factors. As regards the latter, an individual's reaction to fear and helplessness or proneness to shame are likely to reflect procedures developed earlier, perhaps in analogous circumstances, which it will be helpful to identify. The symptoms include anxious re-living of the trauma, intrusive memories or images associated with it, vivid nightmares, avoidance of thoughts or places associated with the trauma and alternations or combinations of emotional numbness, hyper-vigilance, chronic anxiety and depression. Where the trauma has been a single, brief and unpredicted devastating event, hyperarousal, intrusive memories and avoidance are marked. Sustained or repeated stress, such as may be experienced in warfare and in abusive relationships, where helplessness and irrational guilt are commonly experienced, leads to similar initial symptoms but these are likely to be dealt with, with incomplete success, by dissociation which in turn may damage relationships and self-management and may lead to prolonged depression, anxiety and substance abuse. The symptoms of PTSD may last for decades and in chronic cases are associated with neurological and neuroendocrine changes (Van der Kolk et al., 1996; reviewed in Freeman, 1998).

Although the recent 'rediscovery' of the neuropsychological consequences of trauma was prompted by work with Vietnam war veterans, it has become increasingly accepted that a repeated experience of childhood trauma and deprivation has a comparable but more pervasive, damaging effect on the personality. This has come to be conceptualised as 'complex' PTSD (Hermann, 1992), or as a 'disorder of extreme stress not otherwise specified' (DESNOS) as categorised in DSM IV (Van der Kolk, 2000). The concept of 'complex' PTSD is seen as virtually synonymous with borderline personality disorder by these writers given the almost invariably traumatic origins of the latter. This emerging and powerful body of evidence adds weight to the views of those who have historically advocated deficit/trauma theories of psychopathology.

Brewin et al. (1996) suggest that the features of PTSD can be explained in terms of two forms of memory, one automatically accessed in response to contextual cues and one verbally accessible, the former having the quality of re-experiencing the traumatic event and the latter being open to successive editing. In the view of these authors, incomplete emotional processing is manifest in mood disorders and distortions of attention and memory whereas premature inhibition of processing leads to memory impairment, dissociation, phobic states and somatisation. Psychological treatments for PTSD were found to be more effective than medication in a meta-analytic study (van Etten and Taylor, 1998) but medication also has a place and the two may be combined.

Systematic desensitisation to cues or memories which have been avoided and cognitive restructuring methods are the common approaches to fear-based PTSD, with the recent addition of EMDR (eye-movement desensitisation and reprocessing; see MacCulloch, 1999). Where shame as well as fear is an important factor and where long-term symptoms have become associated with pervasive personal and interpersonal problems, a more general therapeutic approach is called for and it is here that CAT may have a part to play. At present there have been no systematic studies although work with PTSD has been undertaken by several practitioners (Evans, Kenny, Haupt and Wilton, personal communication).

Efforts to prevent the development of PTSD by early counselling of those exposed to trauma are common but are of uncertain effectiveness and may be harmful. Thus two studies involving burn victims (Bisson et al., 1997) and road traffic accident victims (Mayou et al., 2000) reported increased symptoms in those receiving debriefing. In many cases it may be more important to mobilise existing personal and social support. On the international scale it can certainly be argued that counselling has been oversold. Summerfield (1999) is particularly critical of the sending of Western-trained counsellors to devastated areas on the grounds that only local communities can offer culturally relevant ways of supporting their members. He suggests that practical and economic aid would be psychologically more supportive.

In the case of 'complex' PTSD, as with severe personality disorder, it may be that early psychological interventions could play a role in minimising or repairing some of the developmental damage inflicted by traumatic early life experiences (Chanen, 2000).

The following brief summaries of two case histories demonstrate the potential value of CAT in this area.

Case example: Richard (Therapist Ceri Evans)

Richard was a man in his early thirties who had been referred by his GP to a traumatic stress clinic. He had been experiencing considerable problems in living since an episode five years previously when he had been threatened with a gun during a robbery in a pub where he had been manager. He was clearly suffering from PTSD as assessed clinically and by standard questionnaires. His symptoms included long 1–2 minute 'video-like', highly distressing, intrusive re-experiencing of the episode when the gun had been held to his head and when he had feared he would be killed. In addition, he suffered from what were described as 'mind rages' (precipitous and explosive outbursts), he had developed a serious drink problem and had become cut off socially and depressed.

He reported symptoms of morbid arousal including insomnia, irritability and hypervigilance. These difficulties had resulted in the break-up of a previously stable relationship and in his losing his job. Richard himself was also able to link these difficulties with a history of childhood victimisation and sexual abuse which he had previously 'coped with'.

His background also included childhood experience of a difficult and abusive relationship with an alcoholic father and an 'absent' mother who was remembered as passive and powerless. In addition, he had had a bad experience of school where he felt lonely and isolated. The sexual abuse he had suffered had been at the hands of a male neighbour from the ages of about 8 to 13.

Given the presence of complicating, pre-morbid personality factors Richard was offered a 14-session course of CAT by the traumatic stress clinic. He engaged well and committed regularly to therapy. Early assessment sessions elucidated childhood coping strategies of cutting off and withdrawal as well as indulging in risk-taking behaviour. He also expressed a sense of shame and guilt about the sexual abuse. Notable procedures which he identified in the Psychotherapy File included the 'trying to please' trap, the dilemma of 'keeping feelings bottled up or risking making a mess' and 'if I must then I won't', as well as most of the dilemmas around behaviours with others (see Appendix 2). He also identified most of the unstable and difficult states of mind. These procedures and role enactments were rehearsed in the written and diagrammatic reformulations where a *need to be in control, threatening and cut-off role* relative to a *feeling victimised or threatened* reciprocal role was noted. It was this precarious control which had apparently been shattered by the more recent traumatic episode. This was also a role which was experienced by the therapist in session and required much attention. The work of therapy subsequently centred to a considerable extent around experiencing and communicating painful emotions, especially his childhood memories, without resorting to these defensive role enactments. Some work was also done on identifying triggers for his intrusive memories. However, most of the work focused on his earlier experiences and their consequences, which had the interesting effect of enabling him to work on later experiences and difficulties himself. He reported a rapid improvement on both his social relations, alcohol consumption and PTSD symptoms although, interestingly, little of the work had focused on these explicitly. The therapist's goodbye letter emphasised that future stress might cause him to revert to old role enactments and that this was something which, with the help of the tools of therapy, he would need to continue to work on. At follow-up after three months he reported considerable improvement in his general well-being as well as in the specific symptoms he had presented with. In addition, he had a new partner and job and overall felt that he had made a 'full recovery'. This clinical impression was confirmed by psychometric testing which showed remarkable improvements on all measures used. These included shifts on the Revised Impact of Events from 65 to 1, the Penn Inventory from 51 to 17 and the General Health Questionnaire from 7 to 1.

Case example: Hannah (Therapist Ceri Evans)

Hannah was a young woman in her early thirties who had been referred to the traumatic stress clinic by her GP because of depression and unmanageable mood states including anger, guilt and shame. These followed an incident when she had been attacked on the street and subjected to an attempted rape. Significantly she had not initially reported this attempted rape to the police, only reporting the theft of her purse. Her father had developed cancer shortly after this event and she had been involved in looking after him at considerable cost to herself.

Other difficulties which she reported were a long-standing lack of assertiveness, a tendency to comfort eat and, more recently, 'rushes of fear' triggered by memories of the attack. These difficulties were also stressful, straining her relationship with her partner. However, she was still managing to work as a junior manager and put on an appearance of coping to the outside world. Her GP had initially refused to offer her counselling on the grounds that she seemed 'too well'. This had resulted in her being quite angry at presentation about how hard it had been to get help. She described how she still overloaded herself at work by agreeing to work overtime and consequently had virtually no time for herself.

Given the predominance of historical psychological issues in her history she was offered a 12-session CAT by the clinic. This included four sessions of 'nested' eye movement desensitision and reprocessing (EMDR—see review by MacCulloch, 1999) which would not have been possible without the prior CAT owing to the existence of complicating personality difficulties (see below).

She described a difficult upbringing with an unhappy and very critical mother who appeared to demand care from her but not to offer it in return. She had been frequently called sullen and miserable by her mother who also criticised the father which resulted in Hannah feeling alienated from him. It was only in later years that she had come to think that perhaps he had been quite a decent man. His illness and death consequently left her feeling cheated of a relationship she might have had with him. She had a younger brother who had often been ill and had, she felt, been very much the favourite with her mother. She had done well academically at school and subsequently at college where she got a good degree in business studies.

During the early sessions it became apparent that the reciprocal role repertoire Hannah had acquired had played an important role in her response to recent events as well as to therapy. These RRPs included, notably, a *striving to please and placate* relative to a *conditionally accepting and loving* role as well as an *idealising/care seeking role* relative to an *actively caring for but denying own needs* role. These had been enacted around the traumatic attack as well as with her therapist. Key procedures which were identified through the Psychotherapy File (see Appendix 2) included notably the placation trap, the dilemmas of 'either keeping things in perfect order *or* fearing a terrible mess', 'either 'being sustained by the admiration of others *or* feeling exposed', '*either* sticking up for oneself *or* giving in and getting put upon by others and feeling cross and hurt', and, very significantly, the snag of feeling limited because of a sense of inadequacy, which sabotages progress.

These procedures were spelled out in her reformulations and worked on in therapy, where her tendency to idealise and placate were prominent. Despite her anxiety about the brevity of therapy she was able to use the insights and understandings she gained to work on her target problem procedures. The therapy also included some role-play on her difficulty with assertiveness, which appeared productive. Despite her initial reluctance to acknowledge the impact of the assault, after work on her RRPs, she eventually decided to have EMDR. This produced a major abreaction dominated by considerable anger and rage. Despite anticipating that she might slip back into re-enacting of old RRPs, she 'chose' not to write a goodbye letter, wishing not to make a fuss and because she 'happened' to be very busy. It was, however, possible to note this enactment helpfully with her. At follow-up she appeared to have done well and reported being less depressed, more confident and assertive, which had been noted at work, and she was able to talk openly about the assault. These impressions were confirmed by reductions in her psychometric measures. These reduced on the Impact of Events Scale from 49 to 14, on the Penn Inventory from 26 to 19 and on the General Health Questionnaire from 6 to 5.

DEPRESSION

The reported massively rising incidence of depression over the past decades (see *Economist*, 1998), if true, almost certainly reflects general social changes. Clinically, patients who are depressed commonly report a sense of exhaustion, existential isolation, hopelessness, the loss or lack of acknowledgement, care and love and the experience or anticipation of criticism, control or abuse from others and from themselves, the latter experienced in the form of irrational guilt. The experience of self-critical and hostile voices by depressed patients can be accounted for as the enactment of early internalised RRPs. Although one consequence of these RRPs may have been 'silencing' of any expression of anger, we see little validity in the traditional psychoanalytic formulation of depression as representing anger turned inwards upon the self. We rather note, certainly in severe cases, exhaustion and the *absence* of affect in conjunction with the other features noted above. Such factors are not necessarily operating in the present, for we do not live only in relation to our current social world, we have internalised the values and rules of that world. Physiological and psychological responses may therefore be initiated by events in the social context by remembered, anticipated or imagined events or by actions or intentions which provoke internal judgements derived historically from the social world.

Experiences which would be distressing to anyone, such as bereavement or loss of employment or status, may provoke more profound and persistent changes in those genetically predisposed to abnormalities of mood control. More severe symptoms such as poor sleep with early waking, low mood in the morning improving through the day, poor concentration, altered appetite, lack of interest in sex and the presence of suicidal preoccupations and irrational self-blame point to physiological changes which make it very difficult for the patient to make any use of therapy. In such cases medication is needed before or in parallel with therapy. Patients keen to avoid medication may be given a few trial therapy sessions, medication being started if there is no response within three or four weeks.

In treating depression, CAT will focus on procedures which maintain negative attitudes to self and submissive tendencies to others. Some of these are discussed in terms of 'self-esteem' and are considered in Chapter 4. There is now extensive, naturalistic evidence for the effectiveness of CAT for depression, both as a presenting problem and as an associated issue in other disorders in settings as various as general practice, student counselling services and health service outpatient departments (Dunn et al., 1997).

SOMATISATION

Depression is frequently accompanied by somatic symptoms but these may also occur independently as manifestations of procedural problems, notably internalised prohibitions on the expression of anger or assertion and associated submissive role procedures. One feature of the complex of procedures enacted in somatisation is very commonly an inability to communicate anxious feelings, often in relation to an internalised role of feeling one 'ought' to cope alone. It has been suggested that this inability may be partly constitutional and represent the complex of temperamental factors referred to as 'alexithymia' or literally, inability to put feelings into words (see Taylor et al. 1991). However, this inability may also reflect the difficulties in self-reflection and self-expression which individuals who have been subjected to childhood trauma or adversity are known to experience. Such internal processes, often acting in concert with ongoing social or interpersonal situations, may produce chronic physiological changes and may cause or exacerbate psychosomatic 'diseases'. These may in turn play a part in controlling interpersonal procedures, as when a depressed, submissive individual develops somatic disturbances which elicit care from others. In persistent or recurrent depression and somatisation, a full procedural analysis of the patient in relation to his or her current relationships is therefore necessary (see also the case example of Susan, in this chapter). The successful trials of brief psychodynamic–interpersonal therapy in 'functional' gut disorders (Guthrie et al., 1991; Hamilton et al., 2000) in our view address and modify these role enactments by means of a therapy which, as has been noted (Margison, 2000), has much in common with CAT.

DELIBERATE SELF-HARM

Deliberate self-harm is a major clinical problem, accounting for 140,000 visits to Accident and Emergency units each year (Hawton et al., 1997) and being the third most common cause of admission to general medical beds in one region of the UK (Gunnell et al., 1996). People who have self-harmed have a risk of suicide far in excess of the general population. Only a small proportion of self-harmers have a formal psychiatric illness but a considerable proportion have borderline traits or meet the full BPD diagnostic criteria and the great majority are experiencing interpersonal difficulties; in these the harm can be seen as a form of angry or help-seeking communication.

Repeated self-harmers are at a greatly increased risk but, even more than first timers, they frequently provoke hostile or indifferent responses from clinical staff, and they seldom receive more than a basic psychiatric screening designed to identify the few cases of severe mental disorder. The generally poor care received by these patients reflects the lack of an adequate psychological under-standing among many medical and nursing staff and the power with which collusive responses—usually of rejection, sometimes of inappropriate concern—are elicited. In this respect they constitute a classic type of 'difficult' patient. Moreover, few A&E departments can offer any continuity of care to these patients (in whose lives themes of abandonment are often dominant), with the result that few return to follow-up appointments when these are arranged, thus reinforcing rejecting or helpless reactions among staff.

Cowmeadow (1994) reported the use of an eight-session CAT in self-harmers and also (1995) reported cases in which assessment was combined with a single session intervention which included the construction of a sequential diagram. Because the scale of the problem is such that the majority of patients will never be seen by trained psychotherapists, Sheard and Evans built on this work and on the CAT model of borderline personality disorder to devise a model of a structured one- to three-session intervention which could be taught to and delivered by staff without any therapy training. They report how they devel-oped a manualised approach which pays particular attention to the feelings evoked in the assessing clinician during the interview with the aim of (1) guard-ing against reactions based on countertransference elicited by the patient and (2) using the recognised elicited feelings as an indication of the appropriate focus for a very brief intervention. The successful delivery of the approach by trainee psychiatrists was also reported (Sheard et al., 2000).

This work is an important example of the introduction of CAT ideas into psychiatric and medical contexts, using the basic reciprocal role model and structural understandings to provide accessible and comprehensible models of the clinician–patient interaction. It provides a further example of the value of 'using' the CAT model as opposed to 'doing' it as formal therapy.

EATING DISORDERS

Eating disorders represent the expression of inter- and intrapersonal problems through an abnormal preoccupation with weight and food. They are always associated with, but may serve to obscure, problems at the level of self processes, predominantly expressed around issues of control, submission, placation and perfectionism. In a proportion of cases there are associated problems, notably depression and substance abuse, and severe cases may meet criteria for personality disorders. Almost inevitably difficulties in communication are involved (usually within the family of origin), with the disorder representing a covert means of communicating or of coping with feelings of not being heard or being pressurised to 'perform'. In many cases these patients cause considerable systemic difficulty with splitting of teams and consequent frustration and burn-out, or alternatively over-involvement on the part of some staff. These are just the sorts of difficulties classically described by Main in the 'The Ailment' (Main, 1957); see also discussion in Kerr (1999). It may be helpful and necessary to work with the whole team and/or family, using individual and contextual reformulations, to create a common understanding of the patient's procedures and to avoid enacting collusive role reciprocations which may 'split' those involved.

Most cases of bulimia nervosa can be treated with the basic CAT approach of achieving a reformulation of the procedural repertoire, using patient self-monitoring to identify the role procedures accompanied by, or replaced by, vomiting or purging and then focusing on these procedures. Common antecedent cues leading to bingeing are fear of abandonment and unexpressed anger or disappointment. Commonsense advice about eating habits may be followed better once the procedural issues are understood. In some long-established cases controlled, anorectic phases alternate with sequences of angry bingeing, purging and vomiting. These cycles can seem self-perpetuating and require symptom-directed CBT methods within the context of the procedural model.

Anorexia nervosa is notoriously difficult to treat; many patients prove hard to engage in the therapeutic work and in severe cases the threat of further starvation puts intense pressures on therapists and other clinical staff. Apart from ensuring that a minimum weight is maintained, psychological treatments should focus on the procedural repertoire and not on the symptom. Both the traditional psychiatric force-feeding approach and cognitive therapy techniques are liable to provoke pseudo-compliance and covert or overt resistance. CAT reformulation is a powerful means of engaging with these patients; by being genuinely collaborative it avoids struggles about control and sets up a reciprocal role pattern which is 'off the patient's map'. All those involved in the treatment programme need to base their interventions on an understanding of the patient's diagram in order to recognise and resist pressures to collude. Such pressures commonly reflect patient-to-therapist roles involving (1) intense (controlling) *neediness* evoking *desperately caring*, (2) (controlling) *passive resis-*

tance evoking *angry control,* (3) (controlling) *emotional unavailability* evoking a *mirroring withdrawal,* (4) *perfectionist striving* leading *to exhaustion.* This is a frequent pattern in the patient's self-management which is often also induced in clinical staff. Patients often evoke different reciprocations from different staff members and without a shared diagram this can be a potent source of staff conflict. This can necessitate the use of 'contextual' approaches as noted above.

The spectrum of role procedures found in 30 eating-disordered patients was reported by Bell (1999). This author proposes a 'stepped care' approach whereby subjects with minimal associated psychopathology receive CBT-based self-help packages or treatments. Beyond that she recommends CAT as the most comprehensive time-limited approach but notes it is also the most complex to learn. As regards effectiveness, Treasure et al. (1995), from the Maudsley eating disorder unit, reported a pilot study in which CAT was compared to educational behaviour therapy; weight gain was similar in the two groups but CAT patients reported greater improvements in global functioning. Treasure and Ward (1997) further reviewed the use of CAT in anorexia nervosa and provide a case study of a severe case. Further research is being carried out in the Maudsley unit.

CAT AND THE MANAGEMENT OF MEDICAL CONDITIONS

A considerable proportion of patients with medical conditions do not adhere to their treatment regimes, even if they are given full explanations and support. Two conditions in which such failure has serious consequences and where the use of CAT has been evaluated are diabetes and asthma, in both of which there is some research support for the value of CAT in improving self-management

Management of insulin-dependent diabetes

Insulin-dependent diabetes is a condition where modern techniques using regular monitoring of blood sugar levels and carefully spaced and adjusted injections of insulin, combined with keeping to a strict diet, can allow the majority of patients to avoid the serious complications of damage to eyes and kidneys, arterial disease and peripheral neuritis. However, a sizeable proportion of patients develop these complications despite being fully educated and supported by diabetic nurses. Proper self-care in insulin-dependent diabetes is a tedious business and the effects of poor control are not immediately obvious, so it is not surprising that many patients take risks.

Work by Fosbury et al. (1997) with CAT has demonstrated that the reasons for failing to adhere to diets, do blood tests, take appropriate doses of insulin and so on are various and in no way specific to the condition. They are often manifestations of more general patterns of self-management and are related to procedural patterns of which the patient is often largely unaware. The CAT approach is therefore particularly appropriate, reformulation allowing the 'symptom' of poor self-care to be set in the general procedural repertoire. CAT does not require the patient to submit to instructions—an important point in that a passive resistance in relation to authority in general and the clinic staff in particular is one common pattern. Other procedures underlying poor management include depressive self-neglect (which can extend to what amounts to slow suicide), eating disorders where, in the pursuit of weight control, omitting insulin can replace or supplement purging and vomiting, and resentment at having the disease expressed in denial or defiance.

Fosbury et al. (1997) demonstrated benefits from CAT compared to nurse education in the reduction of HbA1 blood levels (an indication of the average blood sugar level over past weeks). There were no significant biochemical differences at the end of the 16-week interventions but nine months later the HbA1 levels in the CAT group were significantly lower. It should be noted that these were long-standing patients few of whom had expressed an interest in counselling or therapy. This study suggests that early recognition of damaging self-care and preventive CAT would be humanly and cost effective.

Management of asthma

A broadly similar study relating to asthmatic patients' failure to use suppressive inhalant medication as recommended has been completed by Cluley et al. (2000). In a study of non-compliance with inhaled steroid medication, in which a concealed microchip recorded the actual use of the inhaler, a group of patients with severe asthma was identified and those showing poor compliance were randomised between usual care and CAT. Fourteen of the 17 patients allocated to CAT completed a 16-session therapy. Identified reciprocal role patterns were similar to those found in the diabetic study, notably, patterns of *critical control* to either *crushed or rebellious, neglecting–neglected* and *ideal care* fantasies. At six-month follow-up there were significantly better measures of treatment compliance ($P < 0.05$) and quality of life in the treated group. As with diabetes there would seem to be a case for early identification and treatment of poor self-managing cases. Walsh et al. (2000) report a study of asthma sufferers with poor self-management of their medication, arguing strongly for the value of a CAT-based understanding of the emotional and interpersonal factors responsible.

The studies of diabetes and asthma demonstrate the failure of both authoritarian and 'rational' attempts to achieve good self-management in many sufferers from these chronic diseases. The work reported lends support to the argument made in many parts of this book in favour of CAT as providing a whole person, high level understanding as opposed to the CBT focus on symptoms, behaviours and illness beliefs. The findings suggest that a broadly based understanding of the individual's specific damaging behaviours, locating them within a model of the general reciprocal role repertoire, offers the best chance of avoiding what to the patient is often a slow suicide and what to the Health Service is liable to be a costly palliative exercise. Compared to the resources put into refining the medical treatment of diabetes and asthma (which patients so often undermine) and involved in treating the consequences of poor management, the instituting of preventative and early psychological intervention as a part of specialist medical services would require trivial sums.

It is clear that these approaches could be very usefully applied to a variety of disorders, such as those which present to the consultation and liaison psychiatrist in the form of psychological complications of medical disorder or as physical symptoms arising in relation to psychological problems. CAT may well have an important role to play as a consultation tool in these settings, beyond its immediate use as an individual therapy, as a general model for understanding patients and helping staff treat them. (See also the case example (Brenda) of a 'difficult' patient on an oncology palliative care unit discussed in Chapter 11.)

SUBSTANCE ABUSE

The place of CAT in treating substance-abusing patients is fully reviewed by Leighton (1997) and its relation to the Minnesota 'twelve step' approach is discussed by the same author (Leighton, 1995). As a general statement it can be said that patients continually abusing alcohol or drugs are unlikely to benefit from psychotherapy unless undergoing prior withdrawal. Where abuse is combined with borderline personality disorder (BPD), as it is in a small but possibly increasing percentage of cases, management of withdrawal in inpatient or group settings will be helped by CAT reformulation. A randomised controlled trial of the role of CAT in the treatment of adolescents at risk for developing BPD, the majority of whom are substance abusing, is currently in progress (Chanen, 2000). In this group it may be necessary to offer psychotherapy before withdrawal can be realistically achieved, the sole condition being that patients must come substance-free to their sessions. In older patients therapy is of most need after withdrawal has been accomplished, particularly in those patients for whom alcohol or drugs have served to keep at bay memories and feelings from disturbed early experiences. Many of the borderline patients treated by outpatient CAT have come following succesful treatment for substance abuse which has left them facing the sense of emptiness and unmanageable feelings which the substance had served to suppress. Such patients may not be able to use the supportive group offered by Alcoholics Anonymous and similar organisations and are liable to discharge themselves from most available treatments. Assessment of patients completing withdrawal programmes should routinely seek to identify such patients. The role of drugs and alcohol in general may combine elements of 'perfect care'—states of blissful fusion with the absence of conflict and need—with the enactment in self-management of an *abusing–abused* pattern. It should also be noted that there is also some evidence of a genetic predisposition to addictions with the implication that some of the work of therapy may need to focus on living with such a vulnerability.

CAT IN OLD AGE AND EARLY DEMENTIA

The use of a CAT framework in work with elderly people facing early dementia, and those who have suffered past traumas and are now facing early dementia, has been pioneered by Sutton (Sutton, 1997 and in press; Sutton and Ryder, in press; Hepple and Sutton, in preparation) and CAT in the elderly is now a developing special interest group within ACAT. Sutton (personal communication) has written the following account of how she came to work with the elderly using CAT; it both illuminates what the work implies and has resonances for others who move from other theoretical backgrounds.

> I had been working in old age for a few years after qualifying as a clinical psychologist. I was largely schooled in CBT and was using this framework for my work with older people. While it was good for phobias, anxiety and the like, I didn't know what to do with clients telling me about the long lives they'd lived. I was aware of work elsewhere in reminiscence and life review in ageing. I felt that CBT failed to capture the qualitative perspective of age and, while personal construct theory was better, I was still frustrated by the split between cognitions/constructs and life review/reminiscences. When I first heard about CAT and attended a 2-day meeting I was working in a nursing home and I was astonished to find a model that described my client and her state shifts so well. The SDR we worked out made sense to my client's daughter and to the staff as well as to me and was the foundation for a year's work—the narrative part—in which her behaviour could be understood in terms of her past abuses (see Sutton, 1997).

> Narrative therapy was being introduced into dementia care, based on the stories that people with dementia tell. I began to find these approaches insufficiently critical; although they talked as if they addressed society they were essentially constructivist, not socioconstructivist; what I wanted to emphasise was re-storying (Sutton and Cheston, 1997). Here too CAT appealed through its understanding of how a large part of the human suffering we encounter represents the internalisation of external relations; through its staying at the level of meaning, CAT avoids reifying and biologising human experience, countering the profound biological reduction of ageing. That, I feel, makes CAT, with its base in the historical formation of mind, a suitable framework for attending to the long histories of ageing people, while its dialogical understanding can ensure that the fact that we exist and are conscious and think in and through our relations with others is not forgotten. These points will be central to the book which Jason Hepple and I are preparing (Hepple and Sutton, in preparation) in which we will present the theoretical understandings and practice of CAT in old age, covering trauma, personality disorders, dementia, carers and systems and the need for developing a lifespan psychopathology.

In applying the CAT model to later life this work has drawn on and extended the basic Vygotskian and Bakhtinian elements in CAT theory. Human minds, to the end, are sustained by a continuing narrative and dialogue with others.

GENDER ISSUES

The aim of therapy in CAT is the revision and integration of the damaging procedures identified during the collaborative reformulation. Many role procedures may be expressed in sexual relationships and through sexual practices but, in a way consistent throughout CAT, these will be understood in terms of the basic procedures governing self-management and self–other relationships. These are concerned with giving and receiving acknowledgement and care and with issues of control and submission. It is of course the case that committed sexual relationships are likely to mobilise intense feelings and to generate conflicts between the wish for autonomy and the wish for care. In terms of psychoanalytic theories the CAT emphasis is more on two-person relationships than on three-person 'oedipal' ones, but issues of rivalry, jealousy and sex role identification are also of importance and need to be attended to.

Certain procedural patterns remain tied to gender stereotypes which have a long history and are still instilled and sustained by cultural and economic pressures. They are also to some degree rooted in, although in humans certainly not completely determined by, complex evolutionary predispositions which could be described as archetypal. In our culture, patterns of placation and submissive dependency are much more commonly found in women, helping to maintain continuing social inequalities, while the avoidance of emotional expression and denial of emotional needs remains a largely male characteristic. Procedural change in these respects is a common aim in CAT and fortunately receives more social validation than was the case in the past. Changes in the law and the slow diminution of prejudice have also eased the problems faced by homosexual persons. There are, however, additional problems faced by gay individuals, many of whom have had difficulties in being accepted by their families and all of whom are liable to encounter discrimination. Both of these features may contribute to self-blaming procedures the modification of which would be an appropriate aim in CAT. The problematic relationship procedures found in gay partners differ little from those found in heterosexual couples. Denman and de Vries (1998) provide an interesting case history illustrating many of the above issues.

THE EFFECTS OF CHILDHOOD SEXUAL ABUSE

The incidence of sexual abuse in childhood is higher in most psychiatric diagnostic groups than in the general population. It is particularly high in borderline personality disorder where, in those genetically predisposed, it may be the common initial trigger for dissociation (see Paris, 2000). It is only in recent decades that the high rate of abuse has been acknowledged; discussions in the media served to make it something that could be talked about publicly and this seems to have enabled many people to recall and report experiences which had not been thought or talked about for many years.

CAT is not primarily concerned with the (impossible) task of autobiographical reconstruction but patients who recover or, as is more common, extend their recollections of childhood abuse during therapy need to be helped to make sense of and assimilate these memories. A major focus needs to be on disputing the almost universal irrational guilt suffered by victims of sexual abuse. The common forms of abuse are those involving family members, most often siblings and stepfathers, and those occurring in institutional settings. Within the family there is often associated violence towards the child and between the parents, often combined with evidence of personality disorder and substance abuse, all of which have damaging effects on the development of children. As Zanarini (2000) comments, sexual abuse may be 'the childhood event most horrific to clinicians … it may not be so to patients. Rather, it may be emblematic of the ongoing chaos and insensitivity that they faced on a daily basis'. The effects of the abuse itself are more damaging where it involves penetrative sex, is repeated and is accompanied by threats of, or actual, violence, but sexualisation of an affectionate parent–child relationship and the blurring of generational and gender boundaries can also be a source of confusion and guilt.

The psychotherapy of adult abuse survivors will usually be concerned with the overall distortions of their self-management and relationship procedures. These are likely to take the form of the re-enactment of abusive procedures towards self and others, sometimes but not always including repetitions in the form of perverse sexual practices, or to involve restrictive and avoidant procedures. The narrative reformulation of CAT can help the integration of the many survivors with partially dissociated self states and the diagrams are of particular value in preserving therapeutic relationships in the face of distrust. Pollock (2001) has written and edited a book in which the use of individual and group CAT to treat abuse survivors is described in detail, sometimes in combination with other methods such as 'power mapping' (Hagan and Smail, 1997). The book includes some encouraging case histories and naturalistic studies of the effectiveness of CAT.

True or false recollections of abuse

After many decades in which memories of abuse were routinely interpreted as fantasy by psychoanalysts, the acknowledgement during the past 20 years that it was a common and real event led to a reversal of attitudes and to a general tendency for therapists to accept such memories as being at least based on actual experience. More recently, however, there has been a growing realisation that this is not always so and, more importantly, that therapists can easily suggest, or can seem to offer validation of, false memories.

To have an experience of abuse denied can be abusive, especially where threats and lies had accompanied the abuse, and in the past many patients suffered in this way. But it is also abusive for a parent to be falsely accused of having committed abuse. The fact that recovered memories are liable to surface during therapy and that some therapists had actively sought for (and indirectly suggested the presence of) such memories generated a passionate reaction and divided people, including professionals, into believers and non-believers in the possible truth of recovered memories. The debate about the 'false memory syndrome' was therefore fuelled and obscured by much pain and anger on both sides. It is now generally accepted that most but not all memories of abuse, even those recovered after periods of amnesia, are based on real experience, but that, in line with all the research on memory, what is recalled is a mental construction with a variable and often slight resemblance to what occurred (Brandon et al., 1998; Offer et al., 2000). However, in the absence of corroboration, there is no way of distinguishing between true and false memories; in particular, the latter can be as detailed and vivid as the former. Where adults recall memories after decades of complete amnesia, where the memory refers to very early childhood and where elaborations such as accounts of satanic rituals are reported, the likelihood that the memory is a false construction is greater.

The practical implications of this for therapists have been spelled out by the Royal College of Psychiatrists (Brandon et al., 1998) and the British Psychological Society (1995). Techniques involving hypnosis or powerful suggestion should be avoided, and the suggestive potential of detailed questioning should be borne in mind. It should be made clear to patients that all memory involves selection and construction and that the truth or otherwise of uncorroborated memories cannot be established. Because false memories may be held with great conviction and because their effects on current family relationships can be devastating, responsible therapists will be careful to remain uncommitted about the truth of uncorroborated memories of childhood abuse.

Elaborations of fantasy of the kind emphasised by Freud, distorted interpretations of innocent events, retrospective revisions based on later experiences, sociological changes influencing gender roles, unresolved psychological tensions in the family and other factors may all be the source of partially or totally false recovered memories of abuse and their relative weights and frequencies have not been established.

UNRESOLVED MOURNING

The loss of others whom one needs or values, the loss of one's own health and capacities, the loss of one's beliefs or illusions and the losses imposed by time in the receding past and diminishing future are all unavoidable aspects of life. These issues constitute an important and implicit focus of work in all forms of psychodynamic therapy, and a central and explicit focus in some, notably attachment-theory based approaches (Murray-Parkes et al., 1996; Marrone, 1998). Coping requires acceptance of the fact of loss followed by the assimilation of its meaning. The focus here will be on bereavement but other losses involve similar processes.

The period of early mourning following the death of a loved person is normally marked by emotional instability, with shifts between states of acute distress, of protest or anger at the deceased, of intrusive memories or hallucinations and of denial or disbelief. These fade with time as acceptance is gradually accomplished. In modern industrial societies the social rituals and conventions surrounding illness and death are generally impoverished and we have generated no replacement for the role played by religions in the past of supplying support and giving meaning to the experience. Failures to complete mourning are common and only a few people make their way to the available resources of self-help groups and counsellors. Maybe for these reasons, and also because of the more general loneliness of many people in our individualistic societies, incomplete mourning is frequently an aspect of the difficulties which bring people to psychotherapists. It commonly presents as depression and restriction which serve to avoid or suppress the more powerful affects of grief and rage associated with loss. Sadness may have been intolerable at the time of the loss due to the absence of support or the need to cope and care for others, or there may be anger or resentment reflecting the sense of abandonment which, because irrational and not respectable, has not been expressed. This anger may be redirected at professional carers who are seen to have failed to look after and save the dead person. Whatever coping mode was adopted at the time, the most common ones which involve suppressing feeling and getting on with the practical tasks can become habitual. In some cases the particular relationship with the dead person and the role procedures active in it may further complicate the mourning process, most notably where the subject feels guilt as if the death occurred as a result of his or her hostile feelings or actions.

One experience of loss and mourning requiring assimilation is a product of therapy itself. The reformulation commonly confronts patients with how their own past procedures have restricted and damaged their life so far. The appropriate recognition of this lost possibility is an important step on the road to change. More generally, therapy can reach beyond the defensive dulling of incomplete mourning. The termination of an emotionally powerful therapy relationship can be an emotional recapitulation of past losses which can be supported in ways allowing the revision of the previous restrictive modes. Here, the time limit of CAT, its intensity and the direct focus on loss at termination which is recorded in the 'goodbye letter' are all features which make it a suitable intervention for patients with problems in this area. On the other hand, the reformulation of the patient's role procedures allows the recognition of specific relationship issues and general strategies which may have contributed to the incomplete assimilation of the loss. Issues surrounding the negotiation of death, dying and mourning are explored further from a CAT and Bakhtinian perspective in Kerr (1998a).

CAT IN PRIMARY CARE

CAT is being increasingly used in primary care settings by therapists and counsellors for the range of neurotic and less severe personality disorders encountered there. A further, demanding part of the workload in general practice centres around a number of 'frequent attender' patients (often referred to vividly if rather pejoratively as 'heart sink'). Such patients are estimated to represent about 5% of a typical practice workload. While less disturbed patients tend to recover with many different interventions by GPs or practice counsellors, for this 'difficult', frequent attender group the evidence suggests that CAT is an effective treatment in this setting. In a pilot study reporting on a series of patients ($n = 29$) with a range of disorders, many of whom fell into the frequent attender category (customarily defined as 11 or more attendances per annum), impressive results were obtained both in terms of psychological difficulties as assessed clinically and also by frequency of attendance. The latter reduced from a mean of 11 to 4 per annum across the whole group (Barker, Johnstone, Reidy and Williams, personal communication). Comparable results are also being obtained in a further extended series documented by these workers. Interestingly, however, in the few patients evaluated in the pilot study who received a mean of only six sessions a reduction of frequency of attendance was not seen. This suggests that a full course of CAT may be necessary to achieve clinically significant and lasting results in many patients, although these numbers are of course too small to be significant. This incidental finding raises important questions, however, about the widespread practice in primary care of restricting therapists or counsellors to delivering such a limited number of sessions only and is an issue which requires further, formal evaluation.

Given the sorts of difficulties generated by such patients in primary care, the support of staff through, for example, CAT-based discussion groups, could be a further, useful contribution of the model.

PSYCHOSIS

In recent years there has been a growing interest in the psychological treatment of psychotic illness and a CAT special interest group has been undertaking some work in this field. Out of this, some interesting findings and a preliminary CAT-based model of psychotic disorder has emerged (Kerr et al., 2000; for a fuller account see Kerr and Crowley, 2001). Given that this will be an unfamiliar

psychotherapists, a brief overview of the background to this work
, noting in particular psychosocial aspects of these disorders.
ounts of recent research into psychotic disorders can be found in
es edited by Wykes et al. (1998) and Martindale et al. (2000) and a
consideration of psychosocial issues is offered in a review by Hemsley and
Murray (2000).

Current models of psychotic disorder

The dominant paradigm in addressing psychotic disorder has come to be that of
a stress-vulnerability model as originally proposed by Zubin and Spring (1977).
This paradigm views the occurrence of such disorders as the culmination of
factors representing a vulnerability to the disorder (genetic and/or biological)
acted upon by psychosocial stressors both during development and in the
present. Exactly how vulnerability and, in particular, psychosocial stress is
conceived of varies in different models and is still accounted for in only varying
degrees of adequacy. In particular, the extent to which higher mental function is
understood to be socially formed and subsequently expressed, both in normal
and psychotic states, we would see as a neglected area in most current models.

Neurobiological and cognitive abnormalities in schizophrenia

Evidence from studies of heritability (e.g identical twins adopted and brought
up apart and studies of incidence in first degree relatives) suggests that approximately 50% of the vulnerability to disorders such as schizophrenia and bipolar
affective disorder is inherited. However, this leaves open the important question of what constitutes the remainder of the vulnerability. It is increasingly
accepted that psychosocial factors affect both the development and the course
of psychotic illness over and above the influence of genetic or biological vulnerability. Various neurobiological abnormalities have been shown in the
schizophrenias, many of which implicate some neurodevelopmental abnormal-
ity. These abnormalities include pervasive and long-standing subtle neurological defects in most individuals who develop schizophrenia. The general
consensus is that there exist systemic impairments of 'functional connectivity'
or a widespread 'cognitive dysmmetria' (Andreason et al., 1998). Various
complex but overlapping theories have been proposed to account for both overt
symptoms and underlying neurocognitive deficits. A few studies in this area
have paid attention to the social and interpersonal origins of the personal
meaning of higher mental activities. Thus Bentall and his group (Bentall and
Kindermann, 1998) hypothesise, for example, that persecutory delusions arise
in response to perceptions that appear to represent personal threat and are associated with underlying attributional cognitive biases. Their study of the ways in
which paranoid and delusional thinking is generated is rooted in a more social

constructivist viewpoint than are the monadic and purely 'information process-ing' perspectives implicit in most cognitive accounts.

Neurobiological and cognitive abnormalities in bipolar affective disorder

In bipolar affective disorder the overt symptoms appear to be rooted in a consti-tutional predisposition to lability of mood and disinhibition, with consequent grandiose and deluded thinking and behaviour in the acute phase. Much remains to be discovered about this disorder. It is known that psychosocial stressors are important in the course of the disorder although less is known about their role in its initial development. By analogy with the schizophrenias it seems likely that they play some role.

Secondary effects of psychotic illness

One important consequence of these abnormalities is not only the catastrophic disruption in the sense of self central to the experience of these disorders (Hemsley, 1998) and important in recovery from them (Davidson and Strauss, 1992), but also the profound damage done to the individual often attempting a delicate and difficult life stage and developmental transition from late adoles-cence to, and subsequently through, adulthood. The experience of psychosis may leave an individual with a frank post-traumatic stress disorder, which may require additional therapeutic consideration (McGorry et al., 1991).

Current psychological treatments for psychotic disorders

Psychosocial interventions

The idea that psychosocial stressors are of importance in the course of psychotic disorder has been recognised for several decades since the pioneering work of Brown et al. (1972) on the role of family environment in the outcome of schizophrenia. This work demonstrated the importance of high levels of 'expressed emotion' (i.e. overt criticism and hostility by family members) in determining subsequent relapse rates. Current treatments for this include family and systemic therapy focusing on both psycho-education for the family as well as on high expressed emotion.

Psychological treatments

More recent CBT-based treatments of major psychotic disorders, notably schizophrenia, have tended to focus either on the presumed underlying neurocognitive deficits in, broadly speaking, the areas of information process-ing or, as in the UK in particular, on particular symptoms or difficulties such as delusions or hallucinations. Trials of CBT have now been reported by several groups demonstrating clear effectiveness in the major areas of psychotic symptomatology as well as, to varying extents, in associated problems such as depression, social function, and overall relapse rates. There are encouraging, reports of more psychodynamically informed treatments, notably from various groups in Scandinavia, from the well-known 'need-adapted' psychosocial interventions developed by Alanen in Finland and from the carefully formulated psychodynamic approach developed by Hogarty in the US. Several cognitively based theorists have also developed approaches aimed at normalising and working with experiences of hearing voices, based on an understanding that these are not fundamentally abnormal experiences (Chadwick et al., 1996; Leudar and Thomas, 2000). Significantly, early experience of trauma may adversely affect the way in which voices are internalised, integrated and subsequently experienced. Romme and Escher (Romme et al., 1992) in Holland have pioneered voice hearers' groups which have had apparently powerful therapeutic effects. It can be seen that these approaches represent a form of dialogical understanding and treatment.

Aims of psychotherapy for psychotic disorders

It is clear that treatment may need to be offered at a variety of levels ranging from increasingly specific pharmacological, to cognitive remediation work, individual psychotherapy through to more general social and family support of both a practical and psychoeducational nature. Garety et al. (2000) summarise the threefold aims of therapy as reducing the distress and disability caused by psychotic symptoms, reducing emotional disturbance and helping the person to arrive at an understanding of psychosis in order to promote active participation in the regulation of risk of relapse and social disability. Most authors in the field stress the importance of a detailed and individual formulation of the patient's problems, ideally in conjunction with the patient.

A CAT-based model of psychotic disorder

What CAT may have in particular to offer to the understanding and treatment of psychotic disorders is an account of how development (including its social and cultural dimensions) may, or may not, be stressful both historically and in the present, through the 'internalisation' of role procedures and their associated dialogic voices. Such a Vygotskian and dialogic model would predict that both vulnerability to and also expression of psychotic symptoms and experiences would be determined by an individual's repertoire of internalised reciprocal role procedures, constituting as they do fundamental components of higher mental function. Thus the form of psychotic phenomena such as auditory hallucinations or disturbed or self-harming behaviour, delusions (whether paranoid or grandiose) or extreme self-critical depressed states could be largely accounted for in terms of internalized RRPs and their associated dialogic 'voices'. These would be evident in both internal self–self and self–other enactments, as is the case normally, but in psychotic states, whatever the cause, in a highly distorted, amplified and muddled form due to 'information processing' abnormalities in a vulnerable individual, particularly if stressed. It can be seen that distortion of these self–self procedures or inner dialogue could, for example, result in misattribution of 'voices' to external agencies such as the devil in the case of extremely self-critical or self-harming procedures, or the development of paranoid delusions (see parallel argument by Bentall and Kindermann, 1998).

A further consequence of psychotic states is the damage, as noted by Hemsley (1998), to the sense of self and its continuity. This can be seen as damage at levels 2 and, especially, 3 as described in the CAT developmental model (see also Figures 4.1 and 4.2). One implication of this model is that psychosis may be due to a failure of integration of RRPs and dissociation of self states for whatever reason. Such 'pockets' of refractory psychosis (paranoid beliefs and reciprocal role enactments) have been noted, for example, in BPD (Heather Wood, personal communication).

A CAT-based developmental model of vulnerability to psychosis

Developmentally it can also be seen that vulnerability, for example due to subtle neurological abnormalities, may result in social difficulties and abnormal interpersonal interactions, as well as in a tendency to mis- or over-interpret perceptual phenomena. This could in turn be compounded and exacerbated by difficult experiences *which may have been partly elicited or generated by that vulnerability* in a dialectical process. Thus we would suggest that the psychological internalisation of abnormal interpersonal experience in the form of RRPs could in itself be a 'self-stressful' dynamic which could have serious long-term psychological, and possibly neurobiological, consequences. It has, for example, been suggested that stress hormones could be in part responsible for mediating such pathways at a biological level (Walker et al., 1996). It is also known that neurodevelopmental processes are not complete until early adulthood and these processes may well be affected by such stress and determine the time of onset and severity of an illness. This RRP repertoire we would see as constituting a core aspect of these disorders and its expression, as well as determining how it is responded to by others, both during development and also in terms of current interpersonal difficulty. An important implication of this model is that stress may be generated internally through the prior internalisation of self-critical or restrictive reciprocal role procedures through early interpersonal experiences, informed also by their cultural values and meanings. This stress could be seen as 'internal' expressed emotion, by analogy with the overt expressed emotion addressed by family therapists.

A further implication of this dialogic model is that psychotic states may be viewed as a being 'out of' or 'impermeable to' dialogue, both internally, in terms of disrupted and disordered inner self–self dialogue, as well as in terms of dialogue with others. Interestingly, key risk factors for psychotic states in old age (formerly described as paraphrenia) include social isolation and deafness. Such consideration of the origins of psychotic phenomena appears to provide additional evidence for the validity of a dialogic approach to understanding and working with higher mental functions, whether in psychotic states or not.

Therapeutic implications of a CAT-based model of psychosis

This model implies that working with RRPs and their dialogic voices can inform and assist attempts to make sense of psychotic experiences with the patient. The CAT emphasis on active participation and agency on the part of the patient in generating a joint, meaningful, narrative of their story and experiences would also be expected to have important therapeutic effects given the core disruption of sense of the self. Therapeutic work would, as in CBT, focus on the origins and meaning of psychotic symptoms such as hallucinations or delusions but would pay particular attention to their interpersonal origins. Even with neurotic patients it can be helpful and surprising to consider what the nature of a 'voice of conscience', for example, might be. The CAT model would imply that it would be important for a patient to understand and revise highly 'self-stressful' RRPs to reduce risk of relapse. A key part of such work would be an attempt to get a patient back into dialogue both internally and externally with others as well as to understand the circular nature of maladaptive role enactments. It is clear that isolation of a damaged and disturbed person will exacerbate their problems and stress them and this will have often occurred historically. In part, a CAT-based approach would be explicitly psycho-educational, based on an understanding of the nature of vulnerability to psychotic states. Importantly, any therapist working with such patients would need to become a trusted and reliable other with whom it is possible to have a confiding relationship and develop a dialogue. A further important aspect of any psychotherapy with such disorders would be the talking through and mourning of a life that might have been led but for the illness, an undertaking which will be greatly assisted by the explicitly narrative-based approach of CAT.

CAT would also aim to address the self-sabotaging or 'resistant' RRP enactments which may occur in psychotic disorders. As in the case of various medical disorders, these may lead to the patient being seen as 'difficult' and eliciting unhelpful role reactions from staff and family, particularly if the behaviour is seen as directly due to the illness, rather than as maladaptive coping strategies which may be compounded or amplified by the illness. Mapping out these role enactments, whether individual or contextual, would be expected to be helpful in these instances. What such approaches would effectively achieve would be the diminution of a generalised form of high 'expressed emotion' surrounding such patients in a way that will make sense to the patient and those around.

Two case histories will be described in order to illustrate these points in more detail. The first case describes work with a patient with a long-standing illness in a relatively stable condition, following recent discharge from hospital. The second case, which has been described at length elsewhere (Kerr, 2001) and will only be briefly summarised here, was a patient in a post-acute psychotic state in a locked ward who had become a 'difficult' patient with attendant, characteristic, unhelpful staff team role enactments.

Case example: Sarah (Therapist IK)

Sarah was a young woman in her early thirties, a graduate in fine art from a prestigious university, who was finally referred to a psychotherapy department with considerable reluctance by her community mental health team. She had been asking for psychotherapy for years and saw it as somehow a possible solution to her problems. She had a ten-year history of what was eventually diagnosed as a schizo-affective disorder and had been told by her doctor that she was 'born' with this and would always have it. There was no formal family history of psychotic disorder but her father was said to have been difficult, moody and incapable of intimacy and may have suffered from mood swings. Mother was quiet, rather timid and placatory towards her husband. Although she was described as supportive of Sarah they have never had an intimate or confiding relationship. As a child Sarah related that she kept herself to herself and was often lonely and cried alone in her room upstairs. She was also afraid of the dark. She said that she always *felt* criticised and teased by her father although on closer exploration she appears to have been seldom actually overtly criticised or punished. Her younger sister suffered from severe depression but has also managed to graduate from university.

Sarah had had multiple admissions to hospital, often under a 'section' of the Mental Health Act which involved admission to a locked ward. She described these as frightening and traumatic experiences and she did not feel treated seriously on large ward rounds. Some symptoms during these admissions were described in lurid terms in her case notes as 'very psychotic'. She described hearing the voice of God and of the Devil who urged her to attack people with knives or telling her she was worthless. She took a serious overdose one year prior to referral; she could not remember exactly why she did this. However, she remembered lying on the floor and it not seeming that she had herself done it. She 'coped' in the past with difficult feelings by cutting herself off and drinking heavily. She had an eating problem (bingeing and vomiting) at one point but had become overweight due to medication. She was taking lithium and neuroleptic medication although she was no longer on antidepressants, which she was pleased about. She felt that medication muffles real feelings and 'jollies you up' and would ideally like to have come off it, despite advice from her doctors. She was living in a hostel where she had no intimate friends and was doing some voluntary work in an old people's home. She found this rewarding but would like to do more with her life. She was attending church regularly and seeing some people from there. By her own account she found difficulty in social relationships and had never had a long-term, serious relationship. When she presented for therapy she did so with an intense enthusiasm but with also an obvious wariness and sadness.

She was offered a 40-session CAT-informed psychodynamic therapy as an outpatient which she eagerly if warily took up. She attended regularly and punctually and respected boundaries although was clearly often curious to know a lot more and be involved with her therapist. She joked in fact in her goodbye letter about still not knowing whether he was interested in art although she was sure he was. Her initial concerns appeared to centre around what the therapist's agenda was and what his connection with the community team was. She was also, it transpired, initially very wary about the therapist trying to recover repressed memories and also worried that psychotherapy might be 'dangerous'. She also expressed worries about what she called the 'trip wire' for her 'crashes' and about not really understanding what her illness was. She felt that she had suffered an 'emotional illness' related to the stress of her past. One of her major initial stated aims was to try to find her real self which she felt she had lost. She expressed considerable confusion and lack of confidence about her identity, especially as a woman and in relation to men. She noted that it felt difficult somehow to say 'I' and felt as if somehow she had been adopted. It gradually became clear that she also felt fearful about expressing any intense or angry feelings because in the past she felt that it had led to people thinking she was ill and to her being locked up. She thought there was a lot of 'frozen anger' inside which might be causing a depression. When depressed she felt that she 'ought' to punish herself and felt she had no concept of being comforted and that she had never been 'allowed' to feel despondent or sad. She also slowly discussed her angry but also, it appeared, idealised view of God although she was very reluctant to do so because talking about God too had led to her being locked up. Gradually too she discussed what she adamantly described as 'not schizophrenic' but recurrent 'critical voices'. On exploration it seemed that most of these could be related historically to her father but also to some teachers and a female family friend who continually ticked her off, as well as the culture around the school she attended. She had been frequently told, she said, that she was stupid and worthless and, in an interesting 'Vygotskian' comment, noted that somehow 'you can't do that' had become 'I can't do that' in her head.

Therapy for the first few months consisted very largely of her exploring and testing out the space and relationship offered to her about which, understandably, she remained very wary, appearing apprehensive of rebukes or rejection.

This period culminated before one Christmas in her attending obviously a little tipsy from a party and slightly disinhibited and, it seemed, testing out the therapist's reaction. She agreed subsequently that she had been really very surprised and relieved that she had not been criticised or rejected and that this had constituted an important point in the therapy. Gradually too it became possible for there to be some longer thoughtful silences and occasional tearfulness in reflecting on her life and what had become of it. Given the apparent need for this longer initial phase of building trust, the work of reformulation was not undertaken until about halfway through this therapy. In this respect the written reformulation in particular took the form more of a review letter reflecting on what had gone on in therapy up to then as well as on her story. It was nonetheless, as so often, a very moving and tearful moment. This letter (not shown) focused also in her case on the tentative discussion of her illness and eventual agreement with her therapist to refer to it as a 'vulnerability'. This is referred to in the list of TPPs, or 'key issues':

1. Feeling that you must somehow cope heroically on your own with difficulties, which seems, however, to leave you often feeling isolated, depressed and sometimes full of angry feelings, and so feeling even more that something is wrong with you and that you should keep things to yourself.
   Aim: Think about the costs we have discussed of trying to cope 'heroically' and check out the consequence of trying gradually to share some of your worries and anxieties with other people.
2. Believing your self-critical 'voices' as if they were really true 'reflections' of you, which leads you often to put yourself down and to feel that you don't deserve care and attention, which in consequence leaves you feeling that the 'voices' must be right.
   Aim: Consider where those internalised 'voices' might have come from as we have discussed and check out the evidence especially with other people as to whether you really believe them.
3. Because of being sensitive and having a psychological vulnerability to stress, feeling that life can never work out perfectly and that it is not worth trying, which in turn seems to confirm your worst fears when you don't try things.
   Aim: Consider that anyone with any vulnerability or disability has a right to a fulfilling life despite them and that it might be possible to live well without things having to be 'perfect', which might in any case be an illusory ideal.

Much of this list was concerned with coming to an agreed, joint understanding of her vulnerability and what might lie behind it and on how she might in the future cope with it. She also constructed with the therapist a detailed 'messy' SDR sketching role enactments around a 'core subjective' and 'original' self which was also a moving moment for her. Interestingly, Sarah insisted on writing at the top of the diagram that 'I have a personality', which she then amended to 'I *am* a personality'. Incorporated within the 'core subjective self' was also some description and agreement about what amounted to her psychotic vulnerability. These included a tendency to be 'up and down', to 'turn' and be 'scared of snapping a trip wire' along with a more general description of being 'sensitive' and tending to 'pick things up'. A refined version focusing on what emerged as key reciprocal role enactments and their consequences is shown in Figure 9.3. This also notes those enactments (either self–self or self–other) which might cause, broadly speaking, 'stress'. The key RRP of *criticised* relative to *criticising* (mostly of self, but potentially of others, which she could relate to since she felt her father did just this) proved to be a fundamental discussion point in terms of thinking about where this voice came from and whether she was prepared to 'own' it. It seemed clear that this self-critical voice constituted a major source of 'stress' for her and could be considered, as noted above, a form of internal 'expressed emotion'. In her goodbye letter, Sarah identified her understanding and modifying of this 'voice' as a major achievement in her therapy.

During this period of therapy Sarah remained stable and had no further admissions although these had hitherto occurred on at least an annual basis. She had also managed to move on and out of her hostel. Her team reported that she appeared markedly more communicative, cooperative and less depressed. She remained well at three-month routine follow-up and said that she wanted to get on with her life meantime and did not want any more therapy. Most interestingly, she said that she was for the first time in years now able to 'cry with God', which she felt was an important change. This does seem to indicate how she had moved on to be able to be more in dialogue, not only with staff but also, arguably, internally with some greater aspect of herself.

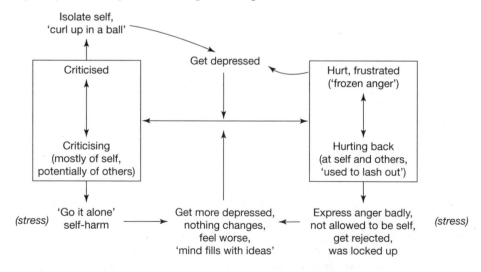

Figure 9.3 Simplified SDR for Sarah showing enactments of key RRPs

Sarah was also enthusiastic about being used as a case example for an article when asked, since she felt very strongly that other people with serious mental illnesses should also have the chance to have psychotherapy and that this might help towards that. This seemed in itself a significant, hopeful and 'dialogic' utterance.

Case example: Andrew

Andrew was a young man in his early twenties who had suffered from a bipolar affective disorder (manic depression) for three years. This had interrupted his studies and his ambitions to be a writer. He had had repeated relapses and compulsory readmissions to hospital due to non-compliance with medication. At the time of his brief CAT he had been admitted to the locked ward and was in 'seclusion' due to his highly disturbed and aggressive behaviour. His behaviour had elicited very different reactions from the staff team who, for the most part, enacted very angry and punitive roles towards him, although a few felt sympathy and had some understanding of how difficult things might be for him. Immediately prior to being offered brief CAT, he had been locked in the seclusion room and had stripped himself naked, torn the mattress apart and was smearing faeces over the walls. Eventually, following medication, he agreed he had 'made a point' and agreed that he might consider meeting to 'talk things through'. This resulted in six sessions of variable length of therapy and the joint construction of diagrammatic and written reformulations. He filled in the Psychotherapy File identifying particularly the dilemma, which he ticked, underlined and added three plus signs to, which states *'if I must not then I will; it is as if the only proof of my existence is by resistance. Other people's rules, or even my own feel too restricting, so I break rules and do things which are harmful to me'*. Key problem procedures described in reformulation included sabotaging of treatment (and so becoming a 'difficult' patient) if he could not be 'perfectly' well, and developing and enacting 'unrealistic' fantasies or dreams about the future to compensate for his illness experience. What emerged from this work was that much of what had been regarded as psychotic behaviour was essentially the enactment of comprehensible if maladaptive attempts at coping with the damaging effects of his illness. These enactments had, however, been compounded and exacerbated by the illness. This was also worsened by the attempts of family and staff to force treatment on him and then reacting in a hostile fashion when he did not 'comply'.

It seemed that a very important aspect of this very brief intervention had been the explicit demonstration that the team were prepared to listen and acknowledge his traumatic story. Interestingly, he too had insisted on writing across the top of his diagram that 'I am more than just my illness'. The reactions of the staff were also mapped onto his diagram as a rudimentary 'contextual reformulation' and this, by their account, not only contributed to a better understanding and working relationship with Andrew but also reduced the stress they themselves had been experiencing. The result was an immediate de-escalation of his disturbed and 'difficult' behaviour and made possible his return a few days later to an open ward. Andrew himself used his reformulation document to negotiate with his community team about his care and in particular his medication regime. This enabled him to return to university and remain stable without further readmission for the year up to follow-up.

What these two case studies illustrate, consistent with the clinical experience of the interest group so far, is that a CAT-based psychotherapeutic approach can be successfully employed with varying sorts of patient difficulties in different settings. In these cases the difficulties were associated with firstly a long-term experience of a severe mental illness and secondly an acute crisis in hospital which resulted in the generation of some of the typical dynamics around a 'difficult' patient. Particular features of the CAT approach which appear to have been important include, notably, a proactive and collaborative stance and the attempt to make, from a coherent theoretical framework, explicit sense (as articulated through reformulation documents) of the patients' distress and difficulties, both present and past. It also appeared that the direct work with these patients had helpful, indirect effects in educating and supporting the teams attempting to treat them, as illustrated in particular by the second case.

It appears that CAT may provide a useful conceptual framework from which to approach the understanding and treatment of psychotic disorders. The abnormal experiences and interpersonal therapeutic difficulties characteristic of these disorders may be understood partly in terms of the internalisation of reciprocal role procedures and their enactments. As such, CAT may usefully extend and amplify some of the more recent, valuable CBT-based work in this field. It may prove especially helpful in engaging patients at an early stage of their illness and so contribute to the prevention of 'secondary' damage. Such a CAT-based model may have an additional, important role to play in team education and support and could serve, as discussed by McGorry (2000), as an integrative platform from which to base treatment for this neglected group of disorders. Clearly formal, controlled evaluation of its efficacy will need to be undertaken on the basis of these encouraging, initial studies and this preliminary model.

LEARNING DISABILITIES

It is well recognised that those with learning disabilities (LD) very commonly suffer from emotional and psychological problems (Szivos and Griffiths, 1990) but treatment for them has been generally neglected. These individuals suffer from a range of problems including depression, anxiety, difficulties with anger and with relationships, personality disorder, experience of abuse and some have forensic histories for offences such as fire setting or inappropriate sexual behaviour. It has been shown that the majority of individuals with learning disabilities do not suffer severe disability but rather mild to moderate forms of it. It is only recently that attempts have been made to provide psychotherapy to this group using cognitive (Dagnan and Chadwick, 1997) and dynamic (Sinason, 1992) models.

It is clear from this work that people with learning disabilities can make use of the simple concepts of cognitive therapy. Experience with CAT (Crowley et al., personal communication) demonstrates that, for individuals with mild to moderate LD who cannot usually read or write, the tools of CAT, with modifications, can be used successfully. Thus the Psychotherapy File has been simplified verbally and symbolisations of traps and dilemmas developed. It has proved possible to represent RRPs symbolically and an SDR can be presented using colours and pictorially in collaboration with the client. The reformulation letter can be audiotaped so that the client can listen to it repeatedly to understand it fully.

Typically, those with learning disabilities have been disabled from an early age, have suffered major losses and have been marginalised and stigmatised by society all their lives, factors which determine their repertoire of RRPs. These commonly include *abused or victim* to *abusing or bully*, *not hearing or understanding* to *not being heard or understood*, *rejecting* to *rejected* and *abandoning* to *abandoned*. Common 'fantasies' are for someone who will perfectly love them, the wish to be perfect and normal and a wish for a powerful or magical care-giver or rescuer. Common procedures enacted include the trying to please trap, the bottling up dilemma, feeling one has to say yes and the snag of sabotaging success or anything good. Frequently such individuals may actually try to appear more disabled than they are. This enactment has previously been described as 'secondary handicap' (Sinason, 1992). However, clients with LD also have similar wishes and needs to those termed 'normal'.

The experience with CAT has been that its descriptive, collaborative, structured and time-limited approach is of great benefit to both clients and therapists. The process of engagement and active participation for the client in creating shared signs and language, in problem solving and in the generation of choices has an empowering effect on a client group that feels usually unheard, powerless and 'stupid'. CAT has appeared particularly helpful in restraining the tendency of therapists to enact the powerful care-giver or magical rescuer, roles which have unhelpful consequences for the client. More generally, CAT has proved to be again useful in this context as a consultative tool in working with staff themselves in both residential and community settings to help them in avoiding collusion with clients' maladaptive RRPs.

The concept of the zone of proximal development (ZPD) is particularly important in working with this client group. Interestingly, much of Vygotksy's own interest in this concept stemmed from his own work in the field of what was then called 'defectology'. Such clients often present with a poor emotional vocabulary, find it difficult to form a narrative and lack the skill of self-reflection. It is interesting to consider that part of these difficulties may have arisen as 'secondary handicap' consequent to inadequate or depriving experiences of care during development. Therapy, to some extent, can aid the development of these skills through the assistance of an enabling other. Not surprisingly these clients require a rather longer experience of therapy, usually around 24 sessions, or up to 32 for those with additional features of personality disorder.

This fascinating work is currently being undertaken by a few practitioners but has clearly important implications for a neglected client group. The CAT approach appears to have much to offer, once the apparent impediment of lack of literacy is overcome by the creative techniques described. This work also confirms and illuminates the relevance of Vygotskian theory whatever the ability of the individual being worked with. It also confirms the importance of helping to create through therapy a meaningful narrative and dialogue whatever the age or ability of the individual concerned. There is now an ACAT special interest group in this area and an extended description of some of this work will be published shortly (Crowley et al., in preparation).

CAT IN GROUPS AND ORGANISATIONS

It would be anticipated that CAT, with its radically social understanding of the formation of mind and its subsequent enactments, could contribute useful insights and understandings into the function and dysfunction of groups and organisations. There is already some experience of running CAT-based therapeutic small groups. In these, patients had individual sessions leading to reformulation before meeting in a group, with diagrams then being shared in the group (Duignan and Mitzman, 1994). In a review of the field, Maple and Simpson (1995) suggest that it is possible to shorten the length of groups, with 24 sessions being found to be effective for many patients. It has also been found in several psychotherapy departments that standard 16-session individual CAT followed by group therapy is effective for patients who may need more therapy and for whom the opportunity to put into practice the lessons of their individual therapy in a group setting is valuable.

The extent to which CAT theory and practice as used in this setting has been genuinely integrated with the theoretical framework of group psychotherapy, of whatever theoretical orientation, has, however, been much more limited. There are clearly conceptual overlaps between these approaches, notably the interest in and therapeutic focus on the individual as a social being. Nonetheless, as is well recognised, complex transpersonal processes are enacted within groups to which the understandings of the CAT model have not yet been rigorously applied and this remains an area of potential exploration. The overlapping and complementary paradigms of CAT and group psychotherapy could certainly both benefit from such work. An attempt to apply Vygotskian insights to the large group processes of a therapeutic community has, more recently, been made (Kerr, 2000).

It would also be anticipated that the CAT model could contribute useful insights to the function and dysfunction of organisations. An account of the usefulness of an innovative CAT-based approach to a dysfunctional organisation (a hospital surgical unit) has been given by Walsh (1996). There are a small number of CAT practitioners with active interest in the area of organisational consultancy who constitute an ACAT special interest group. These workers have found that the CAT focus on the social formation of mind, and on how organisational processes may be conceptualized as reciprocal role procedures, are of some interest and assistance in describing dysfunctional organisational processes (Bristow, Encombe and Walsh, personal communication). They also note many commonalities with existing organisational literature which stresses, for example, systemic thinking, narrative methods, a collaborative, enquiring stance of the part of intervener, and a stress on a capacity for self-reflection (see Senge, 1994). Some writers also emphasise the existence of universal patterns of relating noted by anthropologists such as Bateson (2000).

Clearly, there are major differences in interventions aimed at organisations as opposed to individual patients. The applicability of existing CAT methods of analysis such as diagrammatic reformulation, useful as they appear to be in this context, will require further exploration and integration with existing organisational theory if CAT is to contribute fully to this fascinating area. It should be noted that one implication of such work is to stress the importance of the function and psychological well-being of the individuals comprising an organisation as well as the healthy functioning of the organisation. The original CAT focus on individual psychotherapy may paradoxically re-emerge from such studies of organisational pathology.

FURTHER READING

General problems relating to diagnosis and classification are reviewed in Kendell (1993). A range of psychological treatments of physical illness and of somatisation is described in Hodes and Moorey (1993).

Chapter 10

THE TREATMENT OF PERSONALITY DISORDERS

SUMMARY

Current concepts of personality disorder are confused and frequently unhelpful. Any adequate model must offer a fully biopsychosocial and developmental account of these extreme disorders of self states and function. The CAT multiple self states model of borderline disorder describes increasing levels of damage to the self. Key features of BPD are: (1) a limited repertoire of extreme and 'harsh' RRP's, *(2) a tendency to* partial dissociation *into a characteristic limited number of different self states, (3)* impaired and disrupted capacity for self-reflection. *Narcissistic disorders are described as characterised by two main self states, one described as 'admiring in relation to admired', the other as 'contemptible in relation to contemptuous'. Therapy is difficult because these patients experience neediness as being humiliating and, when faced with their emotional vulnerability, frequently switch to the 'contemptuous' role. All personality-disordered patients are prone to drop out of therapy. It is suggested that some psycho-analytic techniques can inadvertently reinforce dysfunctional procedures, while CBT has no adequate model of how reciprocal role procedures and dissociation may be rein-forced. In CAT, a key therapeutic task with such patients is to map out collaboratively, even in rudimentary form, key RRPs and self states as early as possible in order to create a working alliance and generate an overall understanding of the origins and effects of such state switches and subsequent role enactments. A central aim is to help therapists and others not to collude with the extreme RRPs enacted by such patients. These may occur with bewildering and demoralising rapidity and for apparently imperceptible reasons. Such collusions account for most of the difficulty associated with treating such patients and may easily worsen their condition. An ultimate aim of therapy is to enable*

*patients to reflect on and ultimately revise their RRPs and their tendencies to dissoci-
ated self states. Reformulation with such patients may be assisted by use of the
Personality Disorder Questionnaire (PSQ) and of specially-prepared repertory grids.
The difficulties in working with patients with these disorders are illustrated by material
from two challenging cases.*

THE CONCEPT OF PERSONALITY DISORDER

The evolution of the confused, culture-dependent concept of personality
disorder is usefully reviewed by Berrios (1993). Current diagnostic procedures
such as the DSM IV identify patients as suffering from personality disorders
when their personal difficulties are long-lasting, first evident during
adolescence and are believed either to be persistent (as in obsessive-
compulsive, schizotypal, paranoid and anxious personality disorders) or to
show only slow change (as with antisocial, borderline, histrionic, narcissistic
and dependent personality disorders). These diagnostic categorisations,
modelled on the classification of diseases, depend on the recognition of
syndromes—clusters of symptoms and behaviours which occur together—and
represent a crude and superficial way of describing the complex variations of
human experience and behaviour. Although such diagnostic procedures have
served to clarify the epidemiology and course of personality disorders and
have distinguished them from psychotic illnesses, they are of limited use in
clinical practice in that different diagnoses frequently co-exist in the same individual and in that individuals classified in a given category show wide variations in severity.

None the less, the recognition of personality-disordered patients is of importance to psychotherapists, because they are people who are damaged and
damaging and are usually more difficult to help. In psychotherapeutic practice,
the most frequently encountered are those with borderline personality disorder
(BPD), but cases of narcissistic, histrionic and antisocial disorders (included
with BPD in the 'dramatic–erratic' Cluster B of the DSM IV) are also seen, most
often in mixed forms. The maintaining of a working alliance is particularly difficult with these patients, owing to the instability and extremity of their shifting
states. In forensic practice borderline and sociopathic patients predominate.
People with schizotypal, paranoid and obsessive-compulsive personality disorders are less likely to seek therapy and are more difficult to engage. In this
chapter only borderline and narcissistic personality disorders will be considered; they are the most commonly encountered and have therefore been more
studied. Given the severity of these disorders as they present, at least in health
service practice, it is important to bear in mind that they will usually be 'co-
morbid' with other categories of disorder, and are therefore rarely seen in pure
forms. In many ways it is more helpful to consider such patients as suffering
from 'severe personality disorder' (Berelowitz and Tarnopolsky, 1993).

BORDERLINE PERSONALITY DISORDER (BPD)

Patients qualify for the diagnosis of BPD in DSM IV (American Psychiatric Association, 1994) by having at least five of the following nine traits: unstable, intense personal relationships, identity disturbance, affective lability, inappropriate intense anger, frantic efforts to avoid abandonment, impulsivity, suicidal or self-harming behaviour, chronic feelings of emptiness, and transient paranoid thinking or dissociative symptoms. These features are clearly not independent of each other and they may be present to varying degrees, despite which these criteria do serve to identify a seriously disturbed non-psychotic patient group. When systematically screened (e.g. by a structured interview such as SCID (Spitzer et al., 1987)) most borderline patients also meet the criteria of other personality disorders (the number of diagnoses reached providing a rough indication of severity) and virtually all have Axis I ('clinical disorder') diagnoses. Many patients who do not meet full diagnostic criteria (but who do have unstable relationships, identity disturbances and impulsivity) present similar problems to therapists and are best understood in terms of the BPD model.

The causes of BPD

There is uncertain evidence that the prevalence of BPD is rising (Millon, 1993) and that social factors such as poverty, family violence and instability and the lack of traditional structures may contribute to this. There is abundant evidence for an association of the diagnosis of BPD with extremes of childhood deprivation and abuse. Compared to other diagnostic groups BPD patients have experienced more severe deprivation and more severe forms of sexual and physical abuse. However, while the great majority of sufferers have had such early experiences, only a minority of children so exposed go on to develop BPD or other personality disorders. Other associated or predisposing factors include:

1. Gender. BPD is considerably more common in women. In contrast, sociopathic personality disorder (where similar childhood features are found) is much more common in men. These differences may reflect both biological and cultural influences.
2. Neurotransmitter dysfunctions associated with impulsivity and affective instability are found in BPD (Gurvits et al., 2000) but the assumption that these predispose to, rather than reflect, BPD seems uncertainly established.
3. Other biological factors. These may include responses to chronic stress marked by alternations between increased and diminished responsiveness to stress. There is animal evidence that brain structure as well as neuroendocrine function may be damaged by persistent stress (Silk, 2000) and that neural tracts are, to a degree, socially formed (Eisenberg, 1995).

4. Family members of BPD patients show high rates of personality disturbance but not necessarily BPD (Zanarini et al., 1988). Some genetic predisposition to BPD or similar personality features has recently been demonstrated, although the size of the genetic effect is still unclear (Torgersen, 2000). While psychotherapists will be primarily concerned with the effects of early experience on personality, understood in CAT as reflected in the procedural repertoire and its integration, it is important to recognise that biological factors, whether inherited or acquired, may set limits on what can be achieved psychotherapeutically. This supports the use of carefully managed psychopharmacology; while inadequate on its own, this may be of value when used in parallel with therapy. Different drugs may be effective in diminishing the severity of cognitive-perceptual, affective and impulsive symptoms (Soloff, 2000).

The CAT multiple self states model of BPD

The CAT model of BPD, developed over recent years (Ryle, 1997a, 1997b) builds on basic CAT theory with its emphasis on sequences and reciprocal procedures but adds a structural concept. The multiple self states model (MSSM) is based on the description of three forms of linked damage, as follows:

1. Harsh reciprocal role patterns. Early and extreme patterns, usually derived from relationships with caretakers, of *abusing, neglecting* in relation to *abused, needy* persist in various forms determining self-management and relationships with others. These patterns are at times replaced by symptomatic and avoidant procedures and may be associated with Axis I diagnoses, in particular depression, eating disorders and substance abuse. Not all abused children who develop such reciprocal role procedures (RRPs) become borderline; it seems probable that both the severity of the abuse and a genetic predisposition to dissociation determine the development of BPD. Thus, Zweig-Frank et al. (1994) compared women with BPD and non-BPD disorders and showed that adverse childhood events were equivalent whereas scores on a dissociation measure were significantly higher in the BPD group.
2. Partial dissociation. The coordination, linking and sequencing of reciprocal role procedures is normally carried out automatically by metaprocedures. In BPD these are underdeveloped or disrupted as a result of chaotic parenting and of trauma-induced partial dissociation. As a result, key RRPs are separated to constitute self states which alternate in determining experience and behaviour so that the sense of self and others is discontinuous and access to memory between states may be patchy. Dissociation while experiencing abuse during childhood is commonly reported; this is seen to facilitate subsequent dissociation if further neglect and victimisation were experienced,

perceived or remembered. Such dissociation is not necessarily accompanied by dissociative symptoms. Out of control rage leading to attacks on self or others may occur when such dissociation fails. This may be seen as a primitive reflex or 'defence' of the humiliated, shamed or 'wounded' self (see Kalsched, 1998).

3. Impaired and interrupted self-reflection. The capacity for self-reflection is underdeveloped in BPD due to early neglect and lack of interest from caretakers and what capacity exists is liable to disruption by state switches. Such switches are particularly liable to occur when abuse or neglect is experienced or perceived or when reciprocation to alternative procedures is sought but not elicited, that is to say at the precise moments when self-reflection would be particularly helpful in aiding revision. It has been suggested (Fonagy and Target, 1997) that self-reflective capacity (or 'reflective function') may also be an innate, variable protective factor in the face of such adversity, although we are unaware of any formal genetic evidence for this.

Recognising partial dissociation

When the presence of partially dissociated reciprocal role patterns (self states) is suspected from clinical interviewing or from replies to screening questionnaires the different states must be identified and described. States recur in recognisable form. Switches between them may be triggered by events or by thoughts and images which may or may not be identified by patients; some such switches may be understandable as partially adaptive responses to the context.

Patients will describe their states largely in terms of mood and acts; therapists need to explore the associated role procedures. Borderline patients typically describe a limited number of states; these nearly always include the experience of playing, at different times, both poles of an *abuser–victim* reciprocal role. Abrupt switches may represent (1) role reversal (e.g. the victim turning the tables), (2) response shifts (e.g. switching from *compliance* to *defiance* in response to *control*) or (3) self state switches (e.g. from *caring–cared for* to *bully–angry victim*). The range of states found in borderline patients is not infinite; in a repertory grid study of the partially dissociated states of a series of 20 BPD patients, Golynkina and Ryle (1999) found that 17 patients identified themselves as experiencing ideal states, 14 abuser rage states, 13 victim states, 11 coping states, 8 zombie states and 5 victim rage states. (These states were idiosyncratically named, the above classification being based on the loadings of the states on a range of supplied constructs.)

While the clinical features of partial dissociation are often obvious, some patients may present themselves in emotionally blunted, coping modes, some may be reluctant to describe their dissociative experiences for fear of being seen as mad and, in some, personality features may be overlooked because of the presence of extreme Axis I disorders such as anorexia nervosa or major depression. In practice, the recognition of borderline states is helped by the routine use of screening questionnaires such as the eight-item Personality Structure Questionnaire (Pollock et al., 2001; Appendix 3) or the end section of the Psychotherapy File (Appendix 2). Discussing replies to these when scores are high and initiating patient self-monitoring of states and state switches will usually (but not always) confirm that clear distinctions between recurrent, recognisable, contrasting states are being reported. This can lead on to the process of characterising these states through further self-monitoring and work in the therapy sessions.

The reformulation and therapy of borderline patients

In everyday life the procedural repertoire of borderline individuals resists revision because the pressures on others to reciprocate (collude with) the various roles are intense and often successful, because others are confused by the patient's shifts and cannot respond in an integrating way and because self-reflection is impaired. The available procedures are all liable to generate further experiences of unmet need and unmanageable feelings. The therapist's task is to overcome these reinforcing patterns by working with the patient to create a narrative account which makes some sense of the patient's story and a diagram indicating the repetitive damaging patterns. These can help the patient learn to recognise and control these patterns and avoid the most damaging states and help the therapist to avoid or correct collusive reciprocations. The explicit aim must be to aid integration through the development of self-reflection ('the eye that becomes an I'), by always working with descriptions that include all aspects of the person.

The collaborative construction of diagrams during the reformulation phase is a powerful experience for patients. Preliminary partial diagrams may be roughly drawn from the first session, especially if therapy-disrupting procedures are suspected; the evolution of the diagrams as more evidence is collected is a positive collaborative map-making exercise which establishes a relationship which is 'off the map', that is to say which provides the patient with a new way of being in relation to another. The following guiding principles have evolved over the years:

1. Where clear evidence for discrete self states exists the dissociated RRPs should be located in separate boxes; a single defining RRP is usually adequate.
2. These boxes are heuristic summaries, not pictures of the inner world. Experiences and actions related to, or generated by, each role will be drawn outside the box as procedural loops which will trace the consequences of enactment. Particular relationships may be located on these loops which will also locate symptoms and unwanted behaviours.

3. As a start, the reported historical childhood pattern(s) will usually be recorded in diagrammatic cores. Other patterns evident in current relationships and in self-management will be added as they are recognised.
4. Either pole of the RRP may be enacted; the procedures generated from both poles, in self-management and in relationships, will be drawn in as they are identified.
5. The childhood-derived *abusive–depriving* to *victim–deprived* roles may be re-enacted and re-experienced in some direct form but they may also be replaced by symptomatic, defensive or avoidant procedures. These will be identified and located on the diagram by symptom monitoring and observation.
6. At some point any of the roles drawn out as procedural loops may lead to the experience of unmanageable feelings, often of rage, or of being overwhelmed by the perception of vulnerability and unmet need. This can be represented as a 'crossroads' or 'flashpoint' on the diagram. This may correspond to the point at which dissociation first occurred during abuse. In most cases this leads to a switch to self states (dissociated RRPs) in which the patient plays a coping, 'soldiering on', emotionally blank or in some cases a hyperactive role. In susceptible people such switches become increasingly easily mobilised by memories or reminders of past abuse and they are liable to be provoked by the experience of therapy. Uncontrolled victim rage may be seen as a partial failure of dissociation; when experienced it is often accompanied by dissociative symptoms such as depersonalisation or perceptual distortions.

In concluding the reformulation of patients with partially dissociated self states, it can be of value to get patients to complete a States Grid. In this the patient rates his or her identifed states against a range of constructs describing the mood, sense of self and other and the degree of access to and control of affects of each state and may also indicate which states are accompanied by physical symptoms and which are associated with impaired memory for other states. Patients can usually describe all their states when in their coping or compliant state, but in more severely dissociated patients the memory of some states may be very limited.

   The following case report demonstrates how the use of the States Grid, may be of value.

CASE HISTORY: DEBORAH (Therapist Anna Troger)

Deborah had been treated with CAT four years previously. At that time she had been self-cutting several times each week. She had been involved in a series of relationships with physically abusive men. She returned for treatment on account of very marked mood (state) instability, but she was no longer self-cutting and was holding down a responsible job. Her present partner was submissive and helpful and she was often impatient and bored with him.

Deborah completed the States Grid, the elements being five states which she labelled blank, hopeless, speedy, victim and angry. The grid was analysed in two parts, using 'Flexigrid' (Tschudi, 1990), one based on constructs concerning self-descriptions and the other based on descriptions of self-to-other and other-to-self relationships. Figures 10.1 and 10.2 map out the location of the elements in these two analyses, by plotting the states and the constructs (written in the margins for clarity) in terms of their loadings on the first two principal components derived from the analysis. Closeness on this map implies conceptual similarity and vice versa.

Figure 10.1 Deborah—grid of self descriptions

Others look after me

I give in to others

I try to please others

Hopeless

Blank

I can trust others

People like me

Others look down on me

+

Others threaten me

Others envy me **Speedy**

I do not trust others

Enraged victim

I hurt and blame others

I control others

I am aware of but do not care
about others' feelings

Others ignore and reject me

Figure 10.2 Deborah—grid of self–other relationships

Results

The self-descriptions grid

The abused and angry states are identically located; in the map they are re-described as 'enraged victim'. Deborah commented that any hint of feeling abused now leads to immediate anger. Located in the lower right quadrant, this combined state is described as angry, overwhelmed by feelings and with clear memories of the past. It is contrasted with the blank state in the upper left; this is associated with having few clear memories and with never being angry. On the upper right the hopeless state is described as sad, weak and indifferent to doing things badly, accompanied by physical symptoms and as lacking memory of other states. This state is contrasted with the speedy state in the lower left in which she is more competent than usual, self-righteous, feels well and okay as a person and is in control.

The grid of relationships

The angry and abused states are identical as on the first grid and are labelled enraged victim. In this state she sees herself as threatened and disliked and as indifferent to, and blaming and hurting of, others. In the contrasting hopeless state she can trust, depend on and be looked after by others. In the blank state she gives in to and tries to please others, whereas in the speedy state she controls others and feels they envy her.

The implications of this picture are as follows: to be cared for she has to be hopeless, incompetent, sad and have physical symptoms. Other patterns of relationships involve being either submissive, mutually destructive or very positive about herself but controlling of, and envied by, others.

It is evident that each state carries with it costly implications; therapy must seek to maintain a less fractured sense of self. With integration, the extreme, contrasting qualities of the different states may be mitigated so that both personal strength and mutuality with others may become possible.

The course of therapy

The course of therapy with borderline patients is never smooth. Reformulation and the active shared use of the diagram offer a basis for maintaining or repairing the therapy relationship and for the establishment of an observing eye. But the safety established through the creation and use of reformulation tools is often followed by increasing access to painful memories and by enactments of negative or avoidant procedures in relation to the therapist. Surviving and containing these is personally demanding, as the case reports earlier and at the end of this chapter demonstrate, but it is greatly helped by the reformulation. Patients should never be pressed to enter or extend these severely disturbing feeling states and should be given explicit control of the pace of therapy. Termination involving a weaning pattern of follow-up sessions at increasing intervals is usually helpful and will often involve planning some form of further support.

NARCISSISTIC PERSONALITY DISORDER (NPD)

Narcissistic features are commonly found in association with borderline structures, as in the case of Deborah, and the same methods of mapping self states are applicable. 'Purer' examples of NPD show a predominant preoccupation with issues of surface, appearance, success and status; their search is not for care and love so much as for admiration. The preferred reciprocal role relationship for a person with NPD is to feel admired by an admirable other. Where this is unachievable, the concern is with the relative status of self and other and hence with occupying the more powerful contemptuous role in the reciprocal role pattern of *contemptuous* in relation to *contemptible*. Because emotional neediness is closely identified with the contemptible role, therapy, as an admission of need, is hard to seek or persist with. Extreme sensitivity to criticism and envy are common features. Therapists treating NPD patients may be briefly idealised but will soon have to survive indirect or blatant dismissiveness from the patient who is intolerant of perceived criticism of any sort. The key task is to make it tolerable for the patient to be sad and vulnerable. These main features of NPD are summarised in the 'split egg' diagram (Figure 10.3). Narcissistic patients will identify themselves in terms of the admired state as far as possible, often achieving highly, especially in areas where performance is visible and rewarded. Failing to achieve adequate recognition leaves them in the other self state, in which they will seek to preserve a good opinion of themselves by looking down on others. In mapping such states it is best to illustrate the different roles using the patient's own descriptions as far as possible, but descriptions should always be as general as possible. Because the descriptions offered by the sequential diagram are unflattering it is particularly important to work collaboratively and non-judgementally with narcissistic patients and to

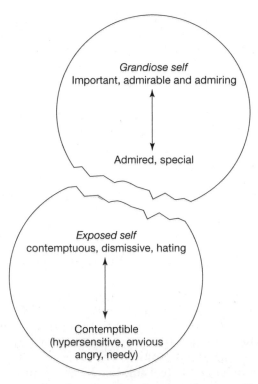

Figure 10.3 Narcissistic personality disorder: the two common self states

acknowledge both their real achievements and their real but feared vulnerability. And because therapists can easily fall from grace and be transformed from admirable helpers to contemptible fools deserving revenge, it is wise to get the patient's signed acknowledgement that they accept the final letter and diagram.

The sources of NPD are often traced to an early childhood in which the requirement was to be pretty or clever and to perform in order to be a good advertisement for the parent, while being deprived of real, consistent care or concern. In other cases, emotional deprivation in the family may be more overt but the child discovers an alternative source of acknowledgement and praise by shining at school, in sport or in some other sphere. The preoccupation with surfaces and with being admired can lead to real achievement, particularly in careers where merit is clearly recognised or performance is the point, and in such cases consultation usually follows some setback or a shortfall in the supply of praise. In less talented narcissists there may be an earlier consultation because loneliness and emotional coldness leave a sense of inner emptiness. Whereas BPD patients evoke a range of powerful and mixed feelings in their therapists those with NPD are more prone to generate irritation, coldness and rejection, responses which reflect their mobilising the contemptuous and critical roles in themselves and in their clinicians.

The textbook descriptions of NPD are also liable to reflect this reinforcing countertransference, emphasising the negative characteristics of envy and coldness and ignoring the underlying neediness which, even when it is well concealed, must be recognised by therapists.

Patients weaning themselves from the need for admiration and acknowledging their neediness must be supported (and can be genuinely admired) through a period of vulnerability and deep sadness; the first tears of a patient with NPD are signals of hope. If sadness is not reached, little changes and the end result may be renewed efforts to extract admiration from the world or the turning of the tables by dismissing the useless therapist.

Owing to the extreme vulnerability of these patients, giving up protective role enactments can be experienced as highly threatening, especially if a therapist is experienced as being more knowledgeable than they are. This can provoke enactment of dismissive or contemptuous roles and in extreme cases can lead to a patient dropping out of therapy, even when conducted as carefully as described above. Rarely, but seriously, such roles may be enacted as litigation towards a therapist who is perceived to have failed or damaged them.

CASE HISTORY: OLIVIA (Therapist Anna Troger)

Olivia, a 28-year-old secretary, was referred for CAT following an admission after an overdose. She met diagnostic criteria for both borderline and narcissistic personality disorders. While superficially lively and attractive she described a feeling of there being a void inside her. In the first half of therapy she was frequently dismissive of the therapist and declared that none of the items in the Psychotherapy File applied to her. In her work and social life she described a desperate wish to please and a related pattern of passive resistance and sabotage. In the early sessions she completed none of the agreed homework tasks, for fear they would be wrong. Her diagram is reproduced in Figure 10.4.

By mid-therapy Olivia could accept the part of her diagram spelling out the *critical dismissive demand* in relation to *irrational guilt and striving* pattern and she became less desperately competitive. She could also acknowledge that the *preoccupied with surface appearances and unprotective* in relation to *empty* self state was typical of her family. It was only in the last three sessions, when the therapist could say clearly how she had felt dismissed and could recognise that she had found it hard to acknowledge the reality of the void, that Olivia could acknowledge a dilemma generated by these two cores, summarised as *either* envy those 'above' *or* dismiss those 'below'. At follow-up, when she reported considerable improvement, she spoke of how difficult and painful it had been to acknowledge the accuracy of this description, in particular of her own dismissiveness. It was only in the last few sessions that she realised that it was true and had been true of her relationship with her therapist; she saw this as the turning point in her therapy.

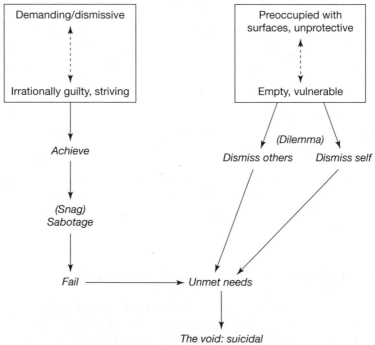

Figure 10.4 Olivia—self state sequential diagram

A fuller account of a therapy will now be offered, demonstrating in more detail how, while diagrammatic reformulation enables therapists to stay in relation to patients showing extreme states and marked state shifts, the process can be extremely demanding of both technical skills and human sensitivity and resilience. Our attention was drawn to this account by the therapist's supervisor. We are very grateful to the therapist Kate Freshwater (a clinical psychologist) for her permission to publish this moving and in many ways intimate account of her work, and to the patient 'Sam' (whose story has been altered in detail), both for the courage and intelligence he displayed in the work of therapy and for his being willing for his story to be told, in order, he said 'to contribute to the education of health care workers regarding the impact of abuse'.

CASE HISTORY: SAM (Therapist Kate Freshwater)

Sam was a 45-year-old man with a mixed Axis II Cluster B diagnosis, who had been in the mental health system since his early twenties and had also spent time in prison for grievous bodily harm. He was attending a day centre full-time and had been supported by a psychiatric nurse for many years; two years previously he had revealed a history of severe sexual abuse to the nurse. He was receiving both antidepressant and anti-psychotic medication. His early childhood had been marked by severe psychological and physical abuse from his stepfather, who had also beaten up his siblings and his mother. He began stealing when aged 11 and subsequently spent four years in an approved school where he was regularly beaten and buggered by older boys until he began to fight back. His mother died in his early twenties, a death he linked to his stepfather's repeated violence and neglect. He had worked intermittently during his twenties at unskilled jobs and was married with a son and a daughter but it was 12 years since he had been in employment.

During his assessment sessions Sam spoke calmly and, to quote the therapist 'frequently made remarks about women which he believed to be charming but left me feeling uncomfortable'. Early sessions ran over time and the therapist felt passive and powerless, struggling to retain control over the process; she felt further muddled by Sam's presentation of himself as having four separate personalities. These were characterised as follows:

1. 71; this was Sam's number in the approved school; he described 71 as gentle, scared, loving, numb and severely depressed.
2. Heartless Sam; described as having emerged when in the approved school and as being fearless and indifferent to pain; he would quickly divide up the world into the abused and the abusers. He would get involved in, but might have little recall of, violent episodes. He was rejected by the other personalities as being too much like his abusive stepfather.

3. Benjamin Sam was a sad, beaten up, spaced out child.
4. Friend of Benjamin. He was described as protective of Benjamin Sam; he was rebellious and had offended as a boy in order to be sent away from home. He would try to calm down Heartless Sam.

The first diagram consisted of four circles standing for these four 'personalities', listing their main attributes. Two intermediate diagrams traced the sequences between and procedures generated by these as they were identified. The final diagram (Figure 10.5) was constructed around two cores, one derived from his painful relationship with his victimised mother, the other based on his many experiences of being abused at home and at school.

Sam sought help for his inability to control his violence and for being emotionally numb and scared of closeness and he wanted his four selves to be on better terms with each other. When offered therapy he said that 'three of us are terrified', having experienced the 'mind games' of psychiatrists. He saw the therapist as a 'sculptress' setting out to work on him as a lump of clay, adding that they would need the water of emotion to achieve change. This metaphor, from the client, gave an opportunity to negotiate the work together and develop the alliance. It could have left the therapist feeling controlling, seductive or

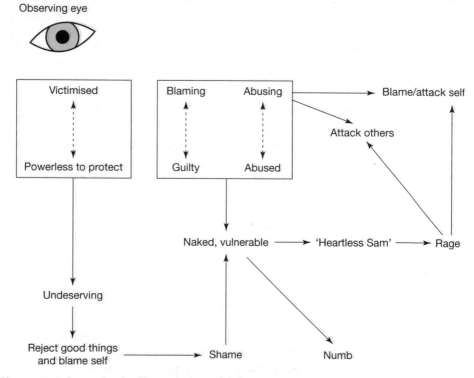

Figure 10.5 Sam—final self state sequential diagram

intimidating but was used to develop a more cooperative style of working as the client accepted the concept of working together to 'mould the clay'.

The therapist considered the possible diagnosis of dissociated identity disorder but the absence of amnesia for any one personality, his ability to switch at will between them and the fact that many features and questionnaire scores were constant across states argued against this. (The presence of both partial dissociation and multiplicity in more severe borderline patients is described by Pollock et al., 2001.) Having listed the main features of each state ('self') as a first step, successive diagrams were constructed over the first 11 sessions. Sam's identity as a case of 'multiple personality disorder' provided an important framework of meaning to him and the therapy involved gentle negotiation over the language used; such as always using 'self states' to describe Sam's different personalities. During this time Sam suffered a bereavement (the death of a loved niece) after which he was involved in picking a fight with seven men. He explained this as being angry at Heartless Sam for having no feelings about the death and as expressing this in anger with others but he could follow the therapist's suggestion that by starting a 'no-win' fight he was also punishing himself.

In the reformulation letter and the developing diagrams the therapist accepted Sam's account of the different selves as a basis for describing self states but continually emphasised that she saw them as aspects of a single person, stressing that the integration of the states would be an important aim of the therapy. Sam was predominantly controlling in the sessions, but after a second bereavement—the suicide of a half-brother—and an initial reaction of self-blame (saying the deaths were punishments for his talking about the abuse) he had an intense experience of grief. At this time he was able to place at the centre of his diagram the description 'nakedness' (a description relating to his abuse experiences) which continued to be important through the rest of the therapy, and from this time he began to stop and think more before reacting with violence. During the next few sessions he showed greater swings in his moods. The therapist described this phase as follows:

...he seemed to swing between feelings of grief and vulnerability, feelings of intense guilt and anger at the 'system' for abusing and failing him, and wanting to take control and protect me from his more traumatic experiences. He came to one session looking dishevelled, saying 'the deaths are catching up on me' and describing how he had been uncharacteristically quiet at the Day Centre. At other times he attacked 'the mental health system' (and myself) for wasting time in working with abusers; although he could now acknowledge his own physical abusiveness, he regarded sexual abusers as despicable animals whom he wished to destroy. He described how he had 'arranged' for a reported pervert to be beaten up. ... I initially felt powerless and outwitted, for this was hardly the safe way of venting his anger which we had been discussing, but I was helped by supervision to avoid my induced self-blame and sense of failure and to challenge Sam to think through the consequences of such vigilante behaviour. We completed

the final diagram at session 11 [see Figure 10.5], adding his sense of having been unable to protect his mother and how this had contributed to his self-blame and to his sense of not deserving anything good, and linking his dismissal of past careworkers with his search for perfect care and its inevitable disappointment. Following this we began to name 'exits'—alternative behaviours—and he recalled his childhood image of a bird which, while he was being abused, would fly away with the pain. This bird image became a fifth 'personality', able to show some compassion towards Heartless Sam. Picturing his granddaughter was suggested as a way to remind him of his own vulnerability and powerlessness as a child.

By this midpoint of therapy Sam was speaking more openly to his wife and his GP, to whom he had shown his reformulation letter, and he was more in touch with the day centre staff. The release at this time of the Department of Health's Consultation Paper 'Managing dangerous people with severe personality disorder', which he read, made him angry with 'the system' and evoked the statement that he would never have come to therapy had this been policy, for fear of being detained. This was used by the therapist to clarify confidentiality, to remind Sam that her concerns about violence had already been shared with Sam's GP in a letter of which he had a copy, and to point out that this concern about his violence was now balanced by the way he was already using therapy to find ways of controlling his abusiveness.

At session 18, Sam read out a letter to his dead stepfather, in which he detailed the abuse of his mother and the terror shared by all the children. The letter concluded:

We carry your name but that is all you ever gave us. Not one ounce of love or affection. Just pain, pain and more pain… You cannot hurt us anymore because a heart attack took you to the devil's door. We will all call upon you there to tell you to your face what an evil cunt you were. Bye bye for now you bastard.

This session continued as follows:

Therapist: You've said you'll meet him at the gates of hell. You've said why he deserves to be there but why do you?
Sam: Well for what happened to us—for being abused—Innocence and everything is taken off you. You no longer have a childhood, they take all that.
Therapist: But why should that be punished rather than comforted?
Sam: It's just the way we think, Kate, just the way we think… It seems to follow naturally that we'll go there.
Therapist: But you know how many people there are who have been sexually and physically abused. Do they all deserve to go to Hell?
Sam: Well, I would say no to that.
Therapist: So why do you?

Sam: Well it just seems to follow… They've taken the goodness off us… it's as if we're evil in our way. I'll give you an example: I can see a plane crash on TV or kids starving and it doesn't touch me—things that should mean something. But to us it don't mean a thing…

Therapist: Isn't that because from a very early age you learnt to cut off from painful feelings because they were so overwhelming…

Sam: Oh yeah, so now it's automatic.

Therapist: Are you saying that because you can do that then it makes you bad?

Sam: Yeah, I'd go along with that, yeah.

Therapist: Well I don't think that makes you evil; It's how you learned to survive as a kid and it still happens. But I don't think it makes you bad.

Sam: Well we do. (pause)

Therapist: But I can see where you are coming from. (pointing to the diagram) Abusing, attacking yourself. (pause). Thinking about—In the letter to your stepfather, I was struck by where you wrote how he never gave you any affection

Sam: He didn't. Not once. Never like I used to do with my son—like ruffle your hair. You know what I mean. … We were always on guard… always afraid we'd start something and then my mother would step in and then she'd finish up getting a whack. If we could avoid his company we did. It was as simple as that.

Therapist: So he didn't show any care and it feels as though you can't show yourself any either—can't be patient with yourself or love yourself.

Sam: I'd agree with that. I think it's beautiful to love yourself and all that. If you love yourself I imagine it means that others might love you too, eventually. But it just doesn't seem to apply to us. I can see what we're missing out on.

Therapist: Mmm.

Sam: There are odd times, a few seconds, when I get like a euphoric state. Just for a few seconds but they're lovely when I get them. But I don't get them every week, maybe every three months. And I don't know what triggers that …

Therapist: Do you remember the last time?

Sam: Oh, it was a few months ago. I can't explain it. It's as if something sweeps through me. It's almost dreamlike, but I'm wide awake and I want to hang on but it goes. It's almost as if … as if I'm brand new. (pause). I don't read the papers or watch TV, you know, because I get tripped back with all the stories of abuse that are coming to light now, all the churches and approved schools. There's a lot more to come through your hands. You know what I mean.

Therapist: Your euphoric state, when you feel brand new… It makes me think about you feeling tainted and marked so much by the abuse, so full of shame and evil … (pause). How do you think I see you?

Sam: (pause) Well, like I said. Tainted. And things like that.

Therapist: Is that really what you believe?

Sam: Yeah. That's how I feel everybody who knows about our abuse thinks. That's the reason why we didn't discuss it. I wouldn't have discussed it with my mother, it would have broken her heart.

Therapist: What does it mean that you are tainted; what does it mean that I think of you?

Sam: Well, we can never be good or anything. Because of what happened to us. They stole everything of decency off us.

Therapist: So how do I feel about being with you?

Sam: Well … the same way… you know… you're just doing your job and through your eyes you see us as tainted. Like we're a couple of classes lower—I don't mean class systems, I just mean lower; like castes. We're right at the bottom. They steal off you your soul. That's why we have no emotion. Soulless. Shell-like.

Therapist: That is not how I see you. People did things to you that were so horrendous that your whole life is affected. But in terms of you as a person, I don't see you as any the less for that, I don't feel that at all. I actually feel that you have shown enormous strength and courage to have got through as you have.

Sam: (jokingly) Without doing serious jail?

Therapist: Just the fact that you have lived. The bits I do not sit comfortably with, as you know, are when you hurt yourself or hurt other people. I want to work with you about getting more control over them. But as I said, I do not see you as less of a person. In fact I see you as having enormous courage. There's a lot about you that I respect.

Sam: Is that right? (pause) I'll try to take that on board. I took on board thinking about the baby… I can see the baby and the baby can't stop anybody raping the baby.

Reflecting upon this important and moving session, the therapist was aware of having been hurt by Sam's saying she was 'just doing her job' and questioned whether this has mobilised her forceful insistence on disclosing her positive feelings and naming his abusive aspects. In supervision she was encouraged not to over-analyse or rubbish what had been achieved by her intervention. At the following session a sadder Sam described how he had been 'talking to Benjamin Sam' about the past and when his wife had noticed his sadness he had been able to give her an account of his experiences for the first time. The therapist wrote:

The pervading feeling of the session was of sadness and Sam went on to describe his shame and fear regarding what he had experienced at the hands of the abusers. He told me that he had been fearful of telling me this at previous sessions and that these events represented his deepest fear that the abusers had left their badness inside him, thus representing the permanence of the damage of his abuse. These images struck me as very powerful with regard to Sam's struggle to fully recognise his own more abusive parts as the ultimate terror was that the abusers who had tortured him sexually were inside him. Thus I became more attuned to his difficulty in discussing the either abused or abusive dilemma and to the need to distinguish his physical abuse of others from his experience of sexual torture.

Towards the end of this session the therapist noted Sam's difficulty in recalling the emotional tone of the previous week as he continued to blame himself and was unable to remember the therapist's disclosure of her positive feelings towards him:

Therapist: I did wonder if you would want to shut down and if it would be hard to take in. I said that I respected you but also that there were parts of you I do not like, as when you were abusive. It seems the urge to block out good things is very strong. And as we have a two-week break now you may need to distance yourself from me.

Sam: You've noticed that?

Therapist: Yes. As with past breaks. Perhaps this time you could think what you've done with what I said about my positive feelings.

Sam: (As they walked towards the door) Can I ask you a question? Why do you never wear skirts? I don't mean to embarrass you ...

In commenting on this, the therapist wrote:

Sam may have felt helpless in the face of my comments on his need to distance himself and so perhaps needed to reassert his power by switching to an exposing position. I wondered if he recognised the intimacy and exposing power of what he had said ... . I was able to revisit this issue at our next meeting (session 20), at which he spoke about his fears regarding the end of therapy, and again in session 21, when he described how an acquaintance had been arrested for molesting a woman he describes as 'jail bait'.

Therapist: Thinking about how you describe her as using sex as a power thing and then about how for you as a child sexual issues were merged with being used and abused ... and being humiliated ... I want to come back to your comment about my not wearing skirts. At first in our relationship you had to be very much in control, not letting me get too close but I feel as we have gone on that has changed, you've let me get closer.

Sam: Oh yeah, there's trust.

Therapist: Well I wondered when you asked me about skirts whether you'd thought I'd felt unable to wear them with you in case I felt vulnerable ...

Sam: It wasn't like that. It wasn't meant in any depth. I just wondered, that was all. You know ... you've got nice bits to go with a skirt. Are you with me? I relate women who wear trousers as a power thing as well. Some like to wear the trousers, to be in charge. But I thought no, she doesn't come over as that type ...

The therapist commented on this:

I was able to talk about the skirt issue and use the diagram to link it with my early need to protect myself from his controlling and dominating behaviour in contrast to the greater trust that had developed. His embarrassed comment about 'nice bits to go with a skirt' felt very different to the arrogant 'charm' of the early sessions. In the rest of the session he acknowledged that there are more 'shades of grey' when it comes to considering sexual power and he was able to speak of the increasing physical intimacy with his wife which had developed during therapy.

The therapy ended with an exchange of 'goodbye letters', read out at the last session. In hers, the therapist reviewed in detail the work done in challenging Sam's sense of being tainted and in resisting his self-attack and finding some ways of being comforted. Various ways of controlling switches into destructive states were rehearsed, namely walking away, counting, reminding himself that it was the present time and not 30 years ago, describing to himself where he was as a way of staying in the present and explaining to others when their behaviour or talk was upsetting him and asking them to stop. The change in the relations between his different 'selves' was noted. In particular in the greater tolerance for Heartless Sam, based on an understanding of how he had been a way of surviving, and noting how Sam, in this state, was far more mellow, with more 'shades of grey', a change clearly experienced in the therapy relationship. To conclude, the therapist's letter spelled out Sam's difficulty of being vulnerable and of allowing good things, reminding him how he had blocked off her affirmations of respect and concluding:

It may have been really hard to hear the positive messages in this letter, as it often was in our sessions, but I hope you will re-read it often and continue to explore ways of soothing your more painful feelings and reducing your attacks on yourself and others.'

Sam's letter, addressed to Dearest Kate, read as follows:

We wonder what to write. I suppose you wondered about us too. Well let us inform you that you have helped us a great deal, i.e. our trigger factors, our mood swings and teaching us about self-harm, which was all news to us. You have also told us that we are not tainted like we all think but that will take time to adjust to, if we can ... We are pleased that you began to understand us. You are the first. Maybe there will be more. It all comes down to trust and you know that doesn't come easy to us ... yet.

The highest compliment we can pay you is to say we trust you, even Heartless Sam. Knowledge without understanding is just knowledge. Understanding without knowledge is just understanding. Put both together, that equals wisdom. Therefore we all bow to your wisdom. Thanks from us all.

The therapist commented on Sam's letter as follows:

His remarks about my 'wisdom' concerned me as possibly idealising me and potentially rubbishing help from others. I discussed this with him gently, being mindful of the need not to minimise his experience of having something with me he had not had before.

In reviewing the whole therapy she reflected as follows:

When I first began working with Sam I felt fearful, intimidated and powerless and doubted whether I had the therapeutic skill to help him. Towards the end, I felt a fondness towards him and a sense of privilege that he had been able to expose his long-concealed vulnerabilities... . As he said goodbye I remained acutely aware of his long-term psychological damage ... but I also felt a sense of hope that he left therapy with new experiences and a desire to explore himself further.

The collaborative and open nature of CAT were central to his ability to trust me and the diagram helped him to look at all his parts rather than remain trapped in one or other 'personality'. The evolving diagram was essential in helping me acknowledge the 'powerfully controlling to exposed and powerless' reciprocal role pattern and so to resist Sam's domination. It also helped me control my tendency to be appeasing in the face of his attacks or protective of him by not naming his abusiveness. And it protected me from feeling self-idealising and grandiose in relation to other staff who did not share my understandings. The diagram also provided me with a link to the comments of my supervisor, reminding me of the range of positions which Sam or I might occupy.

Conclusion

It is to be hoped that the combination of the summarised account, the actual dialogue between the therapist and this eloquent patient and the therapist's sensitive reflections on her work can convey something of the therapeutic process in which the role of theory and of supervision in supporting the therapist's human presence can be seen.

The psychoanalytic concepts of transference and countertransference have been incorporated in CAT theory, located, along with the concept of projective identification, as examples of the more general phenomena of reciprocal role induction through empathic identification and elicited reciprocation. But in CAT these processes are not so much interpreted to the patient as they are incorporated in the explicit shared framework. This allows the creation and maintenance of a carefully defined and circumscribed but genuine human relationship. By working jointly at reformulation and by recognising and avoiding potentially collusive responses, the therapist, in this case, had established the right to offer the direct human affirmation given in session 18 which is likely to have been the critical moment in this therapy.

THE TREATMENT OF BPD: RESEARCH EVIDENCE

Research evidence for the effectiveness of different models of therapy in BPD is scanty, although less negative than is sometimes alleged. Thus Perry et al. (1999) reviewed 15 outcome studies, 6 of which were controlled, of different interventions and concluded that, on average, the treatments were responsible for a sevenfold increase in the rate of recovery. A recent controlled study of the impact of a partial hospitalisation programme combining a range of interventions including psychodynamic individual and group therapy showed significantly better outcome in severe cases of BPD compared to those receiving routine hospital treatment (Bateman and Fonagy, 1999b).

A naturalistic study of 24-session outpatient CAT for BPD has been reported by Ryle and Golynkina (2000); it showed that half the sample no longer met BPD diagnostic criteria six months after therapy ended and that mean scores for the whole sample on a number of questionnaires showed further improvement at 18 months (although one-third were lost to follow-up at that point). Poor response to treatment was associated with greater initial severity. Publications reporting the use of CAT in BPD include the following: Dunn (1994); Marlowe and Ryle (1995); Ryle and Beard (1993); Ryle (1997a, 1997b). Pollock (1997) describes the treatment of an offender with BPD and the same author (Pollock, 1996) described the value of reformulation in allowing women with histories of abuse who had attacked their partners to accept both their victim and abuser roles. Pollock and Belshaw (1998) describe the use of CAT in violent offenders with mixed personality disorders where CAT reformulation offers a means of understanding the offender's relation to his or her victim and provides a guide to treatment and management. Pollock (2001) has edited a book on the role of CAT and the MSSM in survivors of child sexual abuse. Although no formal randomised controlled trial of CAT for adult personality disorder has yet been reported, one is currently under way at Guy's Hospital (despite not receiving funding from health service research sources, even following a successful pilot study). Meantime, the fact that increasing numbers of experienced clinicians are finding that the CAT model is a powerful one suggests that, in a comprehensive outpatient service, CAT would represent a powerful and economical first intervention for a currently poorly provided for group of patients. It can also contribute to clinical management in many settings (see Chapters 9 and 11). It could be lengthened for more disturbed patients and it could be linked with other interventions such as CAT-based CBT aimed at revising identified but persistent problematic procedures. In therapeutic communities or group therapy CAT can offer a concise, accessible way of identifying the ongoing procedures (Kerr, 2000).

THE RELATION OF CAT TO CURRENT MODELS OF BPD

The most influential psychoanalytic models (e.g. Kernberg, 1975) focus on concepts like internal object relations, weakness of the ego and so-called primitive defences and offer a developmental and structural understanding. Few workers nowadays recommend 'pure' psychoanalytic approaches to treatment or, if they do, reserve them for patients who have graduated from lengthy supportive therapy, often recommending intense and prolonged treatment. Kernberg has proposed the model of transference focused psychotherapy (Clarkin et al., 1999), which involves imposing a firm structure and the determining of priorities with a central emphasis on interpreting transference.

Most of the approaches based on cognitive-behavioural theories focus on core beliefs and behavioural strategies which are seen as under- or over-developed. Treatment on this basis is clearly discussed in Davidson (2000) and can be of value for particular aspects of BPD. However, no therapeutic use is made of problems in the therapy relationship and little help is provided to the therapist struggling to establish a relationship with these patients whose key problems are precisely to do with mistrust and interpersonal destructiveness. Where they are effective in containing this destructiveness it is through the imposition of controls (in a way not unlike Kernberg's approach) which, in many cases, echo the authoritarian attitudes of the patient's parents and which therefore risk reinforcing restrictive forces within the self. This approach is exemplified, despite its humanitarian orientation, by Linehan's dialectical behaviour therapy (Linehan et al., 1991, 1993; Koerner and Linehan, 2000) which involves an intense behavioural programme combining individual and group interventions. Small-scale controlled studies show that, in those accepted for and accepting the treatment, it reduces self-harming behaviours but has relatively little impact on the wider personality problems. Beck and Freeman (1990) extended basic cognitive therapy techniques to treat personality-disordered patients by describing both manifest problems and inferred underlying schemas. These latter are articulated in the form of basic themes and beliefs concerning the self and others. The only structural understanding offered is the description of dichotomous thinking.

Most recent commentators agree that any approach to the treatment of BPD must involve a flexible combination of therapeutic methods, and some convergences between hitherto opposed schools of thought are apparent. Stone (2000) proposes a pragmatic approach summarised as ABCD = E, indicating roles for Analytically oriented, Behavioural, Cognitive and pharmacological (Drug) interventions in an Eclectic programme. He accepts that at the present time little firm research evidence exists on which to base decisions in this field.

Livesley (2000) is concerned to develop an integrated rather than an eclectic approach and in his review gives a very accurate account of CAT. He sees BPD as a disorder of the self associated with, and mutually reinforcing of, affective instability and cognitive organisation and is opposed to using 'an array of interventions combined in a piecemeal fashion'; the aim must be 'to promote integration and the development of a more cohesive self-system'. Livesley sees the similarity of the effects of different interventions as pointing to the need to maximise the non-specific or generic elements of treatments; he summarises these as the development of a therapeutic bond and a collaborative relationship linked by the technical aspects of the treatment contract. These views are entirely convergent with CAT, in which the technical procedures serve precisely to foster an emotionally important relationship contained within a collaboratively achieved framework of understanding.

The difference between CAT and Livesley's understandings and those of both psychoanalytic and cognitive-behavioural workers stems from the different theoretical underpinnings. CAT emphasises in particular a full recognition of the dialogic nature of human personality. Psychoanalytic object relations theory offers an important recognition of the fact that relationships with others are internalised to form personality structures, but the preoccupation, in much of the literature, with innate forces, fantasies and defence and its formation of the therapy relationship as an unequal interpretive one constrain or distort the uses made of this understanding. In CAT's (Vygotskian and Bakhtinian) object relations theory the 'permeable' self is seen to have been formed in, and to be maintained through, interactions with others; the internalised relationship dialogue from the past is constantly expressed in, and may be maintained or modified by, current relationships. Much of the stability of BPD reflects the inadvertent collusion with negative procedures elicited by borderline patients from others, including clinicians. The concepts of the zone of proximal personality development (ZPPD) and the idea of the scaffolding role of the therapist are further distinguishing features of CAT. Cognitive models aim to generate a benign teacher–pupil relationship but fail, in our view, to take adequate account of, or to use with adequate complexity, the potential power of the therapy relationship. In CAT, the understanding of sign mediation and internalisation derived from Vygotsky's ideas emphasises how growth and change occur within the dyad and reflect the wider social context.

Persuasive or authoritarian (Magistral) behavioural or psychoanalytic therapists fail to provide a mutual, collaborative relationship within which new meanings of the self and other can be created and the active participation of the patient in psychological change can be promoted. CAT aims to incoporate the strengths of the two traditions in which as much attention is paid to the therapy relationship as is the case in psychoanalytic interventions and in which the cognitive-behavioural practice of accurately describing assumptions and sequences is extended to describe high level self processes. The understanding and descriptive analysis of the main features of BPD (namely the instability of mood, behaviour, sense of self and relationships with others) which the MSSM provides is absent from cognitive and behavioural models. These various distinguishing aspects of CAT theory determine a range of practical activities, notably in the joint creation and use of reformulatory tools, and these techniques in turn serve, we believe, to support therapists in the provision of a focused, powerful and human experience which can allow significant change in a limited time.

FURTIIER READING

Ryle (1997a) presents a full account of the CAT approach to the treatment of borderline personality disorder. Golynkina and Ryle (1999) provide some empirical support for the multiple self states model. Pollock et al. (2001), in describing the Personality Structure Questionnaire, also address the relationship between multiplicity and dissociation. Davidson (2000) summarises the principles and methods of cognitive therapy for personality disorders. Magnavita (1997) offers an account of a short-term dynamic approach which incorporates some cognitive methods and Giovacchini (1993) gives an overview of more conventional psychoanalytic ideas. Livesley (2001), in a review volume, draws on recent developments to propose principles underlying any practical approach to treating personality-disordered patients which are close to CAT practice.

Chapter 11

THE 'DIFFICULT' PATIENT AND CONTEXTUAL REFORMULATION

SUMMARY

The 'difficult' patient is not a diagnostic entity but may be recognised in a variety of patient groups and settings. Although 'difficulty' is usually attributed to the patient, it is invariably a systemic phenomenon and may be accounted for from a CAT perspective in terms of the elicitation of either reciprocating or identifying countertransference role enactments from those around them. Characteristically, these reactions split and demoralise staff teams and may also involve other agencies such as social workers, hospital managers or the police. CAT-based approaches to such patients include the use of the tool of extended, contextual reformulation, mapping out these various, elicited reciprocal role enactments. These are constructed on the basis of discussion with those involved in addition, where possible, to work with an individual patient. This approach can be effective in understanding apparently incomprehensible behaviours as well as containing and illuminating some of the powerful feelings that may be elicited. Use of a contextual reformulation may enable staff to respond therapeutically rather than simply react to such patients. It may also be useful in consultative work around, for example, severe personality disorders and exemplifies a trend towards 'using' CAT in contrast to simply 'doing' it as an individual therapy.

The 'difficult' patient is not a diagnostic entity but rather a label which tends to be applied to patients when particular sorts of interpersonal or professional difficulties are created around them. These may also lead to patients being described as 'hard to help', 'heartsink', 'manipulative' 'attention seeking' 'acting out' and so forth. A point of particular importance in considering such patients is that the difficulty rarely resides in the individual patient, although others might like to locate it there, but rather in a system. It is therefore always germane to enquire whose difficulty it really is. Patients frequently do not regard themselves as having a problem, although this may actually constitute part of the 'difficulty'. This has already been alluded to in the context of the 'frequent attender' patient in general practice who often has underlying psychological distress or dysfunction. Such patients are encountered in various settings and contexts and with various sorts of problems, although some are more likely to acquire such a label than others. The category would include most notably patients with severe personality disorder, eating disorders, those with somatising disorders, some psychotic disorders but also some with neurotic disorders such as anxiety and depression. Similar problems may also arise as a complication in almost any physical illness, especially if chronic.

Tolstoy observed that all unhappy families were different in their own ways. It is also the case that each difficult patient, or rather the difficulty surrounding him or her, is difficult in its own way. Nonetheless, one may attempt to list the sort of ways in which such difficulty manifests. Broadly speaking there are two categories according to whether reciprocating or identifying countertransference responses are elicited from those around them:

1. One group consists of patients who are 'non-compliant' and may sabotage treatment, those who aggressively demand more but may 'rubbish' any attempts to help, or patients who deny any psychological distress or difficulty but who still insist on 'help' on their own terms. These patients typically elicit frustrated, irritated, rejecting and sometimes cynical reactions from some staff who may also criticise other staff who are more sympathetic. These 'reactions' can all be described in terms of reciprocal role enactments.
2. The other group includes the 'helpless', 'needy' patient who elicits often heroic but inappropriate reactions in staff who may become over-involved and helpful beyond appropriate professional boundaries, and who may criticise other staff for not appreciating the patient's plight. Over-involved reactions can perpetuate the 'helplessness' or 'neediness' of a patient, for example by doing shopping for them or negotiating with other professionals such as solicitors. To a point these may be reasonable things to do and may acknowledge a patient's, perhaps very difficult, real life circumstances and sense of powerlessness (see Hagan and Smail, 1997). When this becomes a dominant mode of interacting with a patient, however, it constitutes a largely unhelpful, collusive role enactment.

These elicited reciprocations, or countertransferential role responsiveness (Sandler, 1976), around the 'difficult' or 'special' patient, in particular the way in which counterproductive and divisive reactions are elicited or 'provoked' in staff teams, have been described in the past from a predominantly psychoanalytic perspective. Main's classic paper (1957) 'The Ailment' was an early example and they have been discussed more recently by Pines (1978), Norton (1996), Hinshelwood (1999) and reviewed also in Hughes and Kerr (2000). These consequences include the splitting of teams into those reacting in one of these two countertransferential ways and subsequently, very often, to staff exhaustion and 'burn out'.

As already discussed, the CAT approach of explicit reformulation of the reciprocal role procedures (RRPs) of an individual patient can be useful in working jointly with such patients and their treating teams. In addition, the basic tool of the sequential diagrammatic reformulation (SDR) may be extended into a formal 'contextual' reformulation which describes and maps in addition the responses of treating staff and possibly also the responses, in turn, of other agencies in terms of reciprocal role enactments. These others may include hospital managers, casualty staff, ancillary staff such as receptionists in GP or hospitals, police, social workers or even the general public (Dunn and Parry, 1997; Kerr, 1999). Contextual reformulation may also include the mapping out of interactions with family members who may play a critical role in such difficulty. Clearly such an approach comes close to describing the sorts of interactions addressed, although not formally mapped, in family and systemic therapies. It also has some parallels with the approach advocated by Norton (1996), who describes such clinical transactions as 'complicated', as opposed to 'straightforward', and notes the helpful effects of mapping the personal and public responses of both patient and professional in a 'transaction window'.

One of the important effects of a contextual approach is to locate the difficulty in a dynamic system explicitly describing various role enactments in a way which permits the owning of 'difficult' counter transference *'reactions'* and turning them into collaboratively worked on and jointly understood *'responses'*. Examples of this approach and the principles of constructing such contextual SDRs will be given below. In considering the difficult patient or client, however, it is useful to consider first the background causes of such difficulty and the general principles involved in working with this undoubtedly fraught and 'hard to help' group of patients.

CAUSES OF DIFFICULT BEHAVIOUR

Physical causes

It is important to remember that changed or difficult behaviour, particularly if of recent onset, may be the result of physical factors. These could include serious infections, pain, intracerebral pathology (such as a mild stroke) as well as the effects of medication (see review in Kerr and Taylor, 1997).

Psychiatric causes

Major psychiatric disorder, whether long-standing or of recent onset, may contribute to the appearance of difficulty (e.g. 'sabotaging' treatment), although this may also be due to an acute illness. However, patients suffering from severe or acute psychiatric disorders may also create 'difficulty' for the psychological reasons discussed above, and unpicking these from the effects of a major disorder can be a major and challenging part of work in this area (see Chapter 9). Psychological problems may include such general issues as anxiety or hopelessness, anger, feelings of hurt, being misunderstood or not listened to in the context of illness, whether physical or mental, through to existential issues of meaning and purpose in life.

Staff team dynamics

Finally, it is also important to consider 'iatrogenic' causes of difficulty, including individual staff and/or institutional psychopathology. The latter may include inadequate communication between various members of staff, differences of opinion between staff regarding diagnosis or treatment, or anxiety generated by excessively authoritarian team and management structures as described classically by Menzies-Lyth (1959/1988). These problems may determine the extent to which staff are drawn into, or elicit, antagonistic or apparently sabotaging behaviour on the part of a patient (see Norton, 1996; Hinshelwood, 1999; Kerr, 1999).

GENERAL APPROACHES TO THE 'DIFFICULT' PATIENT

In general, approaches to the 'difficult' patient (bearing in mind the caveats above regarding the systemic aspects of such difficulty) would include the following: (1) use of a firm but empathic, non-confrontational style; (2) jointly agreed definition of common treatment goals and of limits and boundaries (where, for example, the responsibility of a therapist or nurse begins and ends); (3) facilitating the ventilation and exploration of underlying concerns and issues by the primary treating team; (4) drawing patients' attention firmly but gently to the effects of their behaviour on staff and how it affects attempts at treatment or investigation; (5) if necessary, offering specialist psychotherapy individually with the patient in a standard CAT approach; or (6) undertaking a contextual reformulation with the team.

CONTEXTUAL REFORMULATION

Contextual reformulation is an approach which has evolved out of attempts to address more complex processes involved in the perpetuation and exacerbation

of an individual's psychopathology. In part this represents an obvious extension of the pioneering work of therapists such as Walsh, who used CAT-based
approaches to address and work with organisational 'pathology' (Walsh, 1996).
It also has parallels with the theory and practice of family and systemic therapists and, to a lesser extent, with group analysts. The common aim of these
approaches would be to understand and acknowledge the self-reinforcing role
enactments of other individuals and agencies involved around a given patient.
In systemic approaches these would not normally be formally mapped out nor
an explicit account given in psychodynamic terms of various behaviours. In
CAT these would be implicit in an individual SDR, since every patient of course
brings a repertoire of role enactments, each seeking the response of others, both
from their past and in the present. It can be helpful to map out these extended
role reciprocations explicitly, as far as possible in a collaborative manner. One of
the striking effects of so doing is, as noted by Walsh (1996), the location of
various individual reactions in a non-judgemental system of causality. It also
permits the owning of 'negative' emotions and reactions, parallel to those
discussed by Winnicott (1947) under the rubric of 'hate in the countertransference', and permits open discussion of them by a treating team or other involved
agencies. It can stimulate imaginative discussion *of what it is like to be that patient*,
even if the patient remains reluctant to open up or engage. This can in itself be
remarkably illuminating and thought-provoking for staff. Contextual reformulation can also help staff to avoid getting stuck in 'collusive', negative, vicious
circles ('traps') in reaction to 'difficult' behaviour by a patient in the way that a
good SDR can help an individual patient. It can thus have an educative function
for staff and create a shared understanding so, in turn, creating or strengthen-
ing a therapeutic working alliance and communicating that the patient has been
listened to and understood. As with individual SDRs, the effects of these on
staff teams as well as on patients can be both moving and powerfully therapeutic. A good reformulation is a tool which is of use to the whole team.

It is of historic interest that, although Main (1957) was able to identify and
describe the difficulties around the 'special' or 'difficult' patient, he was unable to
propose any systematic course of action from his contemporary theoretical perspective (see discussion in Kerr, 1999). Experience with these techniques suggests that
identifying and mapping out not only the patient's reciprocal role enactments but
also those of others around, can be just such an effective approach. Feeling pressurised or confused is bad for staff morale. Reformulation may be helpful to staff
simply in avoiding 'burn-out' and bad feelings even if it does not always prove
possible to engage and work with a patient who may be too stuck or ill to do so.

CONSTRUCTING A CONTEXTUAL REFORMULATION

One may start with an individual SDR either created with the patient or, sometimes, by asking a team to imagine what the patient's 'core subjective self'

might be like. This can, in itself, be a fascinating and helpful exercise. In our experience the subjective states and role enactments may be described very broadly in terms of two split halves (rather like narcissistic 'broken eggs') (see Figure 11.1). Thus the patient split would typically divide *hurt, misunderstood, needy* and *anxious* roles from *angry, resentful* and possibly *'non-compliant'* and *'sabotaging of treatment'* roles. These should all be familiar polarisations to the CAT therapist. Likewise the staff team split very often runs between *caring, sympathetic, 'wanting to do a good job'* role enactments on the one hand and *feeling irritated, frustrated, angry* and *being rejecting* and *being cynical of other staff* on the other. The identification and acknowledgement of these two splits, if possible, is already a considerable achievement.

In the naturalistic studies conducted so far (Dunn and Parry, 1997; Kerr, 1999, 2001), the explicit detailing of a patient's circumstances and story in relation to the staff team (who are under constant pressure to be part of the 'difficulty') has been powerful, engaging and effective for those concerned. More complex diagrams may be required to map out role enactments and reactions around very disturbed patients such as those with severe personality, psychotic or eating disorders.

These may involve self state switches on the part of the patient and also the involvement of many other agencies apart from the immediate treating team, possibly including family members. An example of a more extended or complex contextual reformulation for a patient with personality disorder being treated by a community mental health team is described in Kerr (1999). This approach may constitute the sole intervention by a consulting therapist or team, for example, within a district service (see Dunn and Parry, 1997). With some 'difficult' patients it is possible to use the patient's SDR in discussion with those involved and to note enactments in the team of roles mapped on the patient's SDR. This can be a very illuminating and containing exercise and has been used to good effect, for example in very disturbed patients with eating disorders (Claire Tanner, personal communication). It should be noted that there may be as many ways of describing these role enactments through contextual reformulation as there are 'difficult patients' and therapists doing them. The two examples below will show relatively straightforward staff team splits and enactments.

EXAMPLES OF SIMPLE CONTEXTUAL REFORMULATIONS

Case example: Brenda (Therapist IK)

A 'difficult' patient on a palliative care unit.

This reformulation was constructed on the basis of an initial diagram of a revised 'subjective self' done with a patient on a palliative care unit, followed by discussion in a team meeting of how they were reacting to what they mostly perceived as a 'difficult' patient. Figure 11.1 shows a simple, basic split between collective 'sympathetic' and 'difficult' aspects of both the patient's subjective states and role enactments and those of the team.

Brenda was a middle-aged woman with an advanced, inoperable tumour who had been recently referred to the unit. She confided to the therapist, who of course had the luxury of time to sit down with her, that she was angry about how this referral had happened without any consultation with her, but said that she was afraid to stir things up by saying so. She did not know the new team and was now reluctant to take her medication. She was also angry that she was no longer allowed to smoke on the ward and had to be accompanied some-where outside, if staff were available to do so. She felt bad about being a burden to others and felt frequently hopeless and suicidal. She tended to feel she 'ought' to keep these feelings to herself but sometimes they 'burst out' at her husband, which made her feel even worse. A few staff were sympathetic to her, but on the whole the team were fed up and irritated with her and could not understand why she was behaving the way she was when they were trying to help. The result of the discussion and the construction with the staff team of the contextual reformulation was firstly of astonishment and genuine upset at seeing what the patient felt. There was also a general feeling of relief that they could understand better what was going on and that it was not directly their fault for doing a bad job. This was clearly a concern for many of the nurses. It also led to the decision that the consultant should take some time to explain why she had been transferred and the nurses decided to fix a time each day to explore and encourage ventilation of how she was feeling.

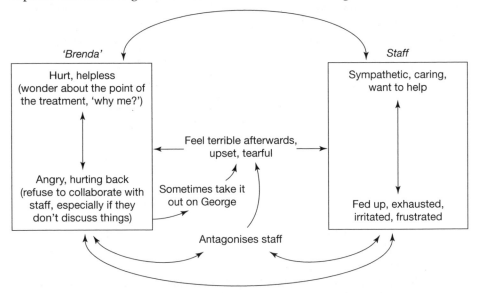

Figure 11.1 Simple contextual reformulation for Brenda developed from the patient's own SDR (left). Team reactions are described in terms of a basic split

Arguably, some of this 'should' have been routine practice on such a unit, but militating against this is the extreme pressure of time on staff, in addition to a residual culture of *doing things to or for* patients rather than *being with* them. In addition, junior staff were neither trained, encouraged nor supported to explore psychological issues with patients. Finally, neither staff nor patient were aware of these processes and they could not have been accessed or understood without some structured exploration. These issues can be explored to some extent in routine staff support meetings, but all too often these discussions are piecemeal and complicated by internal, staff team enactments. In particular, without the top-down, global understanding offered by a diagrammatic reformulation, staff are often left not knowing how things interconnect or how best to proceed. In this particular instance the intervention was identified in a case review as being of considerable usefulness to both patient and team. In addition, Brenda's husband reported that things had improved considerably and that, in particular, she seemed able to talk more openly about 'things' and that this had also helped the family overall.

Case example: Paula (Therapist IK)

A 'difficult' patient on a forensic secure unit; this case also illustrates some general points about the treatment of anxiety-related disorders.

This reformulation was constructed as a consequence of a request from a forensic team on a secure unit for help in managing a 'difficult' female patient. Paula was a young woman of about 30 with a diagnosis of personality disorder and mixed anxiety and depressive disorder. She had been causing considerable chaos and anxiety in hospital where she had been for several months following transfer from prison. The 'difficult' behaviour had consisted in her becoming acutely anxious, panicky and at times 'aggressive', seeking help by rushing around screaming and attacking staff and occasionally resorting to self-harming behaviour such as banging her head on walls. This behaviour caused considerable concern as well as frustration and irritation among staff. This had resulted in several stays on the acute locked ward where she usually calmed down after a few days before being returned to a general ward where, however, the pattern of behaviour would be repeated. Paula's most recent admission to prison had been due to similar behaviour when she assaulted a passer-by on the street because of feeling 'panicky', an act which had broken the conditions of her probation. Her previous admission, which had resulted in her spending a year in prison, had occurred after she had attacked her husband with a knife although this had not resulted in serious injury. It was difficult to determine exactly why she had done this but it appeared in her account to have been because, for once, he had been unable to contain her panicky feelings himself and had worsened her feelings to such an uncontrollable state that she had 'gone for him'. This she bitterly regretted and she was still clearly very fond of him. The issue of the future of her marriage and her anxieties about whether she might ever harm him again were major sources of concern to her at the time of assessment.

By the time of the CAT-based assessment, her mood and behaviour had improved somewhat, although the team were still very worried about further relapses and about the question of long-term management. The staff request was for a consultation rather than for individual therapy. Paula did agree, however, to some exploratory sessions with the therapist with a view to reformulating both her own problems and the systemic 'difficulty', if possible in conjunction with the team. She was now having regular sessions with the team psychologist on the management of her panicky and anxious feelings, as well as regular art therapy sessions where she was able to express some of her more troubled emotions. These, and the more containing atmosphere of the secure unit, all contributed to calming her and making her feel, as she put it, 'safer'. Nonetheless, throughout the initial few sessions she kept asking whether things would eventually be 'OK' and whether she would manage again at home and when that would be. It was very hard to conduct these sessions due to these constant interruptions and for a while it appeared that she might not be able to cooperate with the work at all because of her levels of anxiety. Despite this, and partly through the obviously calming and containing process of sitting down to draw a diagrammatic reformulation, it began to be possible to develop a picture of her background and of the events which had led up to her being on a forensic unit.

Her background included an upbringing in a harsh, working class environment where she was afraid of a violent father (who in addition may have abused her) and a mother whom she described as cold and distant. She herself always felt she 'ought' to cope with things on her own despite nearly always feeling anxious and inadequate about both family life and school. Nonetheless she did complete school and worked for many years as a secretary. She always found relationships with men difficult and her husband had been her first serious boyfriend. Significantly, it appeared, her feelings of anxiety had worsened after they had finally become married several years previously at which time, she said, she had experienced acutely anxious feelings about whether she was 'up to' marriage and possibly having children. However, she had also helped him considerably given that he was not sophisticated (she looked after all the bills and correspondence), and he in turn was a great support when she felt bad and panicky. Nonetheless there appeared to be a part of her (a dialogic 'voice') which 'told' her she ought to cope and keep really difficult feelings to herself. Paula had had an experience of analytically based psychotherapy previously when she had, as she put it, 'gone through all that childhood stuff' and which had been of some help. However, she felt it had not resulted in her difficult feelings or insecurities going away. The picture that finally emerged is depicted diagrammatically in Figure 11.2 and was described in a reformulation letter (not shown) which rehearsed her story, problems and several key target problem procedures (TPPs).

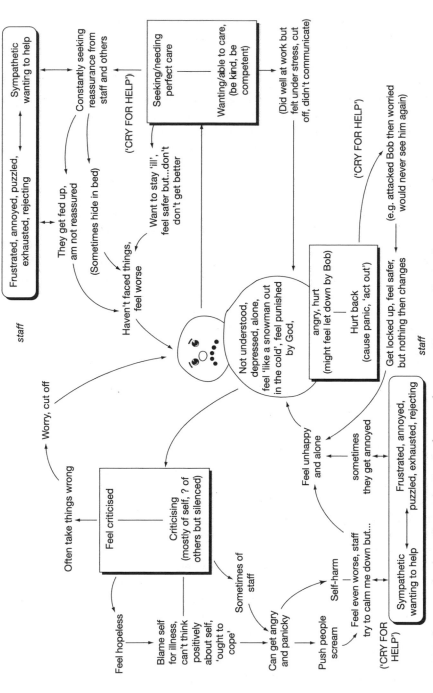

Figure 11.2 Contextual reformulation for Paula showing her own SDR centrally. Staff reactions to her role enactments are mapped collectively at the top and bottom

The contextual reformulation (Figure 11.2) initially centred around Paula's very moving perception of herself as a 'frozen snowman' all alone outside and looking in at everyone else. The initial diagram also depicted her key reciprocal role procedures (RRPs). She herself was able to describe staff reactions to her behaviours and these were confirmed and amplified by discussion with the staff team. These reactions centred around two essentially similar, split sets of role enactments which were mapped on at the top and bottom of the diagram. This appeared to be both illuminating and a relief to members of the staff team who were able to consider their reactions to her and plan future management using these understandings. Interestingly, she was by now having parallel discussions with both her pychologist and art therapist about her 'ought' voice and where it came from and what to do with it. She was also able to consider the idea that she might try to communicate her difficult feelings to others (for example staff) instead of acting on them, and see what happened. The index incident of her attack on husband was explored in the light of the reciprocal role enactments described on the diagram. It appeared that the critical event had been when he suddenly 'jumped', in her perception, from being a helpful, secure person into something like an abuser (with its probable historic antecedents). At this point she dissociated and 'state-shifted' into a *vengeful/attacking* role from a *fearful/abused* role which resulted in her 'going for him'. This, of course, she immediately regretted but had not been able to control. The enactment of similar RRPs has previously been well documented by CAT therapists working with victims of abuse (Clarke and Llewelyn, 1994; Pollock, 1996).

This case shows how attempts to work with symptoms of panic and anxiety may remain relatively ineffective unless the reciprocal role procedures underlying their generation and enactment are addressed and worked with. Wells (1999), working within another conceptual framework, has discussed the need to work with the 'meta-cognitions' underlying such symptoms. Our reservations about the limitations of this approach are discussed in Chapter 9. Paula reported that working on her TPPs had also been of considerable help to her in recognising, understanding and revising her maladaptive procedures. Overall, it appeared that the staff team had been helped by discussion of the descriptions of role enactments in the contextual reformulation. However, they also wanted explicit 'aims' for themselves in terms of what to do if certain behaviours did occur. The advice given was that they should try to recognise where they were on the diagram and what they were enacting, so as to work at not provoking and colluding with Paula's enactments of her maladaptive behaviours. They were also advised to help the patient likewise to recognise where she was on the diagram.

This case represents a further example of *using* CAT as a consultation tool to a team carrying responsibilty for continuing care and treatment of the patient. The work of the therapist in this consultation role was to provide a reformulation to be discussed and handed back to a hard-pressed team and to the patient for further use.

USES AND APPLICATIONS OF CONTEXTUAL APPROACHES TO THE 'DIFFICULT' PATIENT

Work of this sort with the 'difficult' patient, comprising both support, containment and education, may be an application of CAT of some usefulness. For example, one district psychology service in the UK (Dunn and Parry, 1997, and Mary Dunn, personal communication) has developed a consultative service which works with patients suffering from personality disorders. The team routinely uses CAT for assessing and describing relationship processes. They see themselves as employed to identify, name and then step out of the process, handing back treatment to the original team. Usual approaches to risk management can be counter-productive with this client group and they have found that a strong multidisciplinary team with a formulated rationale for its actions can paradoxically reduce risk by taking risk. An example of this is the situation where a client's suicide attempts in hospital seem to escalate as the staff increase their levels of observation and where the client is safer for being discharged. The use of this model has made demands on staff who must ask themselves searching questions about their own role in the relationship. It is seen as turning a traditional medical model on its head to suggest that changes we make in ourselves as health professionals may be important for the client or patient. It is recognised that many of these patients will have had extreme experiences of abuse or deprivation in their early years and may be able to induce similar or reciprocal enactments from everybody they meet. This team, using these contextual approaches, has placed a high priority on changing this experience for these patients within the mental health service.

Experience is still accruing in the use of such techniques of brief consultative interventions, but naturalistic studies completed so far suggest they may be effective tools for use in a range of settings and problems.

FURTHER READING

Main's (1957) classic paper 'The Ailment' describing the difficulties encountered in working with the 'special' patient is still well worth reading, as is Menzies-Lyth's (1959) classic work on anxiety in institutions. A thoughtful account of systemic difficulties in mental health services from an attachment theory perspective is given by Adshead (1998). The systemic application of CAT to organisational pathology was first described by Walsh (1996) and subsequent clinical applications by Dunn and Parry (1997) and Kerr (1999).

AFTERWORD

We set out in this book to offer a new introduction to the principles and practice of the evolving CAT model of psychotherapy. We hope that we have whetted the appetite of those who may wish to take their interest further and consider some form of training and that it will be useful as a guide to those currently undertaking a training. We also hope that it may usefully inform the professional practice and thinking of a wider readership. In this last chapter we recapitulate and consider its distinctive features, the reasons for its rapidly increasing popularity with both clinicians and patients, its research activities and emerging evidence base, and its implicit values.

DISTINCTIVE FEATURES OF CAT

The distinctive features of CAT emerged because it was constructed in a way which sought to include the common factors identified as helpful by Frank (1961) and it set out to integrate ideas and methods from other schools, notably psychoanalysis and cognitive psychology. As a result, many specific aspects of its practice are also to be found in the work of other therapists. What distinguishes CAT are its translations and transformations of these ideas and methods, its addition of some new practical and theoretical features, notably the introduction of Vygotskian understandings, and its seeking to develop a fully integrated model. The coherent and robust psychotherapy theory for which we aim should give an account of people and psychopathology which is compatible with research findings from studies of child development and of effective psychotherapies and from the broader fields of psychology, sociology and anthropology. It should also be fully reflected in practice and be set within an explicit philosophical frame. As such it differs radically from eclectic approaches which address issues of practice and technique but do not seek a common language or theory.

CAT, of course, is not a finalised theory; new experiences, new research findings and continuing arguments will continue to elaborate and refine its ideas and methods. In its present state it can provide a critical perspective from which to view the dominant current schools. As we have argued, we believe that both psychoanalytic and cognitive understandings are restricted by their individualistic assumptions and by their lack of an adequate understanding of the social formation of the human mind or of the social formation of their own theories. This is not to deny that, to a variable extent, the practice associated with them may be dialogic and their individual practitioners may be informed by awareness of social forces and sensitive to broader social considerations, but in this they are not adequately supported by their theories.

The practical techniques employed in CAT, such as the use of written or diagrammatic reformulation, the emphasis on collaboration, the description, recognition and revision of negative procedures and the avoidance of collusive reinforcement, are skills which can be learned through supervised practice. But a full integration of theory with practice demands of therapists a willingness to adopt a genuinely collaborative position, and a capacity to understand each patient by taking account of their temperamental characteristics and of historical, sequential, structural and reciprocal features on the basis of which they may be able to provide a reparative relationship.

THE CONTINUING EXPANSION OF CAT

It would appear that the increasing popularity of CAT has much to do with the appeal of its distinctive features. It has been remarkable to witness this growth. Twenty years ago CAT was essentially a one man band, whereas today in the UK there are 9 trainings in place with 77 trained supervisors, 221 qualified practitioners and 197 trainees. CAT is also established in Finland and Greece and, with the development of distance learning and supervision, trainings are due to start up in a number of other countries. This rapid expansion required the creation of an organisation to replace the very informal methods of the early years. Thanks to a great deal of work by, initially, a few people, the Association for Cognitive Analytic Therapy (ACAT) is now a solid and friendly organisation, maintaining an efficient national structure responsible for maintaining standards of practice and defining an agreed curriculum taught in various ways in the different trainings now established in the UK and abroad. Further information about developments, meetings and the many special interest groups can be found on the website (acat.org.uk).

This rapid expansion occurred, we believe, because CAT, as a way of doing individual therapy, had an immediate appeal to many therapists, clinical psychologists, social workers, community mental health nurses, counsellors and psychiatrists (see Rees, 2000) who were frustrated by the impractical length and doubtful effectiveness of many current treatments and by the lack of human sensitivity offered by many existing therapy models. For those working in underfunded services, confronted by an inexhaustible supply of patients with psychological problems at all levels of severity, the experience of the positive effects of focused time-limited CAT, even in the treatment of chronic and severe conditions, was encouraging. Learning to make rapid sense of their patients' long-term difficulties and the discovery that even severely damaged people can make use of the understandings worked out together in the reformulation process gives a new confidence to therapists. The structure of the model also provides orientation and containment to therapists under supervision who can quickly become clinically effective.

Inevitably, established psychoanalytic and cognitive-behavioural institutions have paid little attention to the ideas of CAT, but it has clearly become a living presence for the current generation of trainees and recent graduates in psychology and psychiatry. Compared to the early days those now seeking training in CAT have increasing levels of prior experience. The expansion of interest in CAT as a model of individual therapy has been accompanied by the increasing use of the ideas in other fields; in particular, the involvement of CAT-trained therapists and practitioners in staff supervision, care planning and in residential and day care settings has provided further evidence of the accessibility and relevance of CAT understandings. As a result, increasing numbers of staff from various disciplines are *using* CAT in their work rather than simply *doing* CAT and are finding that it extends their sense of professional competence and morale. These extending applications of CAT are being accompanied by a continuing process of theoretical development.

THE EVIDENCE BASE AND RESEARCH

CAT arose out of the attempt to evaluate the validity and effectiveness of existing psychotherapy models and has aimed to maintain this as a fundamental component of its own self-evaluation. From its beginning it has reported case studies and naturalistic outcome series in the context of its developing theoretical base and has always stressed the importance of audit and research. It should be noted that this work was initially undertaken by a small number of enthusiastic individuals who had major clinical commitments and who lacked financial or academic support with which to undertake major research trials. These, in the early stages of development of any model, would be, in any case, inappropriate. Owing to its rapid expansion in popularity CAT is now being widely used to treat many conditions very successfully without, as noted recently, having gone through the phase of undergoing strictly controlled randomised trials (Margison, 2000). This is due partly to the popularity of the model and its perceived clinical effectiveness but there are other good reasons, scientific, ethical and political, for this state of affairs. These are further discussed in Appendix 1. Nonetheless, CAT is committed to accumulating comprehensive and robust evidence of the effectiveness of its practice. Many research projects concerning both process and outcome are ongoing and research grant applications have been and are being submitted. (Further details of these for those interested can be obtained though the ACAT website or through the ACAT office and the list of special interest groups.) It should be noted that one of the very major difficulties facing all practitioners in psychotherapy research is the lack of support from government and scientific funding bodies for such work in a field dominated, inappropriately, by biomedical paradigms. Nonetheless ACAT and its research committee continues to stress the importance of such activity, and teaching on both quantitative and qualitative aspects of research is about to be introduced formally into CAT training courses. We would see this position of critical self-reflection and evaluation as being central to the CAT model in terms of both theory building and clinical practice.

THE IMPLICIT VALUES OF CAT

What is most distinctive about CAT, in our view, is something ultimately deeper than details of practice. It is expressed in three distinct but in fact closely related features, namely (1) in its having been developed with the aim of offering a treatment which it could be realistic to provide within the National Health Service; (2) in the collaborative, non-hierarchical nature of the therapeutic relationship; (3) in the inclusion, in descriptions of the psychological processes which therapy aims to change, of the reciprocal relations between the individual and others. These features embody a set of values and assumptions which are little celebrated in the individualistic, consumer-oriented societies of the contemporary Western world but which were expressed famously in John Donne's quotation 'no man is an island, entire of itself; every man is a piece of the Continent, a part of the main; if a clod is washed away by the sea, Europe is the less … any man's death diminishes me, because I am involved in Mankind… .'

In the incorporation of Vygotsky's developmental understandings and of Bakhtin's concepts of the permeable, dialogic self, CAT theory has found a basis both for its mode of working and for its social commitment. In seeing the individual as essentially coming into being through the connection and interaction with others, we underline the responsibility which society (i.e. all of us) bears to offer conditions in which humans can grow and flourish. To blame innate human qualities for the brutality of so many human societies and the tragedies of so many human lives, whether on sociobiological or psychoanalytic grounds, is an evasion of responsibility. To look for the sources of culture in individual psychology while ignoring how individual psychology is socially formed (a tendency we have labelled as cognitive, or more subtly as intersubjective, monadism) is, we suggest, itself an expression of a culture which ignores our collective needs and natures. Our wish to challenge this attitude extends beyond the small world of psychotherapy, for psychotherapists are, to some extent, granted the status of privileged, expert witnesses and the models of man incorporated in our theories have an influence beyond the consulting room. To understand how individual values and assumptions have been socially formed does not imply a deterministic view; it is the only basis on which choice can be extended and oppression in individuals and in society can be challenged.

GLOSSARY

Contextual reformulation   A diagrammatic portrayal of the linked processes and role enactments identified in patients, staff relationships and institutions.

Core   (a) Refers to boxed-in list of reciprocal roles from which procedural loops are drawn in diagrams. (b) Describes or postulates unaccessed or deep feelings, as in 'core pain'. (To avoid confusion best to replace this use of 'core' with 'deep', 'unaccessed' or 'unmanageable'.)

Countertransference   The feelings or actions induced in therapists by their patients; may reflect a general or easily mobilised personal RRP of the therapist but more often is elicited by the patient's behaviour and directly or indirectly conveyed transference. May represent either an identifying response, echoing the affect of one or other of the patient's roles, or a reciprocation to one of the patient's RRPs.

Descriptive reformulation   The transformation of the patient's account into a narrative and/or a diagram which reorders and links the material into a more explanatory and useful form. Carried out with the fullest possible participation from the patient. Creates a shared written and diagrammatic account of the issues to be addressed in therapy.

Dialogic self   A model of the self as based on dialogue/reciprocal roles with external and internalised others.

Dialogic sequence analysis   The analysis of interactions by describing the sequence of roles played and their reciprocals.

Dialogism   An understanding of self formation and processes as essentially derived and expressed in relation to others and to culture. Emphasised by Bakhtin. Contrasted with the Cartesian assumptions of cognitive psychology which places the centre of experience and action 'in the head' of the individual.

Diary keeping   Homework assignments may include diary keeping in relation to particular procedures or may involve noting significant events and then locating them onto the mapped procedures.

Dilemma   A problem procedure: the evident restriction of possible acts / roles etc. to polar opposites, described as *'either … or'*, or as *'if … then'*.

Goodbye letters   Exchanged at the end of therapy as a means of summing up and evaluating what has been achieved and what remains to be worked on.

Internalisation   The process whereby what is learned through interpersonal experience becomes an aspect of the self, a part of the internal dialogue. Distinguished from representation in that it involves the creation and use of mediating signs and transforms the psychological structures which mediate it.

Masochism   See *Motivation*. In CAT it would be described as playing the abused role in an *'abusive (sadistic) to abused'* RRP.

Metaprocedures   The largely unconscious processes whereby the range of RRPs is linked and appropriately mobilised with smooth transitions.

Motivation   An over-used concept which often appears to imply that every action must be explained as initiated by a separate motivating system or a 'motivating ghost in the machine'. Thus, in psychoanalysis submitting to pain and abuse is interpreted as motivated (masochism), and assumed to be 'unconsciously gratifying'. In CAT most maladaptive behaviours, including self-hurting ones, are understood as expressions of one or other of a limited or restricted range of RRPs; people can only mobilise the procedures in their repertoire.

Procedure, procedural sequence   The basic CAT unit of description required to understand the persistence and possible revision of problematic behaviours and experiences. Combines mental, behavioural and external events and other people in a sequence (and hence not equivalent to the cognitive concept of a schema).

Procedural Sequence Model (PSM)   See *Procedure*.

Procedural Sequence Object Relations Model (PSORM)   A development of the PSM with the focus on identifying the reciprocal role procedures of which the enacted procedures are examples.

Projective identification   A psychoanalytic (object relations) concept used to explain the forceful, controlling 'putting' of powerful (usually anxious or hostile) feelings in another. In psychoanalysis this is seen as a defensive process, 'getting rid of the bad by putting it into the other'. In CAT it is seen as a particular example of the general mode of inducing role reciprocation. It is most evident where the dissociated RRPs of borderline patients are concerned: powerful pressures to elicit empathic or reciprocating (collusive) responses are a central aspect of transference–countertransference in such patients.

Rating sheets   Ratings by patients of change in respect of TPs and TPPs, usually made weekly as a means of maintaining the focus and as a way of learning accurate self-reflection. Initial ratings record recognition, later ones revision. Similar ratings may be made of the intensity / frequency with which problem procedures described as procedural loops in diagrams are evident.

Reciprocal role procedure (RRP):   A stable pattern of interaction originating in relationships with caretakers in early life, determining current patterns of relationships with others and self-management. Playing a role always implies another, or the internalised 'voice' of another, whose reciprocation is sought or experienced.

Resistance A psychoanalytic concept implying, or seeming to imply, a motivated opposition to change. In CAT more usefully thought of as either (1) the enactment of one of the patient's procedures (because it is all—or maybe the safest of all—they know), the giving up of which is threatening to the sense of identity, or (2) the failure to change in response to ineffective therapy.

Role Combines action, memory, affect and expectation of reciprocation. See *RRP*.

Self The structure and function of self is seen, in CAT, to include and integrate such functions as memory, affect, perception, thinking, self-reflection, empathic imagination and executive function. It is understood to comprise both subjective and experiential as well as functional aspects. It emerges developmentally from a genotypic self characterised by various innate predispositions, notably to intersubjectivity. The mature, phenotypic self is considered to be fundamentally constituted by internalised, sign-mediated, interpersonal experience and the dialogic voices associated with it. The self is also characterised by a tendency both to organise and be organised by experience.

Self monitoring A homework task. Early in therapy applied to symptoms and unwanted behaviours. After reformulation applied to the recognition of problem procedures or state shifts.

Self state To avoid confusion, these are best described as 'self states: partially dissociated reciprocal roles'. In diagrams, they are drawn in separate boxes as separate sources of procedural loops. A heuristic device. Patients may only know one pole but with reformulation can learn to recognise both. They may sometimes experience the two poles in interaction subjectively, as in a debate between a wish and the voice of conscience.

Sign mediation A key Vygotskian concept describing specifically human modes of learning. Signs convey meanings between people. Infant–mother pairs develop early interpsychological signs; later those of the wider culture, notably language, are adopted. Early experience is internalised through signs rather than stored as representations.

Snags A form of problem procedure in which legitimate and appropriate goals are abandoned or undone either because of the assumed attitudes of others or because of irrational guilt.

State A state of mind or a state of being. Experienced primarily by the dominant mood but accompanied by sense of self and other, degree of access to feeling and control of feeling. The subjective experience of playing a particular role.

State switches or shifts Abrupt changes both experienced and conveyed to others, not always obviously provoked. May reflect (a) role reversal within an RRP, or (b) a response shift between alternative reciprocations to a given role within an RRP or (c) of a switch to a different RRP/self state.

Target problems (TPs) A list agreed early in therapy of the problems which therapy will address. Includes presenting problems and those identified during the reformulation process.

Target problem procedures (TPPs) A list of verbal descriptions of the problem procedures which will be addressed in therapy in the form of dilemmas, traps and snags and/or the repertoire of problematic reciprocal roles.

Transference The (inappropriate) feelings/behaviours elicited or roles experienced or played by patients towards therapists or towards the therapy situation. Usually based on, and hence informative about, the patient's repertoire of RRPs, including those not acknowledged or known consciously. May be identifying with or reciprocating the roles played by or, attributed to, the therapist.

Trap   A problem procedural pattern: self-reinforcing patterns of thought and behaviour. Basically a negative belief generates a form of action which produces consequences that are seen to confirm the belief.

Zone of proximal development (ZPD)   A Vygotskian term. Defined as the gap between current performance and the level which could be achieved with the assistance of a more competent other.

Zone of proximal personality development (ZPPD)   A proposed extension of the concept of the ZPD to apply to the development of self processes.

Appendix 1

CAT-RELATED RESEARCH PUBLICATIONS AND THE EVIDENCE BASE FOR CAT

PUBLICATIONS

Work leading up to CAT

Ryle, A. (1979) Defining goals and assessing change in brief psychotherapy: a pilot study using target ratings and the dyad grid. *British Journal of Medical Psychology*, **52**, 223–233.

Ryle, A. (1980) Some measures of goal attainment in focused integrated active psychotherapy: a study of fifteen cases. *British Journal of Psychiatry*, **137**, 475–486.

Controlled outcome studies

Brockman, B., Poynton, A., Ryle, A. and Watson, J.P. (1987) Effectiveness of time-limited therapy carried out by trainees; a comparison of two methods. *British Journal of Psychiatry*, **151**, 602–609.

Cluley, S., Smeeton, N., Cochrane, G.M. and Cordon, Z. (submitted). The use of cognitive analytic therapy to improve adherence in asthma.

Fosbury, J.A., Bosley, C.M., Ryle, A., Sonksen, P.H. and Judd, S.L. (1997) A trial of cognitive analytic therapy in poorly controlled Type 1 patients. *Diabetes Care*, **20**, 959–964.

Treasure, J., Todd, G., Brolley, M., Tiller, J., Nehmad, A. and Denman, F. (1995) A pilot study of a randomised trial of cognitive analytic therapy for adult anorexia nervosa. *Behaviour Research and Therapy*, **33**, 363–367.

Uncontrolled, naturalistic outcome studies with measured outcomes

Duignan, I. and Mitzman, S. (1994) Change in patients receiving time-limited cognitive analytic group therapy. *International Journal of Short-Term Psychotherapy*, **9**, 1151–1160.

Dunn, M., Golynkina, K., Ryle, A. and Watson, J.P. (1997). A repeat audit of the cognitive analytic clinic at Guy's Hospital. *Psychiatric Bulletin*, **21**, 1–4.

Garyfallos, G., Adamopolou, A., Karastergiou, A., Voikli, M., Zlatanos, D. and Tsifida, S. (1998) Evaluation of cognitive analytic therapy (CAT) outcome in Greek psychiatric outpatients. *European Journal of Psychiatry*, **12**, 167–179.

Kerr, I.B. (2001) Brief cognitive analytic therapy for post-acute manic psychosis on a psychiatric intensive care unit. *Clinical Psychology and Psychotherapy*.

Pollock, P.H. (2001) Clinical outcomes for adult survivors using CAT. In: P.H. Pollock, *Cognitive Analytic Therapy for Adult Survivors of Childhood Abuse*. Chichester: Wiley.

Ryle, A. and Golynkina, K. (2000) Effectiveness of time-limited cognitive analytic therapy of borderline personality disorder; Factors associated with outcome. *British Journal of Medical Psychology*, **73**, 169–177.

Detailed studies of phenomenology and change

Clarke, S. and Llewelyn, S. (1994) Personal constructs of survivors of childhood sexual abuse receiving cognitive analytic therapy. *British Journal of Medical Psychology*, **67**, 273–289.

Clarke, S. and Pearson, C. (2000) Personal constructs of male survivors of childhood sexual abused receiving cognitive analytic therapy. *British Journal of Medical Psychology*, **73**, 169–177.

Golynkina, K. and Ryle, A. (1999) The identification and characteristics of the partially dissociated states of patients with borderline personality disorder. *British Journal of Medical Psychology*, **72**, 429–445.

Pollock, P.H. (1996) Clinical issues in the cognitive analytic therapy of sexually abused women who commit violent offences against their partners. *British Journal of Medical Psychology*, **69**, 117–127.

Pollock, P.H., Broadbent, M., Clarke, S., Dorrian, A.J. and Ryle, A. (2001) The Personality Structure Questionnaire (PSQ); A measure of the multiple self states model of identity disturbance in cognitive analytic therapy. *Clinical Psychology and Psychotherapy*, **8**, 59–72.

Ryle, A. and Marlowe, M.J. (1995) Cognitive analytic therapy for borderline personality disorder: theory and practice and the clinical and research uses of the self states sequential diagram. *International Journal of Short-Term Psychotherapy*, **10**, 21–34.

Sheard, T., Evans, J., Cash, D. et al. (2000) A CAT-derived one to three session intervention for repeated deliberate self harm: a description of the model and initial experience of trainee psychiatrists in using it. *British Journal of Medical Psychology*, **73**, 179–196.

Walsh, S., Hagan, T. and Gamsu, D. (2000) Rescuer and rescued: Applying a cognitive analytic perspective to explore the 'mis-management' of asthma. *British Journal of Medical Psychology*, **73**, 151–168.

Process Research

Bennett, D. and Parry, G. (1997) The accuracy of reformulation in cognitive analytic therapy: a validation study. *Psychotherapy Research*, **8**, 84–103.

Bennett, D., Parry, G. and Ryle, A. (1999) An ideal model for the resolution of alliance threatening transference enactments. (Submitted).

(Note: This excludes individual case studies except those illustrating a new application or methodology.)

THE EVIDENCE BASE FOR CAT

The above list of publications attests to an emerging, although still far from adequate, evidence base for the efficacy and effectiveness of CAT in a variety of clinical settings. The relative paucity of outcome studies so far is due in large measure to the fact that CAT is still a young and developing model and that formal, controlled studies at very early stages of theoretical development are premature and inappropriate. There were no major controlled trials of cognitive-behaviour therapy, for example, 30 years ago but this does not mean that it was not a worthwhile and emerging therapy. Similarly there could have been no trial of CAT for borderline personality disorder until very recently since the borderline model was still being developed. One result of this, however, has been the rapid dissemination and adoption of CAT on the basis of its popularity and apparent effectiveness, without, as noted by Margison (2000), passing through the 'neck' of the hourglass in Salkovskis' model describing the initial development, controlled evaluation and subsequent widespread application of any treatment.

Apart from theoretical issues, there have been and are major difficulties in obtaining resources for most psychotherapy research, the reasons for which we discuss below. In the case of CAT, this affected its early development, which was brought about by a small group of busy clinicians in NHS settings without any formal academic or research infrastructure. In addition, research funding has become increasingly difficult to obtain in this and other countries owing to the hegemony of a largely pharmacological treatment paradigm in psychiatry. This difficulty has been compounded by the need for ever larger trials due to the increasing exigencies of statistical methods used to analyse them.

Given the origins and nature of CAT as an integrative, highly structured, proactive and collaborative therapy with roots in personal construct theory, cognitive therapy, and psychoanalytic therapy, it would be very surprising if its efficacy and effectiveness were significantly different from the generic 'talking treatments' from which it arose. There are additional good reasons to expect that CAT would be in principle, and in practice is, a highly effective treatment. It is well accepted that the question facing psychotherapy in general is not whether it is effective, but rather the detailed problem of 'what works for whom' and also what aspects of what therapy work for whom (Roth and Fonagy, 1996; Parry, 2000), also described as the issue of 'prescriptive matching'. Meta-analyses of outcome studies historically, mostly but not exclusively, based on shorter and cognitively based therapies, indicate that psychotherapy generically has a treatment effect size of the order of 0.8 to 1.0 (Karasu, 1986). In terms of treatments in medicine this is a major effect size and is considerably greater, for example, than that obtained for drug treatments of conditions such as advanced cancer or arthritis, which are nonetheless routinely administered. As noted by Holmes (1993), this is also an effect size considerably greater than that obtained in, for example, trials of aspirin for the prevention of heart attacks where, on the basis of an effect size of 0.32, a trial was discontinued and treatment given to all patients on the grounds that it would be unethical to withhold it (Rosenthal, 1990).

The outcome data collected for efficacy and effectiveness of CAT as cited above is certainly consistent with such a general effect size for psychotherapy. These data include those cases reported in extended, naturalistic studies of neurotic (Dunn et al., 1997) ($n = 135$) and borderline (Ryle and Golynkina, 2000) ($n = 27$) patients, as well as in an earlier comparative trial (Brockman et al., 1987) involving both CAT ($n = 30$) and 'interpretive' therapy for neurotic disorders. In all of these studies significant improvements were reported in standard, as well as CAT-specific, outcome measures. It should be noted, incidentally, that the predominantly naturalistic evidence for the efficacy of CAT does support the rejection of the primary and important 'null hypothesis' in research, namely that the treatment may be doing more harm than good. This has yet to be demonstrated for some other, mostly longer-term therapies.

There are also, as noted above, even stronger reasons for anticipating *a priori* that CAT would be highly efficacious relative to the other therapies reviewed historically. Reviews of the general features of psychological treatments which are effective have stressed that they tend to be focused on achieving a therapeutic alliance and involve targeted goals, guided practice and specific feedback (Luborsky, 1990). In studies reviewed so far, they have, on the whole, also been relatively brief (usually 15–25 sessions) (Marks, 1993), although this may not apply to more disturbed patients or those with personality disorders. A recent review of features of effective treatments for difficult or personality-disordered patients (Bateman and Fonagy, 1999a) suggests that such treatments are longer term, highly structured, have a clear focus, devote effort to treatment compliance, promote a strong attachment relationship and are based on a model comprehensible to both therapist and patient. Virtually all of these are fundamental features of CAT.

EVIDENCE-BASED PSYCHOTHERAPY

Despite this body of naturalistic evidence and preliminary controlled evidence, CAT still lacks evidence from major controlled trials. It is suggested by the protagonists of evidence-based medicine and psychotherapy in this country and by those responsible for managed care in countries such as the USA stressing 'empirically validated' treatments, that therapies should only be purchased and administered on the basis of adequate evidence of efficacy. Clearly this is a position which most self-critical and resource-conscious psychotherapists would subscribe to. There are, however, particular problems with this position which have particular bearing on the attempt by CAT practitioners to validate their work. These relate especially to the placing of the randomised controlled trial (RCT) at the peak of the evidence-based pyramid of evidence, on the basis of which systematic reviews of treatments for given conditions would subsequently be undertaken. This pyramid does imply the existence and validity of other 'lesser' forms of evidence such as uncontrolled naturalistic studies, case-control studies as well as case reports, although these would normally be seen as much less powerful and valid forms of evidence, particularly single case studies. These would normally be considered to be the basis for further extended study or for audit and supervision in the context of accepted indications for a particular treatment. Whilst accepting the necessity and potential power of controlled studies, ultimately required in some form to exclude the possibility that no treatment, or some other treatment, may be more effective than the one being evaluated, it needs to be borne in mind that such studies are crude and imprecise in important ways (Roth and Fonagy, 1996; Parry, 2000). This is important given the importance often inappropriately ascribed to them by funding or research bodies and on the basis of which important decisions may be made.

LIMITATIONS OF THE CURRENT EVIDENCE-BASED PARADIGM IN PSYCHOTHERAPY

The well-recognised problems and limitations of RCTs (Roth and Fonagy, 1996; Parry, 1999) include the inappropriate homogenisation of cases (i.e. treating patients as if they have standard, well-defined problems), the limitations of efficacy studies due to only 'pure' cases being admitted to trials and hence the questionable generalisabilty ('external validity') of such studies. Such issues contribute, for example, to reservations about the findings of small trials such as that of dialectical behaviour therapy for borderline personality disorder (Linehan et al., 1993). Further problems include the assumptions of treatment standardisation when the effective factors in different therapies have not yet been elucidated, raising questions incidentally about the validity of efforts to manualise treatments, and the problems incurred by randomising patients to different treatment conditions about which they may have a preference. This may manifest in 'drop-outs' or poor engagement with treatment. It is also recognised that any placebo condition in psychotherapy cannot be concealed and any active control will have in addition a significant treatment effect size itself (usually estimated to be of the order of 0.3).

One of the most inappropriate and invalid consequences of the employment of an evidence-based paradigm is the premature foreclosure on still developing models of therapy. This may result from the inappropriate conclusion that if there exists no evidence as yet for the efficacy of a treatment, it should then be excluded from consideration for further development, evaluation or application. This tendency has been pithily criticised by noting that 'lack of evidence of efficacy does *not* necessarily imply evidence of lack of efficacy'. Given its youth as a model, as noted above, CAT is particularly vulnerable to this sort of inappropriate evaluation.

Another most important concern in undertaking RCTs is the ethical one of withholding a treatment from a control or alternative treatment group if there already exists some evidence for its efficacy. This concern may be, properly, intolerable and unacceptable to patients as well as ethical committees. In many countries where there is a tradition of strong 'consumer' rights, such pressures make randomised trials virtually impossible to conduct. It also makes it difficult for conscientious clinicians to participate in some trials. Such considerations could be a problem, for example, in evaluating CAT through a randomised controlled trial in, for example, borderline personality disorder where good preliminary evidence (Ryle and Golynkina, 2000) of efficacy now exists.

The RCT approach is also largely based on a quantitative, 'pharmaceutical' model of testing which has questionable relevance to the complex difficulties and issues brought by psychotherapy patients who rarely present with simple and circumscribed problems. This is well demonstrated by the diverse case examples throughout this book. Such studies make, in addition, the flawed assumption that simple factors are responsible and identifiable as the 'active ingredient' in treatment and that this will be directly related to outcome as assessed by easily definable and meaningful measurements. These approaches ignore the complex relationship between process factors in therapy and outcome which, as pointed out by Stiles (1995), is characterised by complex dynamics of ultimately a 'non-linear' nature. That is to say that outcome may not relate directly to the administration or 'quantity' of one ingredient (e.g. an interpretation or an empathic comment). Because of this complexity, psychotherapy outcome research is particularly sensitive to and dependent on an understanding and evaluation of process factors in therapy, some of which may only be amenable to more qualitative research approaches. The latter would include focus, for example, on the exploration of meaning and its social construction and the use of techniques such as discourse analysis or task analysis (Stiles, 1995).

It is accepted (Parry, 2000) that alternatives to the above 'paradigm of excellence' (i.e. the randomised controlled trial) need to be considered. These include evaluation of very large series of uncontrolled treatments and more focused study of the relation of process to outcome in different therapies. In the later respect CAT, given its process research-based evolution, is well placed and indeed has been producing interesting and important research. This has included work on the validity of reformulation (Bennett and Parry, 1998) and, through task analysis, of the significance of therapeutic alliance threatening events and their repair in therapy (Bennett et al., submitted).

We see it as important to highlight the difficulties and limitations inherent in the application of RCTs in this field given their implications whilst at the same time fully accepting the need for controlled evaluation of the efficacy of a treatment model in general and in terms of which aspects of process are effective in particular. The latter is also of importance given the so-called 'equivalence paradox' whereby, so far at least, it appears that therapeutic efficacy of different 'brand name' models tends, very approximately, to be comparable. This suggests that efficacy may depend as much on common factors and on therapist competencies as on the specific package which a model embodies. This again highlights the importance of process research in which CAT, largely through the work of Dawn Bennett and colleagues, has been active. It seems highly unlikely that efficacy will be found to be entirely independent of critical features of different models. Indeed the general evidence, as noted above, suggests that factors such as strength of the therapeutic alliance are critical in determining outcome (Orlinsky et al., 1994) and that those models which emphasize and promote this are more likely to be effective. Clearly CAT would fall into this category. In many ways we see CAT as being in a strong position to promote and undertake further research into its efficacy, bearing in mind the above caveats. We certainly do not, for example, share certain extreme psychoanalytic positions (see Taylor, 1998) that this discourse should not be conducted at all and refuse to engage in it on principle. Although research in this area is complex and involves many factors which cannot easily be conceptualised, operationalised or quantified, we do not see such a methodologically 'Luddite' position as defensible.

CLINICAL EFFECTIVENESS

An important issue in the evaluation of any treatment is how well pure efficacy studies as addressed in RCTs translate into routine settings outside research studies. This will depend on how well a treatment engages and works with patients who may present, as in the majority of cases, with complex personality difficulties in addition to well-defined presenting symptoms. Thus attrition rates or drop-out from therapy are an important consideration since the most 'superior' treatment is of little use if patients will not or cannot stick with it. This appears to be a major problem in trials of psychoanalytic therapy for difficult patients with borderline disorders, for example. There is good evidence for the acceptability of and treatment adherence in CAT for various patients, most strikingly in the borderline personality disorder group where drop-out rates of only 12% have been reported (Ryle and Golynkina, 2000).

Another factor of particular importance in its relevance in the real, clinical world is, of course, its cost. This is not to say that cheaper or short treatment should necessarily be preferred if others are superior, but that if a given treatment if equally effective, cheaper and briefer, then this has important implications. Again the standard, brief format of CAT offers significant advantages in this respect.

RESEARCH RESOURCES

The difficulty of obtaining financial funding for major research projects, including RCTs, in the current climate should also be mentioned. This difficulty stems partly from a still widely held view that psychotherapy is somehow a 'fringe' or luxury activity despite the evidence for the costs of psychological disorder in terms of human suffering as well as in social economics (Gabbard et al., 1997). This view is still frequently encountered despite the evidence that as a treatment modality psychotherapy has an effectiveness as great as or greater than that for many treatments routinely employed in general medicine. Many therapists find themselves in a 'Catch-22' situation of being asked for evidence for their work but denied the means with which to research and substantiate it. In part too this can be seen as a reflection of the dominant biomedical paradigm within psychiatry, encouraged by large pharmaceutical companies who can powerfully promote their own agendas. This unacceptable situation prevails despite the avowedly biopsychosocial base of trainings and practice in the mental health professions and evidence that psychosocial factors are of critical importance in the genesis and maintenance of all psychiatric disorders from the neurotic to the psychotic. It is to be hoped that pressure from psychotherapists, as well as consumers whom we may helpfully encourage and inform, can be brought increasingly to bear on the media and political systems to rectify this alarming and improper state of affairs.

ACAT AND RESEARCH

Despite these difficulties, research is seen within ACAT as a major priority for both scientific and political reasons and, as we have documented, continues to flourish at all levels even without much external support. This has largely been due to the energy and activity of the many practitioners who have contributed to much of what has been reviewed and discussed in this book. Several groups are currently undertaking RCTs or applying for funding for them and the ACAT research committee is involved in actively advising and fundraising to support these and other projects. Training in basic research methodology, both quantitative and qualitative, will shortly be introduced formally onto all training courses in order to encourage further a culture of research literacy and activity.

We believe that the rapid growth of CAT as reflected in the number of its practitioners and trainees, its democratic, patient-empowering principles and the gathering weight of its evidence base, combined with its being cost effective and well adapted for poorly funded public health services, augur well for its continuing development and application.

Further details of research in CAT and of its special interest groups can be obtained either from the ACAT office or from the website www.acat.org.uk.

Appendix 2

THE PSYCHOTHERAPY FILE

An aid to understanding ourselves better.

In our life what has happened to us, and the sense we made of this, colours the way we see ourselves and others. How we see things is for us, how things are, and how we go about our lives seems 'obvious and right'. Sometimes, however, our familiar ways of understanding and acting can be the source of our problems. In order to solve our difficulties we may need to learn to recognise how what we do makes things worse. We can then work out new ways of thinking and acting.

These pages are intended to suggest ways of thinking about what you do; recognising your particular patterns is the first step in learning to gain more control and happiness in your life.

KEEPING A DIARY OF MOODS AND BEHAVIOUR

Symptoms, bad moods, unwanted thoughts or behaviours that come and go can be better understood and controlled if you learn to notice when they happen and what starts them off.

If you have a particular symptom or problem of this sort, start keeping a diary. The diary should be focused on a particular mood, symptom or behaviour, and should be kept every day if possible. Try to record this sequence:

1. How you were feeling about yourself and others and the world before the problem came on.
2. Any external event, or any thought or image in your mind that was going on when the trouble started, or what seemed to start it off.
3. Once the trouble started, what were the thoughts, images or feelings you experienced.

By noticing and writing down in the way what you do and think at these times, you will learn to recognise and eventually have more control over how you act and think at the time. It is often the case that bad feelings like resentment, depression or physical symptoms are the result of ways of thinking and acting that are unhelpful. Diary keeping in this way gives you the chance to learn better ways of dealing with things.

It is helpful to keep a daily record for 1–2 weeks, then to discuss what you have recorded with your therapist or counsellor.

PATTERNS THAT DO NOT WORK, BUT ARE HARD TO BREAK

There are certain ways of thinking and acting that do not achieve what we want, but which are hard to change. Read through the lists on the following pages and mark how far you think they apply to you.

Applies strongly ++   Applies +   Does not apply 0

Traps

Traps are things we cannot escape from. Certain kinds of thinking and acting result in a 'vicious circle' when, however hard we try, things seem to get worse instead of better. Trying to deal with feeling bad about ourselves, we think and act in ways that tend to confirm our badness.

Examples of traps

1. Fear of hurting others trap

Feeling fearful of hurting others* we keep our feelings inside, or put our own needs aside. This tends to allow other people to ignore or abuse us in various ways, which then leads to our feeling, or being, childishly angry. When we see ourselves behaving like this, it confirms our belief that we shouldn't be aggressive and reinforces our avoidance of standing up for our rights.

People often get trapped in this way because they mix up aggression and assertion. Mostly, being assertive—asking for our rights—is perfectly acceptable. People who do not respect our rights as human beings must either be stood up to or avoided.

2. Depressed thinking trap

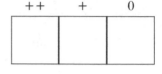

Feeling depressed, we are sure we will manage a task or social situation badly. Being depressed, we are probably not as effective as we can be, and the depression leads us to exaggerate how badly we handled things. This makes us feel more depressed about ourselves.

3. Trying to please trap

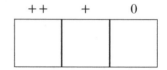

Feeling uncertain about ourselves and anxious not to upset others, we try to please people by doing what they seem to want. As a result: (1) we end up being taken advantage of by others which makes us angry, depressed or guilty, from which our uncertainty about ourselves is confirmed; or (2) sometimes we feel out of control because of the need to please, and start hiding away, putting things off, letting people down, which makes other people angry with us and increases our uncertainty.

4. Avoidance trap

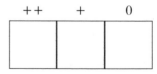

We feel ineffective and anxious about certain situations, such as crowded streets, open spaces, social gatherings. We try to go back into these situations, but feel even more anxiety. Avoiding them makes us feel better, so we stop trying. However, by constantly avoiding situations our lives are limited and we come to feel increasingly ineffective and anxious.

5. Social isolation trap

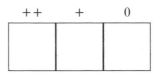

Feeling underconfident about ourselves and anxious not to upset others, we worry that others will find us boring or stupid, so we don't look at people or respond to friendliness. People then see us as unfriendly, so we become more isolated, from which we are convinced we are boring and stupid—and become more underconfident.

6. Low self-esteem trap

Feeling worthless we feel that we cannot get what we want because (1) we will be punished, (2) that others will reject or abandon us, or (3) as if anything good we get is bound to go away or turn sour. (4) Sometimes it feels as if we must punish ourselves for being weak. From this we feel that everything is hopeless so we give up trying to do anything; this confirms and increases our sense of worthlessness.

Dilemmas (false choices and narrow options)

We often act as we do, even when we are not completely happy with it, because the only other ways we can imagine, seem as bad or even worse. Sometimes we assume connections that are not necessarily the case—as in 'If I do "x" then "y" will follow'. These false choices can be described as either/or or if/then dilemmas. We often don't realise that we see things like this, but we act as if these were the only possible choices. Do you act as if any of the following false choices rule your life? Recognising them is the first step to changing them.

Choices about myself

I act AS IF:

	++	+	0
1. Either I keep feelings bottled up or I risk being rejected, hurting others, or making a mess.			
2. Either I feel I spoil myself and feel greedy or I deny myself things and punish myself and feel miserable.			
3. If I try to be perfect, I feel depressed and angry; if I don't try to be perfect, I feel guilty, angry and dissatisfied.			
4. If I must then I won't; it is as if when faced with a task I must either (1) gloomily submit or (2) passively resist. Other people's wishes, or even my own feel too demanding, so I put things off, avoid them.			
5. If I must not then I will; it is as if the only proof of my existence is my resistance. Other people's rules, or even my own feel too restricting, so I break rules and do things which are harmful to me.			
6. If other people aren't expecting me to do things for them or look after them, then I feel anxious, lonely and out of control.			
7. If I get what I want I feel childish and guilty; if I don't get what I want, I feel frustrated, angry and depressed.			
8. Either I keep things (feelings, plans) in perfect order, or I fear a terrible mess.			

Choices about how we relate to others

I behave with others AS IF:

	++	+	0
1. Either I'm involved with someone and likely to get hurt or I don't get involved and stay in charge, but remain lonely.			
2. Either I stick up for myself and nobody likes me, or I give in and get put on by others and feel cross and hurt.			
3. Either I'm a brute or a martyr (secretly blaming the other).			
4. a. With others either I'm safely wrapped up in bliss or in combat;			
b. if in combat then I'm either a bully or a victim.			
5. Either I look down on other people, or I feel they look down on me.			
6. a. Either I'm sustained by the admiration of others whom I admire or I feel exposed;			
b. if exposed then I feel either contemptuous of others or I feel contemptible.			
7. Either I'm involved with others and feel engulfed, taken over or smothered, or I stay safe and uninvolved but feel lonely and isolated.			
8. When I'm involved with someone whom I care about then either I have to give in or they have to give in.			
9. When I'm involved with someone whom I depend on then either I have to give in or they have to give in.			
10. a. As a woman either I have to do what others want or I stand up for my rights and get rejected.			
10. b. As a man either I can't have any feelings or I am an emotional mess.			

Snags

Snags are what is happening when we say 'I want to have a better life, or I want to change my behaviour but ...'. Sometimes this comes from how we or our families thought about us when we were young; such as 'she was always the good child', or 'in our family we never ...'. Sometimes the snags come from the important people in our lives not wanting us to change, or not able to cope with what our changing means to them. Often the resistance is more indirect, as when a parent, husband or wife becomes ill or depressed when we begin to get better.

In other cases, we seem to 'arrange' to avoid pleasure or success, or if they come, we have to pay in some way, by depression, or by spoiling things. Often this is because, as children, we came to feel guilty if things went well for us, or felt that we were envied for good luck or success. Sometimes we have come to feel responsible, unreasonably, for things that went wrong in the family, although we may not be aware that this is so. It is helpful to learn to recognise how this sort of pattern is stopping you getting on with your life, for only then can you learn to accept your right to a better life and begin to claim it.

You may get quite depressed when you begin to realise how often you stop your life being happier and more fulfilled. It is important to remember that it's not being stupid or bad, but rather that:

(a) *We do these things because this is the way we learned to manage best when we were younger,*

(b) *we don't have to keep on doing them now we are learning to recognise them,*

(c) *by changing our behaviour, we can learn to control not only our own behaviour, but we also change the way other people behave to us,*

(d) *although it may seem that others resist the changes we want for ourselves (for example, our parents, or our partners), we often underestimate them; if we are firm about our right to change, those who care for us will usually accept the change.*

Do you recognise that you feel limited in your life:

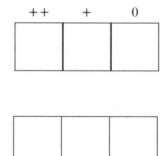

1. For fear of the response of others: for example I must sabotage success (1) as if it deprives others, (2) as if others may envy me or (3) as if there are not enough good things to go around.
2. By something inside yourself: for example I must sabotage good things as if I don't deserve them.

Difficult and unstable states of mind

Some people find it difficult to keep control over their behaviour and experience because things feel very difficult and different at times. Indicate which, if any of the following apply to you:

1. How I feel about myself and others can be unstable: I can switch from one state of mind to a completely different one.
2. Some states may be accompanied by intense, extreme and uncontrollable emotions.
3. Others by emotional blankness, feeling unreal, or feeling muddled.
4. Some states are accompanied by feeling intensely guilty or angry with myself, wanting to hurt myself.
5. Or by feeling that others can't be trusted, are going to let me down, or hurt me.
6. Or by being unreasonably angry or hurtful to others.
7. Sometimes the only way to cope with some confusing feelings is to blank them off and feel emotionally distant from others.

DIFFERENT STATES

Everybody experiences changes in how they feel about themselves and the world. But for some people these changes are extreme, sometimes sudden and confusing. In such cases there are often a number of states which recur, and learning to recognise them and shifts between them can be very helpful. Below are a number of descriptions of such states. Identify those which you experience by ringing the number. *You can delete or add words to the descriptions* and there is space to add any not listed.

1. Zombie. Cut off from feelings, cut off from others, disconnected.
2. Feeling bad but soldiering on, coping.
3. Out of control rage.
4. Extra special. Looking down on others.

5. In control of self, of life, of other people.
6. Cheated by life, by others. Untrusting.
7. Provoking, teasing, seducing, winding-up others.
8. Clinging, fearing abandonment.
9. Frenetically active. Too busy to think or feel.
10. Agitated, confused, anxious.
11. Feeling perfectly cared for, blissfully close to another.
12. Misunderstood, rejected, abandoned.
13. Contemptuously dismissive of myself.
14. Vulnerable, needy, passively helpless, waiting for rescue.
15. Envious, wanting to harm others, put them down, pull them down.
16. Protective, respecting of myself, of others.
17. Hurting myself, hurting others.
18. Resentfully submitting to demands.
19. Hurt, humiliated by others.
20. Secure in myself, able to be close to others.
21. Intensely critical of self, of others.
22. Frightened of others.
23.

Appendix 3

PERSONALITY STRUCTURE QUESTIONNAIRE (PSQ)

The aim of this questionnaire is to obtain an account of certain aspects of your personality. People vary greatly in all sorts of ways: the aim of this form is to find out how far you feel yourself to be constant and 'all of a piece' or variable and made up of a number of distinct 'sub-personalities' or liable to experience yourself as shifting between two or more quite distinct and sharply differentiated states of mind.

Most of us experience ourselves as somewhere between these contrasted ways. A *state of mind* is recognised by a typical mood, a particular sense of oneself and of others and by how far one is in touch with, and in control of, feelings. Such states are definite, recognisable ways of being; one is either clearly in a given state or one is not. They often affect one quite suddenly; they may be of brief duration or they last for days. Sometimes, but not always, changes of state happen because of a change in circumstances or an event of some kind.

Please indicate which description applies to you most closely by shading the appropriate circle

| **Please complete** | **Shade circles like this:** ● | **Shade one circle** |
| **ALL questions** | **Not like this:** ⊗ ⊘ | **per question only** |

THANK YOU FOR YOUR HELP. ALL INFORMATION WILL BE TREATED AS PRIVATE AND CONFIDENTIAL

SHADE ONE CIRCLE PER QUESTION ONLY

	1 Very true	2 True	3 May or may not be true	4 True	5 Very true	
1. My sense of myself is always the same	○	○	○	⊙	○	How I act or feel is constantly changing
2. The various people in my life see me in much the same way	○	○	○	○	○	The various people in my life have different views of me as if I were not the same person
3. I have a stable and unchanging sense of myself	○	○	○	○	○	I am so different at different times that I wonder who I really am
4. I have no sense of opposed sides to my nature	○	○	○	○	○	I feel I am split between two (or more) ways of being, sharply differentiated from each other
5. My mood and sense of self seldom change suddenly	○	○	○	○	○	My mood can change abruptly in ways which make me feel unreal or out of control
6. My mood changes are always understandable	○	○	○	○	○	I am often confused by my mood changes which seem either unprovoked or quite out of scale with what provoked them
7. I never lose control	○	○	○	○	○	I get into states in which I lose control and do harm to myself and/or others
8. I never regret what I have said or done	○	○	○	○	○	I get into states in which I do and say things which I later deeply regret

From: Pollock, P.H., Broadbent, M., Clarke, S., Dorrian, A.J. and Ryle, A. (2001) The Personality Structure Questionnaire (PSQ): A measure of the multiple self states model of identity disturbance in cognitive analytic therapy. *Clinical Psychology and Psychotherapy*, **8**, 59–72. © John Wiley & Sons, Ltd. Reproduced with permission.

Appendix 4

REPERTORY GRID BASICS AND THE USE OF GRID TECHNIQUES IN CAT

Repertory grid technique is derived from personal construct theory, which was developed by George Kelly (1955). It offers a way of exploring how a person makes sense of particular aspects of his or her world. The test consists of a list of elements which are compared by rating how far each is described by a list of constructs. Both elements and constructs are elicited from, or at least must be relevant to, the person doing the test. In the development of CAT, ideas were derived from grids in which the elements were significant people or, in the dyad grid, the relationships between self and significant people, and the constructs were descriptive of psychological characteristics or of patterns of relationship. This work and an outline of the technical and mathematical procedures involved are reported in Ryle (1975).

Completed grids are subjected to a principal component analysis which yields three main types of data: (1) How far any two constructs are used in a similar way is expressed as a construct correlation. For example, people described as strong may be seen as dangerous or as trustworthy, indicated by a positive correlation between strong and dangerous or between strong and trusted. (2) How far any two elements are seen as similar is indicated by a similar measure, namely element distance, calculated around the average value for the whole grid. Thus an element distance of 0.4 between the relationship of self to husband and that of self to father, indicating a high degree of similarity, will carry different implications than would a value of 1.6 indicating extreme dissimilarity. (3) The dispersion of the elements in the construct space can be plotted in a graph which places both elements and constructs according to their loadings on the first two principal components. These can be regarded as maps in which the meaning of the territory is indicated by the construct loadings (usually written in the periphery to avoid clutter) and the elements are located in the 'territory' so defined.

Repeat repertory grid testing can be used to measure change with therapy, predictions of the direction of desirable change in measures, usually construct correlations, being made at the reformulation stage, the procedure being repeated at the end of therapy (Brockman et al., 1987; Ryle, 1979, 1980). The technique was applied to the plotting of changes in transference and counter-transference (Ryle, 1995a). Pollock and Kear-Colwell used the grid technique to investigate the relationship between sexual victimisation and offending behaviour. In the present volume the 'States Grid', involving the rating of states identified in the early stages of the therapy of borderline patients, is described in Chapter 6. A similar use using a standard grid with a series of borderline patients is reported in Golynkina and Ryle (1999).

REFERENCES

Adshead, G. (1998) Psychiatric staff as attachment figures. Understanding management problems in psychiatric services in the light of attachment theory. *British Journal of Psychiatry*, **172**, 64–69.

Adshead, G. (2000) Psychological therapies for post-traumatic stress disorder. *British Journal of Psychiatry*, **177**, 144–148.

Ainsworth, M.D.S., Blehar, M., Waters, E. and Wall, S. (1978) *Patterns of Attachment*. Hillsdale, NJ: Erlbaum.

Aitken, K.J. and Trevarthen, C. (1997) Self/other organization in human psychological development. *Development and Psychopathology*, **9**, 653–677.

Albee, G.W. (1998) Primary prevention of mental disorder and promotion of mental health. *Journal of Mental Health*, **7**, 437–439.

American Psychiatric Association (1994) *Diagnostic and Statistical Manual of Mental Disorders* (4th Edition). Washington, DC: American Psychiatric Association.

Andreason, N.C., Paradiso, S. and O'Leary, D.S. (1998) 'Cognitive dysmmetria' as an integrative theory of schizophrenia: a dysfunction in cortical-subcortical-cerebellar circuitry. *Schizophrenia Bulletin*, **24**, 203–218.

Bakhtin, M.M. (1984) *Problems of Dostoevsky's Poetics*. Edited and translated by Caryl Emerson. Manchester: Manchester University Press.

Bakhtin, M.M. (1986) *Speech Genres and Other Late Essays*. Austin: University of Texas Press.

Bandura, A. (1977) Self efficacy-towards a unifying theory of behavioural change. *Psychological Review*, **84**, 191–215.

Barkham, M., Evans, C., Margison, F., McGrath, G., Mellor-Clark, J., Milnes, D. and Connell, J. (1998) The rationale for developing and implementing core outcome batteries for routine use in service settings and psychotherapy outcome research. *Journal of Mental Health*, **7**, 35–47.

Bateman, A. and Holmes, J. (1995) *Introduction to Psychoanalysis: Contemporary Theory and Practice*. London: Routledge.

Bateman, A.W. and Fonagy, P. (1999a) Psychotherapy for severe personality disorder. *British Medical Journal*, **319**, 709.

Bateman, A. and Fonagy, P. (1999b) Effectiveness of partial hospitalisation in the treatment of Borderline Personality Disorder: a randomized controlled trial. *American Journal of Psychiatry*, **156**, 1563–1569.

Bateman, A., Brown, D. and Pedder, J. (2000) *Introduction to Psychotherapy: an Outline of Psychodynamic Principles and Practice*. London: Routledge.

Bateson, G. (2000) *Steps Towards an Ecology of Mind*. Chicago: University of Chicago Press.

Baxter, L.R., Schwartz, J.M., Bergmann, D.S. et al. (1992) Caudate glucose metabolic rate changes with both drug and behaviour therapy for obsessive-compulsive disorder. *Archives of General Psychiatry*, **49**, 618–689.

Beck, A.T. (1976) *Cognitive Therapy and the Emotional Disorders*. New York: International Universities Press.

Beck, A.T. and Freeman, A. (1990) *Cognitive Therapy of Personality Disorders*. New York: Guilford Press.

Beebe, B. (1998) A procedural theory of therapeutic action: commentary on the symposium 'interventions that effect change in psychotherapy'. *Infant Mental Health Journal*, **19**, 333–340.

Bell, L. (1999) The spectrum of psychological problems in people with eating disorders: an analysis of 30 eating disordered patients treated with Cognitive Analytic Therapy. *Clinical Psychology and Psychotherapy*, **6**, 29–38.

Bennett, D. (1998) *Deriving a model of therapist competence from good and poor outcome cases in the psychotherapy of borderline personality disorder*. Unpublished doctoral thesis. University of Sheffield.

Bennett, D. and Parry, G. (1998) The accuracy of reformulation in cognitive analytic therapy: a validation study. *Psychotherapy Research*, **8**, 84–103.

Bentall, R. and Kindermann, P. (1998) Psychological processes and delusional beliefs: implications for the treatment of paranoid states. In: T. Wykes, N. Tarrier and S. Lewis (Eds). *Outcome and Innovation in Psychological Treatment of Schizophrenia*. Chichester: Wiley.

Berelowitz, M. and Tarnopolsky, A. (1993) The validity of borderline personality disorder: an update and review of recent research. In: P. Tyrer and G. Stein (Eds) *Personality Disorder Reviewed*, pp. 17–41. London: Gaskell.

Berrios, G.E. (1993) Personality disorders: a conceptual history. In: P. Tyrer and G. Stein (Eds) *Personality Disorder Reviewed*, pp. 17–41. London: Gaskell.

Bhugra, D. and Bhui, K. (1998) Psychotherapy for ethnic minorities: issues, context and practice. *British Journal of Psychotherapy*, **14**, 310–326.

Bisson, J.I., Jenkins, P.L., Alexander, J. et al. (1997) Randomised controlled trial of psychological de-briefing for victims of acute burn trauma. *British Journal of Psychiatry*, **171**, 78–81.

Bosma, H., Dike van de Mheen, H. and Mackenbach, J.P. (1999) Social class in childhood and general health in adulthood: questionnaire study of contribution of psychological attributes. *British Medical Journal*, **318**, 18–22.

Bowlby, J. (1988) *A Secure Base: Clinical Applications of Attachment Theory*. London: Routledge.

Boyes, M., Guidano, R. and Pool, M. (1997) Internalisation of social discourse: A Vygotskian account of the development of young children's theories of mind. In: B.D. Cox, and C. Lightfoot, (Eds) *Sociogenetic Perspectives on Internalisation*. Mahwah, NJ: Lawrence Erlbaum Associates.

Brandon, S., Boakes, J., Glaser, D. and Green, R. (1998) Recovered memories of childhood sexual abuse. *British Journal of Psychiatry*, **172**, 296–307.

Braten, S. (1988) Dialogic mind: the infant and adult in protoconversation. In: M.E. Carvallo (Ed.) *Nature, Cognition and System*, vol. 1, pp. 187–205. Dordrecht: Kluwer Academic Publishers.

Brazelton, T.B. and Cramer, B. (1991) *The Earliest Relationship: Parents, Infants and The Drama of Early Attachment*. London: Karnac books.

Bremner, J.D., Randall, P., Scott, T.M. et al. (1995) MRI-based measures of hippocampal volume in patients with PTSD. *American Journal of Psychiatry*, **152**, 973–981.

Brewin, C. (1988) *Cognitive Foundations of Clinical Psychology*. Hove: Lawrence Erlbaum.

Brewin, C.R., Dalgleish, T. and Joseph, S. (1996) A dual-representation theory of posttraumatic stress disorder. *Psychological Review*, **103**, 670–686.

British Psychological Society (1995) Report: *Recovered Memories*.

Brockman, B., Poynton, A., Ryle, A. and Watson, J.P. (1987) Effectiveness of time-limited therapy carried out by trainees; a comparison of two methods. *British Journal of Psychiatry*, **151**, 602–609.

Brown, D. and Zinkin, L. (Eds) (1994) *The Psyche and the Social World: Developments in Group-Analytic Theory*. London: Routledge.

Brown, G. and Harris, T. (1978) *The Social Origins of Depression*. London: Tavistock.

Brown, G., Birley, J.L.T. and Wing, J.K. (1972) Influence of family life on the course of schizophrenic disorders. *British Journal of Psychiatry*, **121**, 241–258.

Bruner, J. (1990) *Acts of Meaning*. Cambridge, MA: Harvard University Press.

Burkitt, I. (1991) *Social Selves: Theories of the Social Formation of Personality*. London: Sage Publications.

Burman, E., Gowrisunkur, J. and Sangha, K. (1998) Conceptualising cultural and gendered identities in psychological therapies. *European Journal of Psychotherapy, Counselling and Health*, **1**, 231–256.

Carroll, M. (1996) *Counselling Supervision. Theory Skills and Practice*. London: Cassell.

Chadwick, P., Birchwood, M. and Trower, P. (1996) *Cognitive Therapy for Delusions, Voices and Paranoia*. Chichester: Wiley.

Chanen, A. (2000) Prevention and early intervention for borderline personality disorder in young people. *ACAT newsletter*, Autumn 2000, p. 9.

Cheyne, J.A. and Tarulli, D. (1999) Dialogue, difference and voice in the zone of proximal development. *Theory and Psychology*, **9**, 5–28.

Clark, R.A. (1978) The transition from action to gesture. In: A. Lock (Ed.) *Action, Gesture and Symbol. The Emergence of Language*. London: Academic Press.

Clarke, S. and Llewelyn, S. (1994) Personal constructs of survivors of childhood sexual abuse receiving cognitive analytic therapy. *British Journal of Medical Psychology*, **67**, 273–289.

Clarkin, J.F., Yeomans, F.E. and Kernberg, O.F. (1999) *Psychotherapy for Borderline Personality Disorder*. New York: Wiley.

Cluley, S., Smeeton, N., Cochrane, G.M. and Cordon, Z. (2000) The use of cognitive analytic therapy to improve adherence in asthma. (Submitted)

Coltart, N. (1988) Diagnosis and assessment for suitability for psychoanalytic psychotherapy. *British Journal of Psychotherapy*, **4**, 127–134.

Costa, P.T. and McCrae, R.R. (1992) Four ways five factors are basic. *Personality and Individual Differences*, **13**, 653–665.

Cowmeadow, P. (1994) Deliberate self-harm and cognitive analytic therapy. *International Journal of Short-Term Psychotherapy*, **9**(2/3), 135–150.

Cowmeadow, P. (1995) Very brief psychotherapeutic interventions with deliberate self-harmers. In: A. Ryle (Ed.) *Cognitive Analytic Therapy: Developments in Theory and Practice*. Chichester: Wiley.

Cox, B.D. and Lightfoot, C. (1997) *Sociogenetic Perspectives on Internalisation*. Mahwah, NJ: Lawrence Erlbaum.

Crits-Christoph, P. (1998) The interpersonal interior of psychotherapy. *Psychotherapy Research*, **8**, 1–16.

Crittenden, P.M. (1990) Truth, error, omission and distortion: The application of attachment theory to the assessment and treatment of psychological disorder. In:

S.M.C. Dollinger and L.F. Dilalla (Eds) *Assessment and Intervention across the Life Span.* Hillsdale, NJ: Erlbaum.

Dagnan, D. and Chadwick, P. (1997) *Assessment and Intervention.* In: B.S. Kroese, D. Dagnan and K. Loumidis (Eds) *Cognitive Behaviour Therapy for People with Learning Disabilities.* London: Routledge.

Dalal, F.N. (1992) 'Race' and racism: an attempt to organise difference. *Group Analysis,* **26,** 277–293.

Davidson, K. (2000) *Cognitive Therapy for Personality Disorder.* Oxford: Butterworth.

Davidson, L. and Strauss, J.S. (1992) Sense of self in recovery from severe mental illness. *British Journal of Medical Psychology,* **65,** 131–145.

Deary, I. and Power, M.J. (1998) Normal and abnormal personality. In: E.C. Johnstone, C.P.L. Freeman and A.K. Zealley (Eds) *Companion to Psychiatric Studies,* 6th edition. Edinburgh: Churchill Livingstone.

Denman, C. (1995) What is the point of a formulation? In: C. Mace (Ed.) *The Art and Science of Psychotherapy.* London: Routledge.

Denman, C. and de Vries, P. (1998) Cognitive analytic therapy and homosexual orientation. In: C. Shelley (Ed.) *Contemporary Perspectives on Psychotherapy and Homosexualities.* London: Free Association Books.

De Waele, M. (1995) A clinical concept of the self: The experiential being. *British Journal of Medical Psychology,* **68,** 223–242.

Donald, M. (1991) *Origins of the Modern Mind: Three Stages in the Evolution of Culture and Cognition.* Cambridge, MA and London: Harvard University Press.

Duignan, I. and Mitzman, S. (1994) Change in patients receiving time-limited cognitive analytic group therapy. *International Journal of Short-Term Psychotherapy,* **9,** 1151–1160.

Dunn, M. (1994) Variations in cognitive analytic therapy technique in the treatment of a severely disturbed patient. *International Journal of Short-Term Psychotherapy,* **9,** 83–92.

Dunn, M. and Parry, G.D. (1997) A formulated care plan approach to caring for borderline personality disorder in a community mental health setting. *Clinical Psychology Forum,* **104,** 19–22.

Dunn, M., Golynkina, K., Ryle, A. and Watson, J.P. (1997) A repeat audit of the cognitive analytic clinic at Guy's Hospital. *Psychiatric Bulletin,* **21,** 1–4.

Economist, The (1998) Spirit of the age: malignant sadness is the world's greatest burden. 19 December, pp. 123–129.

Eells, T.D. (Ed.) (1997) *Handbook of Psychotherapy Case Formulation.* New York: Guilford Press.

Eisenberg, L. (1995) The social construction of the human brain. *American Journal of Psychiatry,* **152,** 1563–1575.

Evans, D. and Zarate, O. (1999) *Introducing Evolutionary Psychology.* Cambridge: Icon Books.

Fairbairn, W.R.D. (1952) *Psychoanalytic Studies of the Personality,* London: Tavistock.

Finlay-Jones, R. and Brown, G.W. (1981) Types of stressful life event and the onset of anxiety and depressive disorders. *Psychological Medicine,* **11,** 803–816.

Fonagy, P. (1999) Memory and therapeutic action. *International Journal of Psychoanalysis,* **80,** 215–223.

Fonagy, P. and Target, M. (1997) Attachment and reflective function: their role in self-organisation. *Development and Psychopathology,* **9,** 679–700.

Fonagy, P. and Target, M. (2000) Attachment and borderline personality disorder: a theory and some evidence. *Psychiatric Clinics of North America,* **23,** 103–121.

Forstelling, F. (1980) Attributional aspects of cognitive behaviour modification. *Cognitive Therapy and Research,* **4,** 27–37.

Fosbury, J.A., Bosley, C.M., Ryle, A., Sonksen, P.H. and Judd, S.L. (1997) A trial of cognitive analytic therapy in poorly controlled Type 1 patients. *Diabetes Care,* **20,** 959–964.

Foulkes, S.H. and Anthony, E.J. (1957) *Group Psychotherapy: The Psychoanalytic Approach*. London: Karnac Books.

Fox, N.A., Calkins, S.D. and Bell, M.A. (1994) Neural plasticity and development in the first two years of life: evidence from cognitive and socioemotional domains of research. *Development and Psychopathology*, **6**, 677–696.

Frank, J.D. (1961) *Persuasion and Healing*. Baltimore: Johns Hopkins University Press.

Freeman, C.P.L. (1998) Neurotic disorders. In: E.C. Johnstone, C.P.L. Freeman and A.K. Zealley (Eds) *Companion to Psychiatric Studies*, 6th edition. Edinburgh: Churchill Livingstone.

Frosh, S. (1991) *Identity Crisis: Modernity, Psychoanalysis, and the Self*. London: Macmillan.

Gabbard, G.O. (2000) A neurobiologically informed perspective on psychotherapy. *British Journal of Psychiatry*, **177**, 117–122.

Gabbard, G.O., Lazar, S., Hornberger, J. and Spiegel, D. (1997) The economic impact of psychotherapy: a review. *American Journal of Psychiatry*, **154**, 147–155.

Garety, P.A., Fowler, D. and Kuipers, E. (2000) Cognitive behaviour therapy for people with psychosis. In: B.V. Martindale, A. Bateman, M. Crowe and F. Margison (Eds) *Psychosis: Psychological Approaches and their Effectiveness*. London: Gaskell.

Gilbert, P. (1992) *Depression: The Evolution of Powerlessness*. Hove: Lawrence Erlbaum.

Gilbert, P. (1997) The biopsychology of meaning. In: M. Power and C. Brewin (Eds) *The Transformation of Meaning in Psychological Therapies*. Chichester: Wiley.

Giovacchini, P.L. (1993) *Borderline Patients, the Psychosomatic Focus, and the Therapeutic Process*. Northvale, NJ: Jason Aronson.

Glover, V. (1997) Maternal stress or anxiety in pregnancy and emotional development of the child. *British Journal of Psychiatry*, **171**, 105–106.

Golynkina, K. and Ryle, A. (1999) The identification and characteristics of the partially dissociated states of patients with borderline personality disorder. *British Journal of Medical Psychology*, **72**, 429–445.

Gordon, R. (1998) Individuation in an age of uncertainty. In: I. Alister and C. Hauke (Eds) *Contemporary Jungian Analysis*. London: Routledge.

Graham, C. and Thavasotby, R. (1995) Dissociative psychosis; an atypical presentation and response to cognitive-analytic therapy. *Irish Journal of Psychological Medicine*, **12**, 109–111.

Greenberg, L.S. (1986) Change process research. *Journal of Consulting and Clinical Psychology*, **54**, 4–9.

Greenberg, L.S. (1991) Research on the process of change. *Psychotherapy Research*, **1**, 3–16.

Guidano, V.F. (1987) *Complexity of the Self: a Developmental Approach to Psychopathology and Therapy*. New York: Guilford Press.

Guidano, V.F. (1991) *The Self in Process*. New York: Guilford Press.

Gunnell, D.J., Brooks, J. and Peters, T.J. (1996) Epidemiology and patterns of hospital use after parasuicide in the south west of England. *Journal of Epidemiology and Community Health*, **50**, 24–29.

Gurvits, I.G., Koeningsberg, H.W. and Siever, L.J. (2000) Neurotransmitter dysfunction in patients with borderline personality disorder. *Psychiatric Clinics of North America*, **23** (1), 27–40.

Guthrie, E., Creed, F. Dawson, D. and Tomenson, B. (1991) A controlled trial of psychological treatment for the irritable bowel syndrome. *Gastroenterology*, **100**, 450–457.

Hagan, T. and Smail, D. (1997) Power-mapping 1. Background and basic methodology. *Journal of Community and Applied Social Psychology*, **7**, 257–267.

Hamilton, J., et al. (2000) A randomised controlled trial of psychotherapy in patients with chronic functional dyspepsia. *Gastroenterology*, **119**, 661–669.

Hawton, K., Fagg, J., Sinkin, S., Harris, L., Bale, E. and Bond, A. (1997) Trends in deliberate self-harm in Oxford, 1985–1995. *British Journal of Psychiatry*, **171**, 556–560.

Hemsley, D. (1998) The disruption of the 'sense of self' in schizophrenia: potential links with disturbances of information processing. *British Journal of Medical Psychology*, **71**, 115–124.

Hemsley, D. and Murray, R.M. (2000) Commentary: psychological and social treatments for schizophrenia: not just old remedies in new bottles. *Schizophrenia Research*, **26**, 145–151.

Hepple, J. (2000) Cognitive analytic therapy for older adults. *Bulletin of Old Age Psychiatry*, **2**, 45–46.

Hermann, J. (1992) Complex PTSD: a syndrome in survivors of prolonged and repeated trauma. *Journal of Traumatic Stress*, **5**, 377–392.

Hinshelwood, R.D. (1999) The difficult patient: the role of scientific psychiatry in understanding patients with chronic schizophrenia or severe personality disorder. *British Journal of Psychiatry*, **174**, 187–190.

Hodes, M. and Moorey, S. (1993) *Psychological Treatment in Disease and Illness*. London: Gaskell.

Holmes, J. (1993) Psychotherapy—a luxury the NHS cannot afford? More expensive not to treat. *British Medical Journal*, **109**, 1070–1071.

Holmes, J. (1994) The clinical implications of attachment theory. *British Journal of Psychotherapy*, **11**, 62–76.

Holmes, J. (1998a) The changing aims of psychoanalytic psychotherapy. *International Journal of Psycho-Analysis*, **79**, 227–240.

Holmes, J. (1998b) Narrative in psychotherapy. In: C. Mace (Ed.) *Heart and Soul*. London: Routledge.

Holquist, M. (1990) *Bakhtin and his World*. London: Routledge.

Hopkinson, P., Oliver, J., Mann, A. et al. (2001) The impact of a cognitive analytic therapy (CAT) training on the Cawley Centre—a day centre therapeutic milieu for the treatment of the 'hard to help' patient: a qualitative study. (In preparation.)

Hughes, P. and Kerr, I.B. (2000) Transference and countertransference in communication between doctor and patient. *Advances in Psychiatric Treatment*, **6**, 57–64.

Innocenti, G.M. and Kaas, J.H. (1995) The evolution of the cerebral cortex. *Trends in Neurosciences*, **18**, 371–372.

James, W. (1890) *The Principles of Psychology*. Cambridge, MA: Harvard University Press.

Jellema, A. (1999) Cognitive analytic therapy: developing its theory and practice via attachment theory. *Clinical Psychology and Psychotherapy*, **6**, 16–28.

Jellema, A. (2000) Insecure attachment states: their relationship to borderline and narcissistic personality disorders and treatment process in cognitive analytic therapy. *Clinical Psychology and Psychotherapy*, **7**, 138–154.

Jenkins, J.M. and Astington, J.W. (1996) Cognitive factors and family structure associated with theory of mind development in young children. *Developmental Psychopathology*, **32** (1), 70–78.

Kalsched, D.E. (1998) Archetypal affect, anxiety and defence in patients who have suffered early trauma. In: A. Casement (Ed.) *Post-Jungians Today*. London: Routledge.

Karasu, T. (1986) The psychotherapies: benefits and limitation. *American Journal of Psychotherapy*, **40**, 324–343.

Kelly, G.A. (1955) *The Psychology of Personal Constructs*. New York: Norton.

Kendell, R.E. (1993) Diagnosis and classification. In: R.E. Kendell and A.K. Zealley (Eds) *Companion to Psychiatric Studies*, 5th edition, Edinburgh: Churchill Livingstone.

Kernberg, O.F. (1975) *Borderline Conditions and Pathological Narcissism*, New York: Jason Aronson.

Kerr, I.B. (1998a) Art therapy, psychological support and cancer care. In: C. Connell *Something Understood*. London: Wexham Publications.

Kerr, I.B. (1998b) A response to rehabilitation in schizophrenia: a psychoanalytic viewpoint. *European Journal of Psychotherapy, Counselling and Health*, **1**, 55–59.

Kerr, I.B. (1999) Cognitive analytic therapy for borderline personality disorder in the context of a community mental health team: individual and organisational psychodynamic implications. *British Journal of Psychotherapy*, **15**, 425–438.

Kerr, I.B. (2000) Vygotsky, activity theory and the therapeutic community: a further paradigm? *Therapeutic Communities*, **21**, 151–164.

Kerr, I.B. (2001) Brief cognitive analytic therapy for post-acute manic psychosis on a psychiatric intensive care unit. *Clinical Psychology and Psychotherapy*, **8**, 117–129.

Kerr, I.B. and Crowley, V. (2001) Cognitive analytic therapy and psychosis: a preliminary model. (Submitted).

Kerr, I.B. and Taylor, D. (1997) Acute disturbed and violent behaviour: principles of treatment. *Journal of Psychopharmacology*, **11**, 271–277.

Kerr, I.B., Crowley, V., Beard, H. and Simpson, I. (2000) Cognitive analytic therapy (CAT)-based approaches to psychotic disorders: a preliminary model. *Acta Psychiatrica Scandinavica* (Suppl. No. 404), **102**, 6–7.

Khan, M. (1973) Cumulative trauma. In: *The Privacy of the Self*. London: Hogarth.

Koerner, K. and Linehan, M.M. (2000) Research on dialectical behaviour therapy for patients with borderline personality disorder. *Psychiatric Clinics of North America*, **23**, 151–168.

Kohut, H. (1977) *The Restoration of the Self*. New York: International Universities Press.

Kohut, H. and Wolf, E.S. (1978) The disorders of self and their treatment: an outline. *International Journal of Psychoanalysis*, **59**, 413–425.

Krause, I. (1998) *Therapy Across Culture*. London: Sage Publications.

Lee, R.L. and Martin, J.C. (1991) *Psychotherapy after Kohut; A Textbook of Self Psychology*. Hillsdale, NJ: The Analytic Press.

Leighton, T. (1995) A cognitive analytic understanding of 'twelve step' treatment. *New Directions in the Study of Alcohol Group*, **20**, 31–41.

Leighton, T. (1997) Borderline personality and substance abuse problems. In: A. Ryle, *Cognitive Analytic Therapy and Borderline Personality Disorder: The Model and the Method*. Chichester: Wiley.

Leiman, M. (1992) The concept of sign in the work of Vygotsky, Winnicott and Bakhtin: Further integration of object relations theory and activity theory. *British Journal of Medical Psychology*, **65**, 209–221.

Leiman, M. (1994a) The development of cognitive analytic therapy. *International Journal of Short-Term Psychotherapy*, **9**, 67–82.

Leiman, M. (1994b) Projective identification as early joint action sequences: A Vygotskian addendum to the Procedural Sequence Object Relations Model. *British Journal of Medical Psychology*, **67**, 97–106.

Leiman, M. (1995) Early development. In: A. Ryle (Ed.) *Cognitive Analytic Therapy. Developments in Theory and Practice*. Chichester: Wiley.

Leiman, M. (1997) Procedures as dialogical sequences; A revised version of the fundamental concept in cognitive analytic therapy. *British Journal of Medical Psychology*, **70**, 193–207.

Leiman, M. (2000) Ogden's matrix of transference and the concept of sign. *British Journal of Medical Psychology*, **73**, 385–397.

Leudar, I. and Thomas, P. (2000) *Voices of Reason, Voices of Insanity*. London: Routledge.

Linehan, M.M. (1993) *Cognitive Behavioral Treatment of Borderline Personality Disorder*. New York: Guilford Press.

Linehan, M.M., Heard, H. and Armstrong, H.E. (1993) Naturalistic follow up of a behavioral treatment for chronically parasuicidal patients. *Archives of General Psychiatry*, **50**, 971–974.

Livesley, W.J. (2000) A practical approach to the treatment of patients with borderline personality disorder. *Psychiatric Clinics of North America*, **23**(1), 211–232.

Livesley, W. J. (Ed.) (2001) *Handbook of Personality Disorders*. New York: Guilford Press.

Logan, R.D. (1987) Historical change in prevailing sense of self. In: K. Yardley and T. Honess (Eds) *Self and Identity: Psychosocial Perspectives*. Chichester: Wiley.

Luborsky, L. (1990) Theory and technique in dynamic psychotherapy. Curative factors and training therapists to maximize them. *Psychotherapy and Psychosomatics*, **53**, 50–57.

Luborsky, L., Singer, B. and Luborsky, L. (1975) Comparative studies of psychotherapies: is it true that 'everyone has won and all must have prizes'? *Archives of General Psychiatry*, **32**, 995–1002.

Luborsky, L. and Crits-Christoph, P. (1990) *Understanding transference: The CCRT Method*. New York: Basic Books.

Lyons-Ruth, K. (1998) Implicit relational knowing: its role in development and psychoanalytic treatment. *Infant Mental Health Journal*, **19**, 282–289.

McCormick, E.W. (1990) *Change for the Better: A Life Changing Self-Help Psychotherapy Programme*. London: Unwin.

MacCulloch, M.J. (1999) Eye movement desensitisation and reprocessing. *Advances in Psychiatric Treatment*, **5**, 120–125.

McGorry, P. (1992) The concept of recovery and secondary prevention in psychotic disorders, *Australian and New Zealand Journal of Psychiatry*, **236**, 3–17.

McGorry, P. (2000) Psychotherapy and recovery in early psychosis: core clinical and research challenge. In: B.V. Martindale, A. Bateman, M. Crowe and F. Margison (Eds) *Psychosis: Psychological Approaches and their Effectiveness*. London: Gaskell.

McGorry, P., Chanen, A. and McCarthy, E. et al. (1991) Post traumatic stress disorder following recent onset psychosis: an unrecognised post psychotic syndrome. *Journal of Nervous and Mental Disease*, **179**, 253–258.

McGuire, M. and Troisi, A. (1998) *Darwinian Psychiatry*. New York: Oxford University Press.

Magnavita, J.J. (1997) *Restructuring Personality Disorders*. New York: Guilford Press.

Main, T. (1957) The ailment. *British Journal of Medical Psychology*, **30**, 129–145.

Malan, D.H. (1976) *The Frontiers of Brief Psychotherapy*. London: Hutchinson.

Mann, J. (1973) *Time-limited Psychotherapy*. Cambridge, MA: Harvard University Press.

Maple, N. and Simpson, I. (1995) CAT in groups. In: A. Ryle (Ed.) *Cognitive Analytic Therapy: Developments in Theory and Practice*. Chichester: Wiley.

Margison, F. (2000) Editorial. Cognitive analytic therapy: a case study in treatment development. *British Journal of Medical Psychology*, **73**, 145–150.

Marks, I. (1987) *Fears, Phobias and Rituals*. Oxford: Oxford University Press.

Marks, I. (1993) Psychotherapy—a luxury the NHS cannot afford? Unevaluated or inefficient approaches are hard to justify. *British Medical Journal*, **309**, 1071–1072.

Markus, H.R. and Kitayama, S. (1991) Culture and the self: implications for cognition, emotion and motivation. *Psychological Review*, **98**, 224–253.

Marlowe, M. and Ryle, A. (1995) Cognitive analytic therapy of borderline personality disorder: Theory and practice and the clinical and research uses of the self states sequential diagram. *International Journal of Short-Term Psychotherapy*, **10**, 21–34.

Marrone, M. (1998) *Attachment and Interaction*. London: Jessica Kingsley.

Martindale, B.V., Bateman, A., Crowe, M. and Margison, F. (2000) *Psychosis: Psychological Approaches and their Effectiveness*. London: Gaskell.

Mayou, R.A., Ehlers, A. and Hobbs, M. (2000) Psychological debriefing for road traffic accident victims. Three year follow-up of a randomised controlled trial. *British Journal of Psychiatry*, **176**, 589–593.

Meares, R. (1993) *The Metaphor of Play: Disruption and Restoration in the Borderline Experience*. Northvale, NJ: Jason Aronson.

Meares, R. (1998) The self in conversation: on narratives, chronicles and scripts. *Psychoanalytic Dialogues*, **8**, 875–891.

Menzies-Lyth, I. (1959) The functioning of social systems as a defence against anxiety. Reprinted in *Containing Anxiety in Institutions*. London: Free Association Books, 1988.

Miller, G.A., Galanter, E. and Pribram, F.H. (1960) *Plans and the Structure of Behavior*. New York: Holt.

Millon, T. (1993) The borderline personality: A psychosocial epidemic. In: J. Paris (Ed.) *Borderline Personality Disorder: Etiology and Treatment*. Washington DC: American Psychiatric Press.

Mitzman, S. and Duignan, I. (1993) One man's group; brief CAT group therapy and the use of SDR. *Counselling Psychology Quarterly*, **6**, 183–192.

Mollon, P. (1993) *The Fragile Self: the Structure of Narcissistic Disturbance*. London: Whurr Publishers.

Mrazek, P.J. and Haggerty, R.J. (Eds) (1994) *Reducing risks for Mental Disorders: Frontiers for Preventive Intervention Research*. Washington, DC: National Academy Press.

Mueller, N. (1996) The teddy bears picnic: four year old children's personal constructs in relation to behavioural problems and to teacher global concern. *Journal of Child Psychology and Psychiatry*, **37**, 381–389.

Murray, L. (1989) Winnicott and the developmental psychology of infancy. *British Journal of Psychotherapy*, **45**(3), 333–348.

Murray, L. (1992) Intersubjectivity, object relations theory and empirical evidence from mother–infant interactions. *Infant Mental Health Journal*, **12**, 219–232.

Murray-Parkes, C., Laungani, P. and Young, B. (1996) (Eds) *Death and Bereavement across Cultures*. London: Routledge.

Neisser, U. (1967) *Cognitive Psychology*. New York: Appleton.

Nesse, R.M. and Lloyd, A.T. (1992) The evolution of psychodynamic mechanisms. In: J. Barkow, L. Cosmides and J. Tooby (Eds) *The Adapted Mind: Evolutionary Psychology and the Generation of Culture*. Oxford: Oxford University Press.

Nijenhaus, E.R.S., Vanderlinden, J. and Spinhoven, P. (1998) Animal defensive reactions as a model for trauma-induced dissociative reactons. *Journal of Traumatic Stress*, **11**, 243–260.

Norton, K. (1996) Management of difficult personality disordered patients. *Advances in Psychiatric Treatment*, **2**, 202–210.

Offer, D., Kaiz, M., Howard, K.I. and Bennett, E.S. (2000) The altering of reported experiences. *Journal of the American Academy of Child and Adolescent Psychiatry*, **39**, 735–742.

Ogden, T.H. (1983) The concept of internal object relations. *International Journal of Psychoanalysis*, **64**, 227–241.

Ogden, T. (1990) *The Primitive Edge of Experience*. Northvale, NJ: Aronson.

Oliviera, Z.M.R. (1997) The concept of role and the discussion of the internalisation process. In: B.D. Cox and C. Lightfoot (Eds) *Sociogenetic Perspectives on Internalisation*. Mahwah, NJ: Lawrence Erlbaum.

Orlinsky, D.E., Grawe, K. and Parks, B.K. (1994) Process and outcome in psychotherapy. In: A.E. Bergin and S.L. Garfield (Eds) *Handbook of Psychotherapy and Behaviour Change*, 4th edn. New York: Wiley.

Paris, J. (2000) Childhood precursors of Borderline Personality Disorder. *Psychiatric Clinics of North America*, **23**, 77–88.

Parry, G.D. (2000) Evidence based psychotherapy: an overview. In: N. Rowland and S. Goss (Eds) *Evidence Based Counselling and Psychological Therapies*. London: Routledge.

Perner, J., Ruffman, T and Leekham, S.R. (1994) Theory of mind is contagious: you catch it from your sibs. *Child Development*, **65**, 1228–1238.

Perris, C. (1994) Cognitive therapy in the treatment of patients with borderline personality disorder. *Acta Psychiatrica Scandinavica*, **89**, Suppl. 379, 69–72.

Perris, C. (2000) A conceptualisation of personality-related disorders of interpersonal behaviour with implications for treatment. *Clinical Psychology and Psychotherapy*, **7**, 97–117.

Perry, J.C., Banon, E. and Ianni, F. (1999). Effectiveness of psychotherapy for personality disorders. *American Journal of Psychiatry*, **156**, 1312–1321.

Pines, M. (1978) Group analytic psychotherapy of the borderline patient. *Group Analysis*, **11**, 115–126.

Pines, M. (1996) Dialogue and selfhood: discovering connections. *Group Analysis*, **29**, 327–341.

Piper, W.E., Hassan, S.A.A., Joyce, A.S. and McCallum, M. (1991) Transference interpretations, therapeutic alliance, and outcome in short term individual psychotherapy. *Archives of General Psychiatry*, **48**, 946–953.

Plomin, R. (1994) *Genetics and Experience; The Interplay between Nature and Nurture*. Thousand Oaks, CA: Sage Publications.

Plotkin, H. (1997) *Evolution in Mind: An Introduction to Evolutionary Psychology*. London: Penguin Books.

Pollock, P.H. (1996) Clinical issues in the cognitive analytic therapy of sexually abused women who commit violent offences against their partners. *British Journal of Medical Psychology*, **69**, 117–127.

Pollock, P.H. (1997) CAT of an offender with borderline personality disorder. In: A. Ryle (Ed.) *Cognitive Analytic Therapy for Borderline Personality Disorder: The Model and the Method*. Chichester: Wiley.

Pollock, P.H. (Ed.) (2001) *Cognitive Analytic Therapy for Adult Survivors of Childhood Abuse. Approaches to Treatment and Case Management*. Chichester: Wiley.

Pollock, P.H. and Belshaw, T. (1998) Cognitive analytic therapy for offenders. *Journal of Forensic Psychiatry*, **9**, 629–642.

Pollock, P.H., Broadbent, M., Clarke, S., Dorrian, A.J. and Ryle, A. (2001) The Personality Structure Questionnaire (PSQ): A measure of the multiple self states model of identity disturbance in cognitive analytic therapy. *Clinical Psychology and Psychotherapy*, **8**, 59–72.

Post, R.M. and Weiss, S. (1997) Emergent properties of neural systems: how focal molecular neurological alterations can affect behaviour. *Development and Psychopathology*, **9**, 907–929.

Povinelli, D.J. and Preuss, T.M. (1995) Theory of mind; evolutionary history of a cognitive specialisation. *Trends in Neurosciences*, **18**, 418–424.

Power, M. and Brewin, C. (Eds) (1997) *The Transformation of Meaning in Psychological Therapies*. Chichester: Wiley.

Premack, D. and Woodruff, G. (1978) Does the chimpanzee have a theory of mind? *Behavioral and Brain Sciences*, **4**, 515–526.

Prochaska, J.O., Norcross, J.C. and DiClemente, C.C. (1994) *Changing for Good*. New York: William Morrow.

Racker, H. (1968) *Transference and Countertransference*. London: Hogarth Press.

Rees, H. (2000) Cognitive analytic therapy—a most suitable training for psychiatrists. *Psychiatric Bulletin*, **24**, 124–126.

Rehm, L.P. (1977) A self-control model of depression. *Behaviour Therapy*, **8**, 787–804.

Robertson, I. (2000) Compensations for brain deficits. *British Journal of Psychiatry*, **176**, 412–413.

Romme, M., Honig, A., Noordhorn, E. and Escher, A. (1992) Coping with voices: an emancipatory approach. *British Journal of Psychiatry*, **161**, 99–103.

Rose, S. (1995) The rise of neurogenetic determinism. *Nature*, **373**, 380–382.

Rosenthal, R. (1990) How are we doing in soft psychology. *American Psychologist*, **76**, 775–777.

Roth, A. and Fonagy, P. (1996) *What Works for Whom? A Critical Review of Psychotherapy Research*. New York: Guilford Press.

Roth, S. (1980) A revised model of learned helplessness in humans. *Journal of Personality*, **48**, 103–133.

Rotter, J.B. (1978) Generalised expectancies for problem solving and psychotherapy. *Cognitive Therapy and Research*, **2**, 1–10.

Rutter, M., Dunn, J., Plomin, R., Simonoff, E., Pickles, A., Maughan, B., Ormel, J., Meyer, J. and Eaves, L. (1997) Integrating nature and nurture: Implications of person–environment correlations and interactions for developmental psychopathology. *Development and Psychopathology*, **9**, 335–364.

Rycroft, C. (1991) 'On selfhood and self awareness'. In: *Viewpoints*, pp. 147–162. London: The Hogarth Press.

Ryle, A. (1975) *Frames and Cages*. London: Sussex University Press.

Ryle, A. (1979) Defining goals and assessing change in brief psychotherapy; a pilot study using target ratings and the dyad grid. *British Journal of Medical Psychology*, **52**, 223–233.

Ryle, A. (1980) Some measures of goal attainment in focused, integrated, active psychotherapy: a study of fifteen cases. *British Journal of Psychiatry*, **137**, 475–486.

Ryle, A. (1982) *Psychotherapy: A Cognitive Integration of Theory and Practice*. London: Academic Press.

Ryle, A. (1985) Cognitive theory, object relations and the self. *British Journal of Medical Psychology*, **58**, 1–7.

Ryle, A. (1987) Problems of dependency on doctors: discussion paper. *Journal of the Royal Society of Medicine*, **80**, 25–26.

Ryle, A. (1990) *Cognitive Analytic Therapy: Active Participation in Change*. Chichester: Wiley.

Ryle, A. (1991) Object relations theory and activity theory; a proposed link by way of the procedural sequence model. *British Journal of Medical Psychology*, **64**, 307–316.

Ryle, A. (1994) Persuasion or education? The role of reformulation in CAT. *International Journal of Short-term Psychotherapy*, **9**, 111–118.

Ryle, A. (Ed.) (1995a) *Cognitive Analytic Therapy; Developments in Theory and Practice*. Chichester: Wiley.

Ryle, A. (1995b) Holmes on Bowlby and the future of psychotherapy: a response. *British Journal of Psychotherapy*, **11**, 448–452.

Ryle, A. (1996) Ogden's autistic-contiguous position and the role of interpretation in psychoanalytic theory building. *British Journal of Medical Psychology*, **69**, 129–138.

Ryle, A. (1997a) *Cognitive Analytic Therapy and Borderline Personality Disorder: The Model and the Method*. Chichester: Wiley.

Ryle, A. (1997b) The structure and development of borderline personality disorder; a proposed model. *British Journal of Psychiatry*, **170**, 82–87.

Ryle, A. (1997c) Transferences and countertransferences; the CAT perspective. *British Journal of Psychotherapy*, **14**(3), 303–309.

Ryle, A. and Beard, H. (1993) The integrative effect of reformulation: cognitive analytic therapy with a patient with borderline personality disorder. *British Journal of Medical Psychology*, **66**, 249–258.

Ryle, A. and Golynkina, K. (2000) Effectiveness of time-limited cognitive analytic therapy for borderline personality disorder: Factors associated with outcome. *British Journal of Medical Psychology*, **73**, 197–210.

Ryle, A. and Lunghi, M. (1970) The dyad grid: a modification of repertory grid technique. *British Journal of Psychiatry*, **118**, 323–327.

Ryle, A. and Marlowe, M. (1995) Cognitive analytic therapy of borderline personality disorder: Theory and practice and the clinical and research uses of the self states sequential diagram. *International Journal of Short-term Psychotherapy*, **10**, 21–34.

Ryle, A., Spencer, J. and Yawetz, C. (1992) When less is more or at least enough; two case examples of 16-session cognitive analytic therapy. *British Journal of Psychotherapy*, **8**, 401–412.

Safran, J.D. and McMain, S. (1992) A cognitive-interpersonal approach to the treatment of personality disorders. *Journal of Cognitive Psychotherapy: An International Quarterly*, **6**, 59–68.

Salkovskis, P. (Ed.) (1996) *Frontiers of Cognitive Therapy*. New York: Guilford.

Samuels, A. (1985) *Jung and The Post Jungians*. London: Routledge.

Sandler, J. (1976) Counter transference and role-responsiveness. *International Review of Psychoanalysis*, **3**, 43–47.

Sandler, J. and Sandler, A-M. (1998) *Internal Objects Revisited*. London: Karnac Books.

Sandler, J., Dare, C. and Holder, A. (1979) *The Patient and the Analyst; the Basis of the Psychoanalytic Process*. London: Karnac Books.

Schacht, T.E. and Henry, W.P. (1994) Modelling recurrent relationship patterns with Structural Analysis of Social Behavior: The SASBY-CMP. *Psychotherapy Research*, **4**, 208–221.

Schafer, R. (1992) *Retelling a Life: Narrative and Dialogue in Psychoanalysis*. New York: Basic Books.

Schneider, M.L., Clarke, S.A., Kraemer, G.W. et al. (1998) Prenatal stress alters brain in biogenic amines levels in primates. *Development and Psychopathology*, **10**, 427–440.

Schore, A.N. (1994) *Affect Regulation and the Origin of the Self; The Neurobiology of Emotional Development*. Hillsdale, NJ: Lawrence Erlbaum Associates.

Schwartz, J. (1999) *Cassandra's Daughter: A History of Psychoanalysis*. London: Allen Lane The Penguin Press.

Senge, P. (1994) *The Fifth Discipline Field Book*. London: Nicholas Brealey.

Sheard, T., Evans, J., Cash, D. et al. (2000) A CAT derived one to three session intervention for repeated deliberate self harm: a description of the model and initial experience of trainee psychiatrists in using it. *British Journal of Medical Psychology*, **73**, 179–196.

Shweder, R.A. and Bourne, E.J. (1982) 'Does the concept of the person vary cross-culturally?'. In: A.J. Marsella and G.M. White (Eds) *Cultural Conceptions of Mental Health and Therapy*. Dordrecht: Reidel.

Silk, K.R. (2000) Overview of biological factors. *Psychiatric Clinics of North America*, **23**, 61–76.

Sinason, V. (1992) *Mental Handicap and the Human Condition: New Approaches From the Tavistock*. London: Free Association Books.

Slavin, B. and Kriegman, M. (1992) *The Adaptive Design of the Human Psyche*. New York: Academic Press.

Solms, M. (1995) Is the brain more real than the mind? *Psychoanalytic Psychotherapy*, **9**, 107–120.

Soloff, P.H. (2000) Psychopharmacology of borderline personality disorder. *Psychiatric Clinics of North America*, **23**, 169–192.

Spence, D. (1982) *Narrative Truth and Historical Truth*. New York: Norton.

Spitzer, R.L., Williams, J.B.W. and Gibbons, M. (1987) *Structured Clinical Interview for DSM-III-R, Patient Version*. New York: New York State Psychiatric Institute.

Stanton, M. (1990) *Sandor Ferenczi: Reconsidering Active Intervention*. London: Free Association Books.

Stern, D.N. (1985) *The Interpersonal World of the Infant; A View from Psychoanalysis and Developmental Psychology*. New York: Basic Books.

Stern, D.N., Sander, L.S., Nahum, J.P., Harrison, A.M., Lyons-Ruth, K., Bruschweiler-Stern, N. and Tronick, E.Z. (1998) Non-interpretive mechanisms in psychoanalytic psychotherapy: the 'something more' than interpretation. *International Journal of Psychoanalysis*, **79**, 903–921.

Stevens, R. (Ed.) (1996) *Understanding the Self*. London: Sage Publications, Open University Press.

Stevens, A. and Price, J. (1996) *Evolutionary Psychiatry, a New Beginning*. London: Routledge.

Stiles, W. (1995) In what sense does outcome depend on process? *Changes, An International Journal of Psychology and Psychotherapy*, **13**, 219–224.

Stiles, W. (1997) Signs and voices: joining a conversation in progress. *British Journal of Medical Psychotherapy*, **70**, 169–176.

Stiles, W.B. and Shapiro, D.A. (1994) Disabuse of the drug metaphor: Psychotherapy process-outcome correlations. *Journal of Consulting and Clinical Psychology*, **62**, 942–948.

Stone, M.H. (2000) Clinical guidelines for psychotherapy for patients with borderline personality disorder. *Psychiatric Clinics of North America*, **23**, 193–210.

Stricker, G. and Gold, J.R. (1993) *Comprehensive Handbook of Psychotherapy Integration*. New York: Plenum Press.

Sullivan, H.S. (1953) *The Interpersonal Theory of Psychiatry*. London: Tavistock Publications.

Summerfield, D. (1999) A critique of seven assumptions behind psychological trauma programmes in war-affected areas. *Social Science and Medicine*, **48**, 1449–1462.

Sutherland, J.D. (1980) The British object relations theorists. *Journal of the American Psychoanalytic Association*, **28**, 829–859.

Sutton, L. (1997) 'Out of the Silence' When people can't talk about it. In: L. Hunt, M. Marshall and C. Rowlings (Eds) *Past Trauma in Later Life: European Perspectives on Therapeutic Work with Older People*. London: Jessica Kingsley.

Sutton, L. (in press) When late life brings a diagnosis of dementia and early life brought trauma. A cognitive analytic understanding of 'loss of mind'. *Clinical Psychology and Psychotherapy*.

Sutton, L. and Cheston, R. (1997) Rewriting the story of dementia: a narrative approach to psychotherapy with people with dementia. In: M. Marshall (Ed.) *State of the Art in Dementia Care*. London: Centre for Policy on Ageing.

Symington, N. (1999) *Emotion and Spirit*. London: Karnac Books.

Szivos, S.E. and Griffiths, E. (1990) Group processes in coming to terms with a mentally retarded identity. *Mental Retardation*, **28**, 333–341.

Tacey, D. (1997) *Remaking Masculinity: Jung, Spirituality and Social Change*. London: Routledge.

Taylor, G.J., Bagby, R.M. and Parker, J.D.A. (1991) The alexithymia construct: a potential paradigm for psychosomatic medicine. *Psychosomatics*, **32**, 153–164.

Tooby, J. and Cosmides, L. (1992) The psychological foundations of culture. In: J.H. Barkow, L. Cosmides and J. Tooby (Eds) *The Adapted Mind: Evolutionary Psychology and the Generation of Culture*. Oxford: Oxford University Press.

Torgensen, S. (2000) The genetics of patients with Borderline Personality Disorder. *Psychiatric Clinics of North America*, **23**, 1–10.

Toth, S.L. and Cicchetti, D. (1998) Remembering, forgetting, and the effects of trauma on memory: a developmental psychopathology perspective. *Development and Psychopathology*, **10**, 589–605.

Treasure, J. and Ward, A. (1997) Cognitive analytical therapy in the treatment of anorexia nervosa. *Clinical Psychology and Psychotherapy*, **4**, 62–71.

Treasure, J., Todd, G., Brolly, M., Tiller, J., Nehmed, A. and Denman, F. (1995) A pilot study of a randomised trial of cognitive analytic therapy vs. educational behaviour therapy for adult anorexia nervosa. *Behaviour Research and Therapy*, **33**, 363–367.

Trevarthen, C. (1993) Playing into reality: conversations with the infant communicator. *Journal of the Squiggle Foundation, Winnicott Studies*, **7**, 67–84.

Tronick, E.Z. (1998) Dyadically expanded states of consciousness and the process of therapeutic change. *Infant Mental Health Journal*, **19**, 290–299.

Tschudi, F. (1990) *'Flexigrid'*. University of Oslo.

Tseng, W.S. (1999) Culture and psychotherapy: review and practical guidelines. *Transcultural Psychiatry*, **36**, 131–179.

Tudge, C. (1996) *The Day Before Yesterday; Five Million Years of Human History*. London: Pimlico.

Van der Kolk, B.A. (2000) The assessment and treatment of complex PTSD. In: R. Yehuda (Ed.) *Traumatic Stress*. Washington, DC: American Psychiatric Press.

Van der Kolk, B.A., MacFarlane, A.C. and Weisaeth, L. (1996) (Eds) *Traumatic Stress: the Effects of Overwhelming Experience on Mind, Body and Society*. New York: Guilford Press.

Van Etten, M.L. and Taylor, S. (1998) Comparative efficacy of treatment for post-traumatic stress disorder: a meta-analysis. *Clinical Psychology and Psychotherapy*, **5**, 126–144.

Volosinov, V.N. (1973) *Marxism and the Philosophy of Language*. Cambridge, MA: Harvard University Press.

Vygotsky, L.S. (1934) Thought in schizophrenia. *Archives of Neurology and Psychiatry*, **31**, 1062–1077.

Vygotsky, L.S. (1978) *Mind in Society; The Development of Higher Psychological Processes*. Cambridge, MA: Harvard University Press.

Walker, E.F., Neumann, C.C., Baum, K. et al. (1996) The developmental pathways to schizophrenia: potential moderating effects of stress. *Development and Psychopathology*, **8**, 647–665.

Walsh, S. (1996) Adapting cognitive analytic therapy to make sense of psychologically harmful work environments. *British Journal of Medical Psychology*, **69**, 3–20.

Walsh, S., Hagan, T. and Gamsu, D. (2000) Rescuer and rescued: Applying a cognitive analytic perspective to explore the mis-management of asthma. *British Journal of Medical Psychology*, **73**, 151–168.

Wedderburn, D. (1996) The superiority of collective action; the case of the NHS. In: P. Barker (Ed.) *Living as Equals*. Oxford: Oxford University Press.

Wells, A. (1999) A metacognitive model for generalised anxiety disorders. *Journal of Clinical Psychology and Psychotherapy*, **6**, 86–95.

Wertsch, J.V. (1985) *Vygotsky and the Social Formation of Mind*. Cambridge, MA: Harvard University Press.

Wertsch, J.V. and Tulviste, P. (1992) L.S. Vygotsky and contemporary developmental psychology. *Developmental Psychology*, **28**, 548–557.

White, M. (1995) *Re-authoring Lives: Interviews and Essays*. Adelaide: Dulwich Centre Publications.

Winnicott. D.W. (1947) Hate in the countertransference. In: D.W. Winnicott. *Through Paediatrics to Psychoanalysis*. London: Hogarth Press (1975).

Winnicott, D.W. (1971) *Playing and Reality*. London: Tavistock Publications.

Wood, D., Bruner, J.S. and Ross, G. (1976) The role of tutoring in problem solving. *Journal of Child Psychology and Psychiatry*, **17**, 84–100.

World Health Organisation (1992) *The ICD-10 Classification of Mental and Behavioural Disorders*. Geneva: WHO.

Wykes, T., Tarrier, N. and Lewis, S. (Eds) (1998) *Outcome and Innovation in Psychological Treatment of Schizophrenia*. Chichester: Wiley.

Young, J.E. and Lindemann, M.D. (1992) An integrative schema-focused model of personality disorders. *Journal of Cognitive Psychotherapy: An International Quarterly*, **6**, 11–23.

Zanarini, M.C. (2000) Childhood experiences associated with the development of borderline personality disorder. *Psychiatric Clinics of North America*, **23**, 89–102.

Zanarini, M.C., Gunderson, J.G. and Marino, M.F. (1988) DSM III disorders in the families of borderline outpatients. *Journal of Personality Disorders*, **2**, 292–302.

Zubin, J. and Spring, B. (1977) Vulnerability: a new view of schizophrenia. *Journal of Abnormal Psychology*, **86**, 103–126.

Zulueta de, F. (1993) *From Pain to Violence*. London: Whurr.

Zweig-Frank, H., Paris, J. and Guzder, J. (1994) Dissociation in female patients with borderline and non-borderline personality disorders. *Journal of Personality Disorders*, **8**, 203–209.

INDEX